Michael Matthews

November 1971

To Pierce & Diana
    with much love
        from
Xmas 1971   Alan & Mama

THE EAST ANGLIAN BOOK

*For
John and Mary Welbon,
With love*

THE EAST ANGLIAN BOOK

A PERSONAL ANTHOLOGY

edited by

MICHAEL WATKINS

EAST ANGLIAN MAGAZINE LTD IPSWICH SUFFOLK

S B N 900227 05 2
Printed and published in Great Britain by
EAST ANGLIAN MAGAZINE LTD
IPSWICH   SUFFOLK

© THE AUTHORS 1971

contents

LETTER TO A NEPHEW	7
THE REASON WHY by *Michael Watkins*	9
THE ESSENTIAL EAST ANGLIA by *James Wentworth Day*	21
EAST ANGLIAN IN EXILE by *Arthur E. Simmonds*	29
AN EAST ANGLIAN CHILDHOOD by *Spike Mays*	31
WHERE MY HEART LIES by *Norah Lofts*	43
A TRAVELLER RETURNED by *Hammond Innes*	55
THE VICTORIANS by *Allan Jobson*	59
THE EAST ANGLIAN HOUSE by *John Hadfield*	67
A PARTICULAR HOUSE by *Mary Gilliatt*	77
PLANTSMAN'S PIE by *Alan Bloom*	85
THE RICH LAND by *Rintoul Booth*	95
THE CHURCH by *the Bishop of St. Edmundsbury and Ipswich*	103
SOME CHURCHES by *Simon Dewes*	107
A PLACE TO PAINT by *Edward Seago*	113
THE PAST by *W. G. Arnott*	121
THE MUSIC by *Peter Pears*	127
THE TWO SUFFOLKS by *Adrian Bell*	133
THE WILD LIFE by *Alan Savory*	139
THE SEA by *A. W. Roberts*	149
THINGS ANTIQUE by *John Steel*	153
THE NEW EAST ANGLIA by *Eldon Griffiths*	159
THE SUFFOLK SETTLER, CRABBEWISE by *Paul Jennings*	165
EASTWARD HO! FOR SPORT by *Logie Bruce Lockhart*	169
WHO ARE WE? by *Ronald Blythe*	173
THE CRAFTSMEN by *John Stannard*	180
THE HAUNTED PLACES by *Eric Rayner*	185
mrs. a. woods	195
HARRY BECKER	198
GONE AWAY by *John Seymour*	201

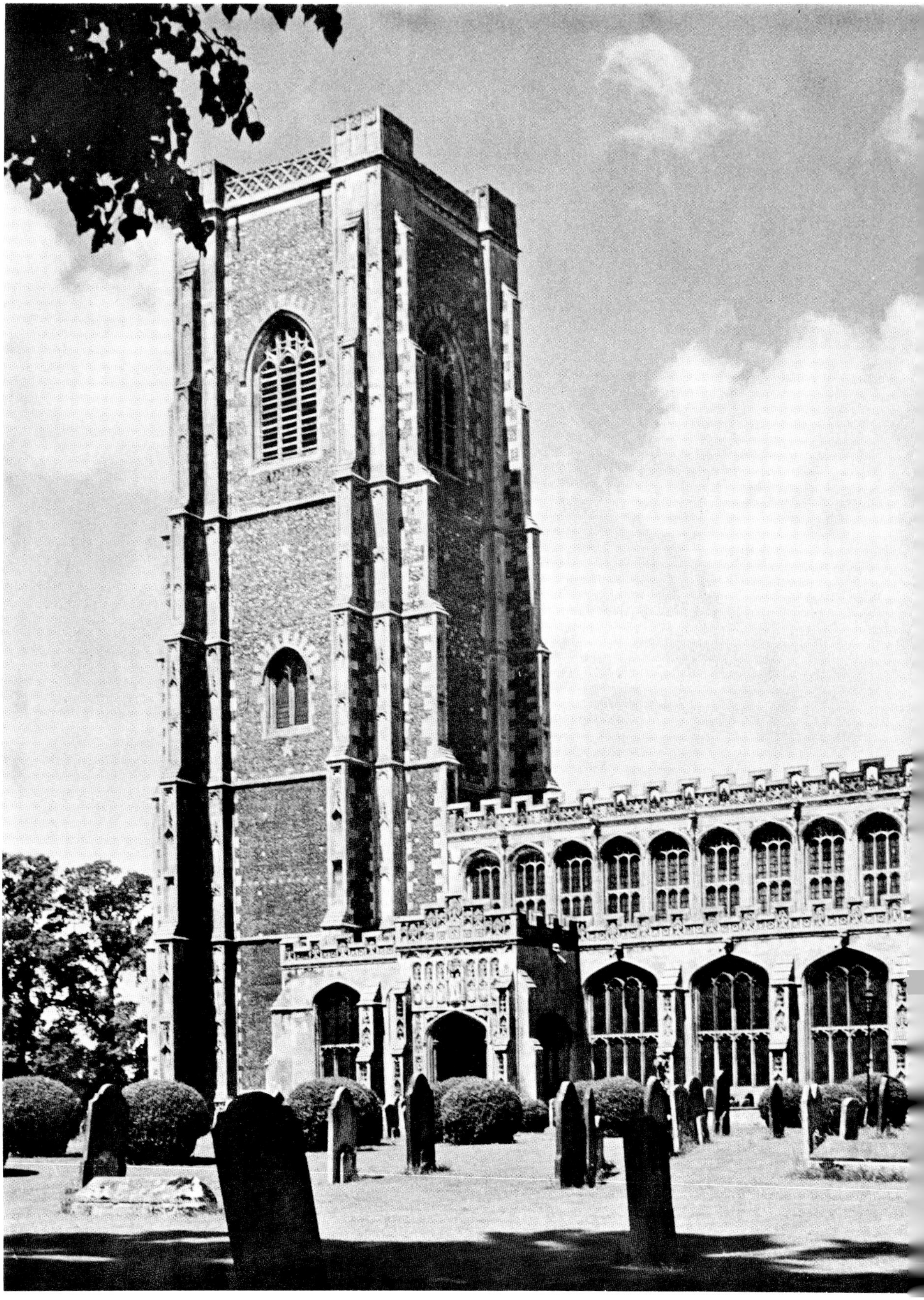

My dear Richard,

SO they've set you a project to write about 'The Character of East Anglia', have they? You're lucky. When I was at school I got 'Elizabethan England' — and no help from Glenda Jackson and Keith Michell in those days.

You've been told, you say, that East Anglians are dour, suspicious, insular, guileful, crafty. Even servile! Who told you? No East Anglian, I'll bet. My own experience tells me that the chief differences between an East Anglian and a Devonian or a Lancastrian are mythical and, like most myths, have their roots in fantasy rather than reality. I believe that an East Anglian will offer his friendship and his loyalty as readily as anyone. Patronise him, woo him with less than the truth, and his reactions will be those of any free man.

Try to get hold of Julian Tennyson's Suffolk Scene. *It's out of print now; but it's worth hunting down — a real classic. Sadly, he was killed in the War. He would agree with a couple of the things you were told, but suggests that this slight animosity of the East Anglian '... attracts the right people and repels the wrong ones'. You might think it a bit smug of me to mention this — but your evidence was fairly damning.*

I'm sending you a copy of The East Anglian Book. *(It can be your birthday present in advance!) It's a new anthology and I don't think there have been many publications covering the region quite so thoroughly: history, churches, farming, village life, the sea, music, wild life, the houses — and so on. You can crib great chunks of it and have your project done in no time.*

One more thing. I'll drop a line to my old friend James Wentworth Day — he lives not far from the school — and ask him to take you out to lunch. He's written 43 books, many about East Anglia, and knows more about the Fens than anyone since Hereward-the-Wake. You'll like him. He'll tell you lots of good stories too: only you'll have to pick your audience carefully before passing them on — some will be pretty ripe.

Yours affectionately,

Michael

Left: Lavenham Church

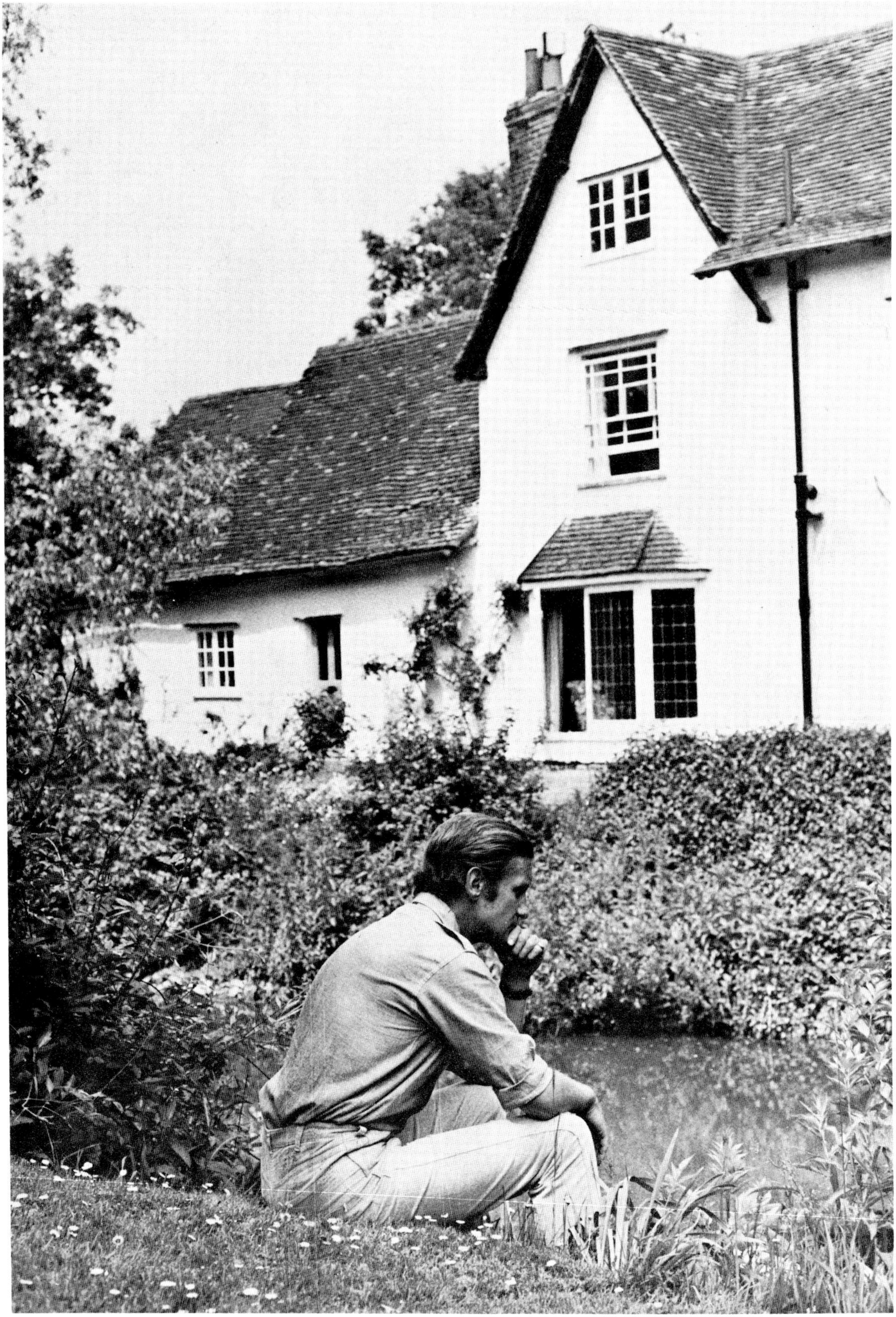

Michael Watkins

The Reason Why

THERE must be other islands. Smaller islands, accessible islands, islands temperate politically if not climatically: not castles-in-the-air islands which one longs for with the kind of wistful passion reserved for dreams and fantasy, but islands which actually come on to the market. Hillier, Parker, May and Rowden islands wouldn't be suitable either — *they'd* be nine miles off the west coast of Scotland or bobbing remotely in the Gulf of Kutch or the Bight of Benim. And Messrs. Hillier, Parker etc. would want £327,000 for them, whereas all *I* could afford was the odd seven.

The idea had been in the antipodes of my mind for a long time. I have always loved islands and would pore longingly over maps showing Fernando Poo and Novaya Zemlya, wondering if the natives ate paw-paw for breakfast and what they'd do if they got appendicitis. The notion of self-imposed exile was attractive — provided one could *lower* the drawbridge as well as raise it. The only thing I should miss radio and television for would be the news; but since it is always *bad* news I'd soon recover.

It was ten years ago when I finally made up my mind. There were, I suppose, peripheral reasons for my defection from London to Suffolk: coagulating traffic, proliferating parking meters, lunar architecture and lunatic conversation. But basically I felt that city life was becoming de-humanised — and I wanted no part of it.

What I did want was to live in East Anglia which, for me, has a distinct island-like quality that exists nowhere else in England. There is something pugnacious, inviolable in the way it juts its great jaw into the North Sea; there is something undefiled and inward-looking about its people — as indeed there is with all island races. It has an immense privacy which you sense the moment you get to Liverpool Street and ask the porters which platform the 5.30 to Ipswich leaves from. There is, it seems, something almost Masonic about their reticence; but it's not that at all: they're simply East Anglians who don't want the place cluttered with unnecessary visitors.

You have the same feeling of being diverted when you travel by road. It's all right going through Stratford and Leytonstone, and then you're just settling into a cosmic mood of inevitability over the eerie Wanstead Flats when you pass a sign soliciting a detour to Stamford-le-Hope. And there's this enormous *camion* thing in front with *Fruehauf: Attention — Freins puissants* written all over its swaying continental backside.

Suddenly the Gallic influence is banished by another highway proclamation: HAVERING-ATTE-BOWER. It has an Arthurian ring to it; a note of chivalry. One can almost hear exultant cries rising from the tournament stands as mounted knights thunder down the lists towards each other, lances extended ... Havering-atte-Bower! It is a happy moment, for soon you will be in the land of Good Easter, Chignell Smealy and Shellow Bowells leading, via the A12, to Camelot.

Tarston and Rodin-esque pose.

Everyone has a friend called Harblow or Pyecraft or something. Well, I have one called Stacpoole. Leading a life of almost mythical indolence in Suffolk gives him a chance to be useful in matters of irrelevance. For a year or two he had known, for instance, of my absurdly romantic wish to live on an island and, in an inert kind of way, it amused him to follow the property columns, inspecting at a distance the plausibility of Pacific atolls appearing for sale.

One day he telephoned me. 'Found just the place for you, dear boy,' he growled sleepily. 'Not exactly an island, but surrounded by water — a moat, actually — about two miles up a goat track. You'll never get anyone to deliver the papers. Should suit you very well. I'll get them to send particulars.'

The part of the estate agent's euphoria I found irresistible read: 'Tarston Hall, mentioned in Domesday Book, is situated at the end of a two mile drive, and is easily found by following the telephone wires.' (I haven't checked the entry in Domesday Book — which I refuse to buy until they do it in paperback — but the estate agent's blurb I have before me at this minute.) Visions of returning home to Tarston Hall after bibulous dinner parties, sense of direction blurred, points of the compass confused. Ah! but here's the telephone wire. Grasp it on tall tip-toe and, like Theseus in pursuit of the Minotaur, grope one's way through the labyrinthine dark of beet furrows.

I bought Tarston for £7000, inheriting a housekeeper called Mrs. Edge, a taciturn gardener called Arthur, an ancient and mangy cat whom I re-christened Domesday — and a ghost called Hannah. The moat was stocked with golden carp and along its banks paraded hungry queues of mallard. So voracious were the latter that I named them after the less mildly mannered Roman emperors: Tiberius, Caligula, Nero .... but one duck is much like another and soon I compromised, renaming them all Smith. They respond well to this and now feed from my hand. I'm rather proud of that.

While plumbers did something about the small fish-like creatures emitted from the taps (somehow misconnected to the moat) and Mrs. Edge tackled cobwebs embracing the beams, Arthur and I set about clearing two acres of equatorial wilderness. Hannah motioned her disapproval by smashing occasional pieces of china, but secretly was rather enjoying the newly-installed central heating. With a little patience and a lot of love, Tarston became a home again.

It is said that the original house, locally pronounced and sometimes spelt Tarsen, was built upon what is now an island. When eventually it fell into decay, Tarston Hall rose again in 1546, overlooking, across the moat, the site of its predecessor. The ruined island is now a wild garden, a Smith-sanctuary and, beneath the suppliant branches of a pear tree, last resting place of the cat, Domesday. Alas, he could withstand the weight of his 885 years no longer and passed away, mewing his feeble protest, a short while ago. Of the old house, nothing remains.

Although undeniably spectral, Hannah is no less real to me than, in life, was Domesday. Sceptical always of the supernatural, the occult and 'inexplicable happenings', I nevertheless would feel traitorous to deny Hannah. I have lived with her too long and know her gentleness, her moods of wilfulness, her sorrow, her gaiety and her femininity.

Hannah's father, Edward Boldry, whose altar-tomb in Darmsden churchyard describes him as 'an Honest and Charitable Man', died in 1771, bequeathing Tarston to his daughter. Hannah shortly married an Ipswich silversmith, John Ward; but the gods must have favoured him, for he died young. Hannah, who did not remarry, survived her husband 40 years, living quite alone at Tarston until 1826. Let 'Rambler', writing in *The East Anglian Daily Times* on 29th September 1928, continue the story: 'By way of a stackyard I enter a meadow and pass Tarston Hall. The house, with its

pink-washed walls, its jumble of mellowed roofs and chimneys, makes a restful picture, partially enclosed as it is by a moat and set amid shapely trees .... perhaps Hannah's ghost haunts this remote spot, and still (as I picture her in life):

> *Like a cloistress, she will veiled walk*
> *And water once a day her chamber round*
> *With eye-offending brine.*

So far as I can trace, no woman has remained mistress of Tarston for any measurable period since Hannah's reign; and there is even a brief history of broken marriages in the house. The curious thing is that it is always the man who remains to care for the place. To become so lyrical on an afternoon's walk makes one suspect that even Rambler succumbed a little to Hannah's charms. Perhaps we are all a bit in love with her.

11

Tarston is in the parish of Barking-cum-Darmsden and if that doesn't mean a thing to you, it is hardly surprising. Darmsden — or Bermesdena, Dermesdena, Dermodesdon, Dermodesduna, Dormesden, Dormesdon, Dormonnesdem — is marked by an R.D.C. post 'No through road for vehicles' at the brow of a hill on the A45, nine miles from Ipswich. There are other announcements, the work of feudalism, 'Private Road' and 'Strictly Private'. Cars snarling by at 70 miles an hour, or Leviathan container vehicles grinding from Ipswich docks to the Midlands, would be unlikely to notice the turning. But there it is, an 'unadopted' farm lane meandering upwards and curving, amid a pine plantation, high above the Gipping Valley and into the folds of nowhere. 'Nowhere' because I have come to regard Darmsden as a sort of limbo: not as a damnable region for lost souls, but as a place for souls who still have time to stand and stare.

The first house you come to, half a mile from the main road, is Darmsden Hall, its economical Georgian facade staring over the valley. There are barns and grain dryers and a mint-new factory edifice for doing something to potatoes. Just storing them, maybe. Across the farmyard is where Mrs. Edge lives, in a pretty, low cottage with thatch a little unruly at the edges, like a Beatle haircut. Then there's Rose Cottage where the major lives. He owns, in partnership with his nephew, about a thousand acres of this land which, in the days of land depression, changed hands for £20 an acre. Last time the farm was up for sale, the figure was over £300 an acre. They say the major is very rich, but I wouldn't know about that: he walks his dogs, knows his port and rejoices in the best cook for miles around.

There are a few other houses: Burnt Cottage, Rose Farmhouse, Bridges, Daisy Farm, Clay Hall Cottage and Tarston Farm, swelling the population to 32, including children away at school. In an age of population explosion, it is comforting to see that there were 40 Darmsden inhabitants in 1674 and a congested 64 in 1861. There is no pub in Darmsden; neither is there a village shop. There is no street lighting, no bus service, no newspaper delivery. Occasionally I see the refuse collection van in the hamlet, but rarely does it make the safari as far as Tarston. The two miles to Tarston sometimes seem like 22 and, when the drive reaches the stackyard, it simply gives up the unequal struggle. Mr. Gooding, the postman, used to cycle up with the mail each day; but four years ago he was mechanised and now navigates a bright red Royal Mail van along the track. I have the feeling somehow that he still prefers his bicycle: the way he lets in the clutch, spurting a vicious shower of gravel on to my lawn, is more the result of angst than ineptitude.

Another sign of the times is the way in which the very landscape has changed. Even in my time. The drive from Tarston to join the main road used to be through leafy tunnels, luxuriant foliage overhead and hedgerows clinging to the verge. May was the best month, for when you turned the corner by the church, the cherry orchards spread a quilt of snow-white blossom over the land. The orchards have now vanished, grubbed out five years ago in favour of higher yielding crops; gone too are the hedgerows and many of the trees, so that the fields are planted to the very edge of the lane and the view nowadays is like that of an undulating prairie reaching to the horizon.

John Vane, my good neighbour who farms Tarston land, once managed the Darmsden estate. When he arrived, straight from the army, he could never rely on his harvest. In those days before compound fertiliser, the light land was normally unprofitable, while the menace of rabbits could destroy half the crops. It has been said that if you can farm Darmsden, you can farm anywhere, so varied is the geological structure of the estate. Down by the road to Needham Market there is a strata of light land overlying chalk while, in the stream-coursed valley, the soil is as good as any in Suffolk. On the top fields there is ugly boulder clay, so that in spring you can be drilling the silt land, while the higher fields are nowhere near ready. The main crops now at Darmsden are cereals, sugar beet, potatoes. At Tarston John Vane farms cereals and soft fruit: he has the reputation for knowing more about strawberries than any other Suffolk farmer.

For a semi-recluse like me, August is a wicked month because it is the tail end of the picking season when convoys of motor cars block the lane as the strawberry-jammers descend on the fields like locusts to strip the remaining fruit. But I'm well compensated, being allowed special dispensation to pick those luscious Red Gauntlets and succulent Cambridge Favourites for my supper each evening. So, in the interest of gastronomy and pure greed, the trespassers are welcome.

When Mr. and Mrs. Vane arrived at Darmsden Hall in 1948, there was no mains water in the village. Their's was the only motor car and their's the only telephone; so for a while their role was squirearchical in a manner which the intervening years of Progress have made redundant. With one car and one telephone among an entire community, all emergencies were routed to civilization and assistance through the Hall. Births, deaths, illness, accidents, were all communicated by that one telephone line. Yet it doesn't seem to have imposed a strain upon the hamlet's communal longevity and St. Andrew's churchyard — an all man's land between devotion and the hereafter — is full of old 'uns. There's Stanford Avis, 83, and Ellen Knock, who missed her century by only six years, and Luke Lockwood, 85, and Herbert Chaplin, 82. And many more besides. Peace, perfect peace.

In those days there was a good turn-out on a Sunday morning and Hubert, appointed Darmsden's first rector in 1146, wouldn't have grumbled at the size of the congregation had he been able to preside over the services in the early years after the war. The present rector must be dispirited every now and then: many is the time when he has preached his sermon to Mr. and Mrs. Vane and old Tom, who rings the bell, and me. And many is the time he has listened to John Vane read the first lesson to me, followed by me reading the second lesson to John Vane. There's still no lighting in St. Andrew's and no heating either, and when the winter wind moans across the fields from Badger Wood and one's fingers turn blue clutching *Hymns Ancient and Modern,* it's a bit of an effort to pray. You can hardly blame the villagers if they're down at the Lion or genuflecting before other idols with twin carburettors and chrome-wire wheels. For the villagers of Darmsden are, like me, newcomers whose roots, if roots we have at all, are not inextricably woven into the hamlet's past. Newcomers we are — and yet I like to think that it is Darmsden that changes us and not the other way round.

Of all the families in Darmsden, there is only one whose lives are threaded into the tapestry of this corner of East Anglia — the Chaplins. Herbert, head of the family, rests, as we have seen, in the churchyard of St. Andrew's. Ellen, his widow, now aged 83 still lives at Clay Hall Cottage, the house they moved into when they married in 1910. With her live boy Jim and boy Dennis. John is away farming in Australia. Peter is in Felixstowe, while Rosie, Dorothy, Muriel and Nan are married and scattered throughout different parts of Suffolk. And Albert, boy Albert who worked up at the cowsheds, never did make it back from El Alamein.

Mrs. Chaplin came from Orford and went into service in London at seventeen for 6d. a week. By the time she was 22 she was earning £24 a year; but then she met Herbert, who sang in the choir at Baylham Church, a mile across the fields from Darmsden. Herbert's parents lived at Baylham where his father was shepherd to Mr. Wilson at Baylham Hall. So Herbert went to work for the Wilsons too, as back'us boy, when he was nine. Until, that is, he married Ellen: he needed the money then and went on to the land for nine shillings a week 'and no wet weather'. By the time they had nine children he was up to 25 shillings a week; but they had a free cottage and Mrs. Chaplin baked the bread and brewed the beer, while her husband tended a vegetable garden and kept a pig or two. Somehow they managed. It helped that coal was 12 shillings a ton, that a bushel of malt cost seven and six, and that you could buy two dozen eggs for a shilling. It also helped that there was a family rule: 'if you can't afford it, you don't have it'.

'Clothes was the problem,' Mrs. Chaplin says. 'We had to patch an' mend — and a strong pair of boots cost 18 shillings. My husband's luxury was his 20 cigarettes a week. I didn't have a luxury. Too busy for luxuries .... too busy to be unhappy. We never did have a holiday. Master Jim and Master Paul say I can stay on here at the old rent.'

Master Jim and Master Paul are Mr. Wilson's sons, who farm the Baylham land as their father did and his father before him. The old rent for Clay Hall Cottage is four shillings a week.

Mrs. Chaplin has lived in her cottage for 61 years, not having much and not wanting much either. There's a coronation picture on the wall of her spotless sitting room; not the 1953 coronation, the one before that. Her cooking range is jet black and I've never seen it unlit. And there's always an apple crumble in the oven and a row of sausage rolls cooling in the scullery. And there's always a bottle of elderberry wine at Christmas.

In November 1964 the spirit of our 12th century rector, Hubert, together with those of his next known successor, Thomas de Castro Bernardi, and the ensuing 43 incumbents of the living, were invoked to attend an extraordinary meeting of the parochial church council. Suppressing their doctrinal differences, they concentrated unanimously on the Central Electricity Generating Board's proposal to dangle another 41 miles of overhead power cable across the Suffolk landscape. If these proposals were enforced, Darmsden and the lovely Valley of the Gipping at Bosmere would, the reverend gentlemen averred, become part of a spawning ground for some Coptic rite of electrical insemination. It was suggested that certain parishioners should express their apprehension about the spoilation of the countryside by addressing correspondence to the newspapers.

One of the results of this literary salvo was that a television company invited me to script a documentary film about the effect the advancing hordes of pylons would have on Darmsden. The script written and accepted, I was then asked to present the film on location. It simply meant that for three days Darmsden was a mass of cables, lights, cameras, recording equipment, bearded men in baseball caps shouting through megaphones, and an astonishingly pretty girl with a whistle and a clapper-board. All in all it was pretty good fun. We 'shot' Mr. Gooding wobbling by to deliver the post at Clay Hall Cottage (this was in his pre-combustible era); we got Jim Chaplin all shy and tongue-tied before the cameras; I forgot the very lines I myself had written, which inspired the megaphone-man to shout 'cut' with increasing hoarseness; and we all ate lots of sandwiches and drank quantities of beer which the astonishingly pretty girl dispensed from an enamel jug.

When the film was eventually screened on television, we thought it rather splendid. One or two of us even felt we were wasting our time mucking out pigs and hammering typewriters when Hollywood was obviously more in need of our services.

The pylons, of course, were erected.

"Harry was only whistling 'All things bright and beautiful' when over comes this vicar and dings him a beaut."

We were visited by sympathetic men from the Ministry and courteous, reasonable men from the Electricity Board. They were frightfully apologetic and said what hell it must be for us; but that they were absolutely certain we'd get used to them — the pylons, that is — in time. I tried very hard, but I'm afraid I'm not used to them at all. Six hundred yards from Tarston one of these giants virtually straddles the drive, a vast confection of tubular knitting. I more or less have to drive under it every time I go to the village.

But I suppose it's a cheap price to pay for culture, for the pylons have brought us Civilization and Coronation Street; and those 19 square inches of flickering grey dots keep us in touch with the horrors of My Lai and help us share, however vicariously, the delights of Mr. Whicker's world. And the current makes the electric toasters pop, the kettles sing, and the washing machines froth: so life in Darmsden has become that much more comfortable and that much more acquisitive.

People who say 'you'll get used to it' remind me of London friends who murmur how they envy me for getting away from it all, as if country living is like retreating from some emotional Moscow. 'Getting away from it all' is a cliché sounding like surrender, a devious kind of escapology. Or it may sound idyllic. I see it as neither: more as an awareness. For one thing you have to work harder for a living. When I telephone these envious friends, it's no earthly good trying to get through to their offices before ten o'clock because they haven't arrived; and from 12.30 to 3.30 p.m. they're lost causes because they're still at the Mirabelle draining their Martell Cordon Bleu.

In the country you are brought face to face with an almost frightening integrity and innocence; and there is nothing *ersatz* about country living: frost is not simply a word you hear on the weather forecast — it is an exquisite decoration which, in May, can destroy a thousand acres of fruit. Snow is something which can turn me into the Yeti; marooned for days, wondering why-I-did-it. And yet ....

Darmsden has changed; but not that much. The view that pious Hubert saw as he stood by his church all those hundreds of years ago is uninterrupted. And the same marvellous clouds that Constable painted, still go scudding across an East Anglian heaven — reminding me somehow that I was born in London, somewhere under those dishcloth grey skies squeezing their gritty juice over a dejected city. But Suffolk is where I should like to die.

When my turn comes I should be happy to join the others in St. Andrew's churchyard: Stanford and Ellen and Luke and Herbert. But most of all, and not because I'm really anti-social but simply because I should feel more at home, I think I'd like to be buried on the island at Tarston, under the boughs of my old pear tree. I don't think Domesday would mind.

Michael Watkins was educated 'erratically'. Served in a foot regiment in the army; transferred to Intelligence: mostly in Far East. Graduated from army to Fleet Street. Then to America, where he sold Christmas trees along the Pennsylvania state highway; taught water ski-ing in Florida; worked in a Texas department store; put lipsticks into lipstick cases in Brooklyn. Is terrified of the 'American Way of Life', yet feels the U.S. cannot be entirely without hope to have produced Dorothy Parker, Scott Fitzgerald and Louis Armstrong. Likes contrasts: such as drifting down the Ganges in a rowing boat or shooting the rapids on a bamboo raft on the Rio Grande in Jamaica — and living 'two miles up a goat track' in Suffolk. Achieves both by dividing his life between co-editing the East Anglian Magazine *and travelling abroad several days each month to gather material for his articles which appear in* Harpers Bazaar International, The Guardian *and* The Sunday Times. *No hobbies. No clubs.*

Winter sunset.

These two studies of Ramsholt have a strong Visconti-like quality.

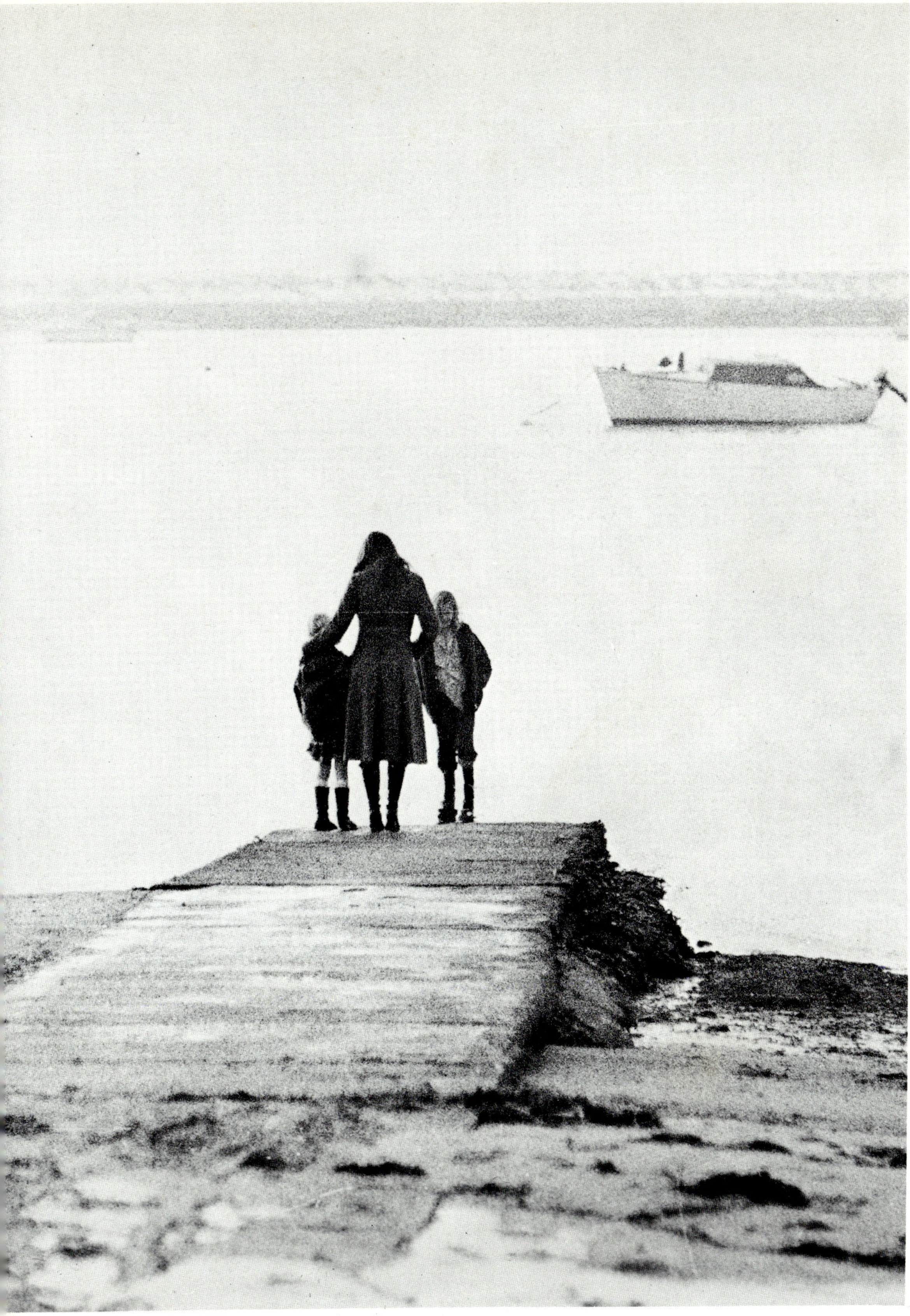

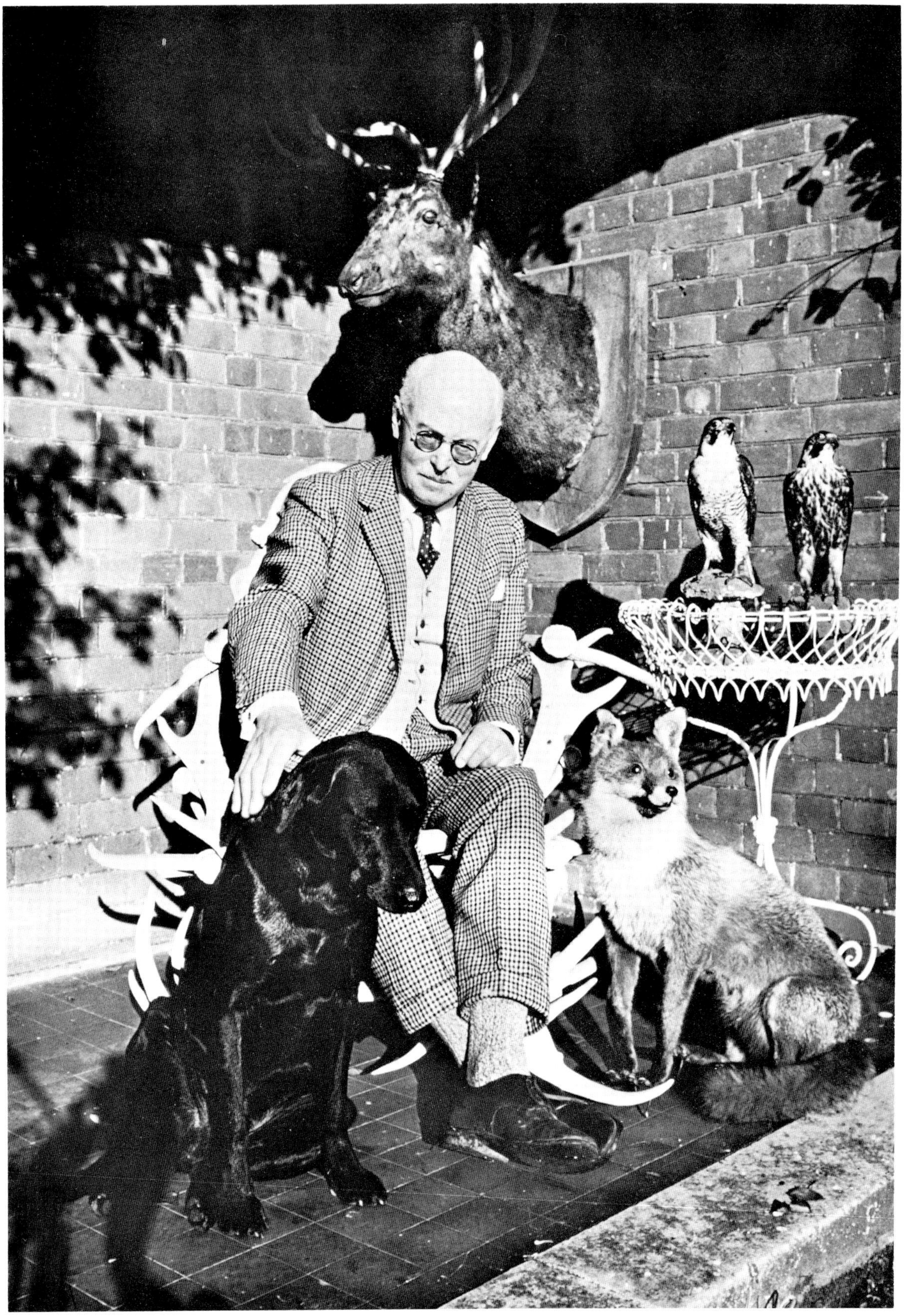

James Wentworth Day
The Essential East Anglia

THE East Anglian is an odd bird of varying plumage. He resembles the pheasant, his avian patron saint. There are at least 11 different species of pheasants running wild in this country. All are of exotic origin. Some have interbred so much that mongrel pheasants are now legion. This applies, almost exactly, to the average East Anglian.

The true East Anglian is, as we had it dinned into us at school, an inhabitant of either Norfolk or Suffolk. He is of the North Folk or the South Folk. The Essex man is not an East Anglian at all. He is an East Saxon, just as a Wessex man is a West Saxon.

We of the Fens where I was born are a rum lot. The men 'from up in the Sheers', whom we regarded as dull clodhoppers relieved by a few bright fox hunting sparks, always called us 'Fen Tigers'. That is because your true Fenman loves a scrap. If he can bust up his neighbours' village feast at the peak of its gaiety, he is delighted. The pugilistic qualities of the average pre-1914 Fenman had to be seen — or suffered — to be believed. They fought with fists, sticks and, worst of all, hobnail boots. They did not, however, use knives, razors, broken glass, studded belts or any of the other small-arms of the long haired louts of today.

This pugnacious quality also marked the Norfolkers and the Suffolkers. Their 'camping' matches, in which two picked sides lined up, charged and then kicked each other in the shins until the wounded were carried off the field on hurdles, sometimes lame for life, were quite as brutal as the Fenman's 'bandy' matches on ice, a sort of ice hockey which usually ended up with half a team being laid out by bandy-sticks.

The Essex man, on the other hand, is on the whole a kindly creature. He is brave enough, God knows. Witness the long line of gallant seamen and great skippers of merchantmen and world-famous yachts which the Essex coast has produced. But in all the local lore of Essex I find no marked parallel to the organised scraps, turn-ups or feuds which marked the Fenman in particular and the men of Norfolk and Suffolk to a lesser degree.

For the purpose of this chapter I have been asked by the Editor (whom God preserve) to include the Fens and Essex as part of East Anglia. So be it. I do almost anything for money.

Consider therefore the background and marked characteristics of these four divisions of the Eastern Counties *vis-à-vis* the pheasant. Consider the breeds of foreign blood which have made East Anglia. The Norsemen dominate the scene. They are the tall, big-boned, blue-eyed, fair-haired giants whom you find all over Norfolk, Suffolk and Essex. They have the Viking blood and the Viking names. There are plenty of Macros in Norfolk who would, if they wished, trace their roots right back to the days of Sweyn Forkbeard. The Kettles, Thirkettles and Thirkells came over in the long-ships, under the raven banners of Odin, as Ketyle. Their ancestors fought the equally tall, fair-haired, blue-eyed Saxons who bore such names as Gurton (The Big One) and Gunaric, whose descendants today in farming Essex are the Wymarks,

Left: James Wentworth Day at home.

Gurtons and the Gunarys. Algar is pure Danish. So are Woolgar and Woolsey, the first deriving from Aethelgar, the second from Wulfgar and the third from Wulfsige. And so one could go on with a few hundred other names of equal ancientry. The Anglo-Norman names are legion.

After the Vikings came the Dutch drainers to the Fens, and the Dutch seamen and merchantmen to the coast, the Flemish weavers in Colchester and mid-Suffolk, the Breton fishermen up all the Essex coast. I think of one of my salt water mates, Algar Mussett, who combines a Danish Christian name with a straight Huguenot surname, originally De Musset. There were Dutch De Witts in the Fens just as there are Dutch D'Wits on Mersea Island in Essex today. I know of a farm labourer who is proud of his name of Bohannon because the parson told him that it is a version of De Bohnn, that puissant Norman Baron who held a fistful of manors in Essex, Suffolk and elsewhere. The Wymarks of Essex, whose name lives in farm-names, derive from Fitz-Wimarc, the Norman.

Plenty of Norman-French names still surviving throughout the Eastern counties, but, oddly enough, few of German origin. Nor are there many Jews, except in the large towns.

The most recent injection of 'foreign' blood into Norfolk, Suffolk and Essex was the 'Scotch invasions' in the latter half of the last century. The Scots came south to the fat farmlands of Essex and parts of Suffolk and Norfolk as a result of the Agricultural Depression. Many a landowner had farm after farm thrown on his hands because his English tenants could not afford to cultivate them. The picture of derelict acres, roofless barns and decaying farm-houses was horrifying. We saw much the same picture between the two World Wars when the policy of importing cheap foreign food at cut prices pretty well cut the throats of half our own farmers. That was a political betrayal of the lowest sort.

When the same blight hit farming in the last century, the late Joseph Coverdale, a shrewd man of North Country origin who was agent to the 19,000 acres of the then Lord Petre's estate, had the bright idea of advertising thousands of acres of vacant farms in the lowland newspapers, particularly those circulating in and around Stirling, Falkirk, East Lothian, Midlothian and the Border Counties. They were offered at peppercorn rents for the first few years provided the tenants agreed to put the land in good heart and farm it properly. The Scots have never been backward in teaching us the values of hard work and thrift. Moreover they produce first rate farmers. Hence the crop of such good farming names in East Anglia as Macaulay, Keith, Hodge, Fleming, Barr, a host of Browns and a regiment of Macs.

All those strains have contributed to the diversive qualities and contradictory quirks which make up the mainstream of East Anglian characteristics.

Broadly speaking — which means diving into dangerous generalisation — one may say that the average Norfolk man is as sharp as his own wind off the sea. Suspicious of strangers, intensely and rightly proud of his county, he, like the more lethargic and softer spoken Suffolker, sees himself as very much a race apart from the rest of England.

Norfolk and Suffolk have almost everything short of mountains, coalmines and salmon rivers which comprise the beauty and natural riches of this country.

There are wide heaths as purple as Scottish moors, splashed with gold of gorse and ling where within living memory red grouse flourished. They were on the Sandringham Estate and to a lesser degree at Elveden in the Breckland. The latter is, or was, until the Forestry Commission smothered it with hideous plantations of unimaginative gloom, a last great relic of England, as neolithic man knew it. His flint pits and underground warrens of mining tunnels still exist at Grimes Graves near Thetford, and all the way to Brandon. Here the Great Bustard, the largest landbird in Britain, as big as a turkey, ran in droves and was hunted on horseback in grandfather's day. They are now extinct. I had in my collection five East Anglian specimens which were sold at Sotheby's with other rare birds for very high prices in 1970.

The Breckland of Norfolk and Suffolk was, until a few years ago, a vast expanse of rust-red brown and purple heath and moorland, about 60 miles long and perhaps 20 miles wide in places. It was unique in England. Today the Forestry Commission plantations cover some 40,000 acres of it. Many other thousands of acres were ploughed up and reclaimed in the last war. Luckily certain tracts of virgin heath such as Thetford Heath, Weeting Heath near Brandon, and East Wretham Heath near Thetford have been preserved by that excellent body The Norfolk Naturalist Trust, the best county naturalist trust in England. Private land-owners have preserved other stretches, but in the main the old wild Breckland, in my youth the most sparsely inhabited part of England south of the Pennines, has largely vanished. Where you can find it, as at Santon Downham and on the Elveden Estate, the primeval magic lingers.

The same primeval magic lingers also on the Broads, another area unique in England. In summer insufferably crowded, with rivers polluted, pubs packed, fleets of boats which would put the Chinese navy to rout, packed with amateur sailors who, by guess and by God, miraculously avoid mass murder. Go to the Broads in spring when the brown winter reeds turn to tender green and cattle marshes are lit by the brassy glint of marsh marigolds and then gentle cuckoo flowers. Then redshank ring their carillon of aerial bells and the courting snipe plunges earthward. The slipstream from his wings vibrates the outspread fan of tail feathers until they drum on the air with a note you can hear half a mile away.

Bitterns boom on indigo nights under the stars. They, like the Great Bustard, were extinct when many of us were boys. Today, thanks to the protection given by land-owners and the many reserves of the Norfolk Naturalists Trust, the Bittern is back in fair numbers. They came over from Holland, heavy winged, to find sanctuary in the ancient Fens which bred their forefathers. Today, the tawny striped yellow-eyed 'budleybump', with his dagger beak and plummed breast and crest, stalks the reed beds as they did when St. Guthlac, the Saxon saint, tossed in feverish delirium on his sheepskin bed in a thatched hut on a Fenland isle and thought them the midnight voices of 'Swart devils'.

That tiny jewel of a bird, the bearded tit or 'reed pheasant', whose song is a chime of tiny bells, has come back from the mists of near-extinction. They and the weeping, wailing plover, the clanking mad-headed coots, comfortable mallards and jewelled teal, with a host of other wildfowl, make the music and the magic of Broadland in spring, autumn and winter when the trippers have folded their tents and stowed away their fancy hats and gone home to the cinema and the telly.

Then, in the reedy wilderness of Broadland, on pewter-coloured rippled waters, where great pike plunge and wild geese and white swans come in high over the North Sea on a windy threnody of wing-born music, the harp strings of the Arctic, the Broads will lift your soul.

There is also that lost and silent land of the sea verges, the immense purple 'moorlands of the sea' between Wells and Salthouse, where the sea thunders on lonely beaches and great clouds of waders wheel and skirl up the lonely coast. From Wells-next-the-Sea to Thornham is another stretch of equally enchanted sea-marshes, with mile upon mile of tawny sand-dunes plumed with marram grass. All or most of this coast is protected from development, either by great land-owners such as the Queen at Sandringham and Lord Leicester at Holkham or by the Norfolk Naturalists Trust and the National Trust who, by the grace of God and the generosity of their supporters have clapped their protective hands on miles of bird-haunted beauty. One has only to go to Caister, near Great Yarmouth, to see how the bungalow-developer can ruin the face of nature. The proposed 'holiday development' at Sea Palling may well turn that lonely fishing village of austere beauty into Appalling-on-Sea.

Suffolk has its full share of this triple beauty of heathland, marshland and lonely sea verges. You find it at its best between Kessingland, south of Lowestoft, all the way down the coast to Felixstowe. There again great land-owners have worked together to preserve the beauty which has enchanted generations of artists and lovers of unspoiled England. The bird-sanctuary at Minsmere, albeit run on somewhat selfconsciously precious lines, is a supreme example of natural marshland, a paradise of wildfowl, waders and harriers, which belongs to a private land-owner and is administered protectively by the Royal Society for the Protection of Birds.

Southwold, Walberswick, Orford, Shingle Street and Bawdsey are coastal towns and villages which have kept their souls. Aldeburgh is a little precious at Festival time but human the rest of the year. Thorpeness is a good example of a well-planned Edwardian holiday village, ideal for children. Inland, round about Westleton Walks, which are still pure heath, Theberton, Sudbourne, Chillesford, Butley, Boyton, Hollesley and Sutton — where the unbelievably beautiful Sutton Hoo treasure was discovered — the old beauty and spirit of the heathland remain. The world of today stops at the A12. Eastward of that high road of traffic you are in undesecrated England.

Mid-Norfolk and Mid-Suffolk have a rich agricultural quality, a tapestry of great woods, an unending panorama of flat, and sometimes dull, plough land and a constellation of lovely villages. It is trite to pinpoint Kersey and Lavenham, Long Melford and Debenham, but they are places of lucent beauty with a host of tiny villages about them which are of equal account.

In mid-Norfolk the heart is warmed by Hingham and Merton with its old, old park and round Saxon church above the little lake with the 'Moot Oak', under whose branches the Saxons held their local parliament. I love Aylsham and Blickling for the Jacobean splendour of the great mansion in which I have slept and listened for a ghost who never came. Swaffham in West Norfolk has all the Georgian calm and quality of a town which, in the 18th century, was the 'Little London' of its surrounding squires. There they held their winter balls and routs and had their town houses. Thus they could cock a gentle snook at the more sophisticated — and far more expensive — lures of London.

Norwich has the great qualities as a splendid city of churches and chiming bells, with its soaring white Norman castle of Blanchtower. Cambridge has also its anthem of evening bells and the heartcatching beauty of colleges old as time with halls of splendour, courts of grace, cloisters of history and alley-ways of mystery, all of it set in and about the green and liquid enchantment of The Backs. These, to my mind, are the two cities of splendour. King's Lynn in its salty Dutch-like way, Colchester with the greatest Norman castle keep in the country and winding streets of beauty; Maldon at the head of the Essex Blackwater where they fought the three day battle against the Danes which decided the fate of England and inspired the epic 'Song of Maeldune', the first great epic poem in the English language, still unspoiled in its rare jumble of Saxon, Norman, Tudor, Queen Anne and Georgian architecture; Clare, blandly beautiful, exquisitely patrician, the unselfconscious jewel of mid-Suffolk; Fakenham, in North Norfolk, which the developers are doing their utmost to ruin; Bures and Nayland and that village gem of the Constable Country, Dedham, with a church of splendour, houses of grace and a couple of pubs, The Sun and the Marlborough Head, of medieval warmth; Wickham Market which keeps the mind and face of a true country town of corn and cattle — full of fat-Suffolk ladies luscious as winter apples. These are among the jewels of beauty which light the face of East Anglia.

I think of Saffron Walden with street after street of splendid Tudor houses, of high-pitched eaves with their carved bressumers and that equally medieval prize, Castle Hedingham, where a tiny square and an entire street remain today almost as they were 400 years ago when the de Veres, Earls of Essex, held kingly court in the castle whose gigantic keep still dominates the little town, huddled at its gates, and commands a sweep of bright fields of corn and the massed greens of woodlands.

Audley End, the dominant house of Saffron Walden, has none of the gaunt strength of Hedingham Keep. It is a Tudor house of singular grace and magnificence, quite one of the best in England, and, luckily, open to public view. Dunmow epitomises the farming prosperity of the Essex countryside in which it sits comfortably, like a mother-duck dozing in the sun. It has a lovely timbered Guildhall, long broad streets of coloured houses, a great village pond in which they ducked the last witch in Essex not so many years ago, and followed it up by trying out the first 'unsinkable' lifeboat.

When I first knew Dunmow, old Lady Warwick, one-time mistress of Edward VII and mother of a very dear friend with whom I stayed, lived at Easton Lodge in the heart of a great park just outside the village. It was a Jacobean house of notable beauty; equally notable was the morning drive of a still-beautiful woman in her little basket carriage drawn by white ponies with white doves fluttering about her, white poodles yapping behind, and, if I remember rightly, a white monkey. The estate was then about 8,000 acres, and in the park of 700 acres was a herd of 570 red deer and fallow deer with 50 goats to liven them up.

Today, death duties have reduced the estate to less than 3,000 acres. The house has been pulled down. The park, during the Second World War, was abominably mutilated by the British Army, who are experts at destroying the beauty of England when once they can get their hands and tanks on it. The deer were shot down ruthlessly by oafs authorised to do so by the War Agricultural Committee. Luckily many escaped into the surrounding woodland where their descendants flourish today in a wild state. Easton Park is a sad place to those who knew it between the two Wars, but the villages of Great Easton and Little Easton still preserve many lovely cottages, some of them self-consciously 'titivated' up by weekenders.

Gosfield, not far off on the road to Cambridge, has lovely cottages with the great four-square Hall of the Wentworths gazing serenely at a lake nearly a mile long. The Tudor part of the court-yarded house was built by Sir John Wentworth in 1550-60 and there, according to our family records, he entertained Queen Elizabeth I on August 19-21st in 1561. The expenses, daily entered in the Household Book, are listed under the following headings: 'Dispens., Buttil., Gard., Coquina., Pullia., Scuttil., Salsar., Aula et Camera., Stabulum, Vadia, et Elimozina;' in plain English, Pantry, Buttery, Wardrobe, Kitchen, Poultry, Scullery, Salt-Meats, Hall and Chamber, Stable, Vails or Presents, and Charity. And the totals at Gosfield were, for 19 August, £107. 9s. 11¾d and for 20 August £104. 12s. 11d.

In 1566, the year before his death, Sir John was troubled with the custody at Gosfield of an illustrious state-prisoner, the Queen's cousin, Lady Katharine Grey, Countess of Hertford, and sister of poor Lady Jane, 'the ten days' Queen.'

Our Elizabethan branch of the Wentworths who derived from the Yorkshire House were settled originally at Nettlestead in Suffolk in about 1420, where the great stone gateway still stands. A branch moved later to Codham Hall which still dominates the valley below Shalford and moved from thence to Gosfield. Their estates covered in all about 25,000 acres. Not one acre remains today. Gosfield Hall is now a residential home for elderly gentlepeople. There was a proposal to pull it down between the two World Wars but fortunately I was able to give this diabolical scheme full publicity in the *Daily Telegraph*, with the result that the house was safe and pigs which had been put in some of the state rooms (believe it or not) were ejected.

East Anglia has a scattered chain of more or less unknown castles, some of them standing out in the fields, others over-lording remote villages and little towns, as at Orford, on the Suffolk coast, which has the only 16-sided Norman keep in the country. Wingfield Castle, rising from a broad moat, like Oxburgh Hall one of the best semi-fortified manor-houses in Norfolk, comes sheer out of the water.

There is Castle Rising, a splendidly preserved shell not far from Sandringham, and Caister Castle, a little north of Great Yarmouth, with the split towers of Hadleigh Castle standing mightily on a high down between Leigh-on-Sea and Benfleet, with a stupendous view across the glittering tides of the Thames Estuary. Among great gatehouses and lesser towers, there is Kirtling Tower, not far from Newmarket, and the splendid Deanery Tower at Hadleigh in Suffolk. Look down the by-lanes and you will find places of moated peace — Parham Hall in the deep heart of Suffolk, Tolleshunt D'Arcy Hall, east of Maldon in Essex with some of the best 16th century panelling in England; and Chatham Hall, half-timbered with rose-red brickwork rising from its walled moat within a few miles of Chelmsford. St. Clere's Hall, not more than a hand-gallop from St. Osyth, whose Priory is perhaps the finest monastic building in East Anglia, has an aisled Saxon hall, as has Tiptofts near Wimbish in the high cornlands of Essex. Horham Hall, near Thaxted, is altogether more baronial and imposing, with not only a splendid moat but one of the few hunting-towers in East Anglia.

My heart was captured in days of youth by the serene beauty of Madingley Hall, a few miles out of Cambridge, in a county which, God knows, has few enough lovely houses.

The truth is that Essex, Suffolk and Norfolk are so rich in small and lovely places that we take them too much for granted. Cambridgeshire villages have been ruined, all too many of them, by hideous white brick which turns to dirty grey, and Welsh slate roofs which hold no warmth of sunlight but merely look like slum-roofs.

Turn your eyes from such Victorian horrors and look for the humbler houses, remote and unrecorded in the antiquarian journals, bare, black-boarded farmhouses lying, treeless and stranded like great ships gone ashore, far out on the endless marshes, with the bitter smell of the sea — Smallgains and Bitchunters, Twinklefoot and Twizlefoot; Marks and Packards and Weatherwick and, lovelier, gentler placed, Reeves Hall and Barling Hall, and the old decoy-house on Old Hall marshes where we ate and slept and cooked our food and hung up strings of fowl while the bullocks gazed with great eyes and lowering horns in at the door.

Loveliest and noblest of all is Layer Marney, aloof and alone in its terraced garden with the benison of chanting rooks, gazing across silent fields and far marshes to the farther sea — a house of enchantments. There is in all England no lovelier herringbone brickwork than in that tall, many-windowed tower which was reared when Hampton Court was built and, I will swear, no more truly Essex home with its old trees and ancient church and great refectory. And in all Norfolk is there a more captivating moated house than Elsing Hall, an early nest of Astleys?

The Eastern Counties have a full tale of the great names of English history — from Boadicea to Nelson, from 'Old Crome' and his luminous School of Norwich Painters to Alfred Munnings, Constable, Gainsborough and those others who learnt to know beauty and paint it in the valley of the Stour. We produced the two greatest names in farming, Coke of Norfolk and 'Turnip' Townshend, with Jonas Webb, the sheep-breeder of a century, and Thomas Tusser who, with John Clare, ranks for all time as a poet of East Anglian earth and sky, hedgerow and marsh.

It would be easy to add a hundred names of splendour to this short list, but I think more particularly of those humbler men of the farms and the humbler villagers whose names alone are guarantee of their lineage, of pedigrees longer and blood more ancient than that of half the upstarts who add strange decoration to our peerage.

D'Wit and Mussett, the one Dutch, and the other Huguenot, and their descendants to-day are fishermen-fowlers, oystermen and yacht skippers, village capitalists who own their own small ships, their own oyster 'lays', and call no man master. Pewter and Cant, Hedgecock and Spitty, Heard and Lèvett, Sycamore and Turner — here are names that are pure Essex and coastal Essex, too. That great yacht skipper, Captain Sycamore of Brightlingsea, has written his name forever in the salty annals of the America's Cup Races, even as Captain Turner, skipper of *Britannia*, that lovely and royal craft which now lies sunk at rest on the floor of the Channel. It was Captain Heard who mastered the Atlantic crossing in the dismasted *Endeavour,* a feat of superb seamanship at which all the world wondered and of which he merely said to me: 'Ah! it was nothing. You know what these newspapers are!'

Was it not old Captain Spitty of Bradwell Waterside who sprang overboard in a January wind at the age of 80 odd and saved a drowning man, his fourth or fifth, I never knew which? As for that, my dear old friend, the late 'Admiral' Bill Wyatt, that artist among shipwrights, when 80, would tell you that he could still bicycle to London, walk 10 miles, drink a gallon of ale, ride a donkey, build a boat, shoot a duck — and sail and win a race in his famous 50-year-old smack *Unity*. These are men indeed.

The deeds of the younger ones of their names will shine forever in the tales of the sea, whenever men of minesweeper and destroyer talk together of the bitter years we have shed behind us.

James Wentworth Day was born on 21 April 1899 at the Marsh House at the bottom of Duck Lane, Exning, Newmarket, where he was Lord of the Manors of Exning Hall and Landwade Hall — his maternal grandfather's place. He is proud of the fact that he has kept one foot in a marsh and the other in a duck-punt ever since. Although 72, he takes an infantile pride in the fact that he can still turn a double somersault backwards and take a cold bath for nine months of the year. This batrachian quality is perhaps induced by the fact that his web-footed maternal forbears have owned land in the Fens since 1320.

He was a right-hand man to Lord Beaverbrook at the age of 23 and later edited The Field, The Illustrated Sporting and Dramatic News *and* The Saturday Review. *He is the author of 43 books including biographies of King George V, HRH Princess Marina, Duchess of Kent and* The Story of the Queen Mother's Family, *which were approved by the Royalties concerned. Princess Marina told him that he 'understood the spider's web of my genealogy better than I do myself'.*

He was on active service in both World Wars in the Army, in the Advanced Striking Force of the RAF and in minesweepers and was semi-paralysed for ten months. He then set out to ride a thousand miles on a horse through the Eastern Counties to describe the transition from the farm horse to the tractor, and set up a national record of 1,330 miles on horseback. The resultant book Farming Adventure *was a bestseller. He has written much on shooting, fishing, dogs, farming and natural history.*

He is married, lives at Ingatestone, Essex, has an enchanting daughter and a notable collection of Old Master Portraits of his Wentworth paternal ancestors including the State Papers, school-books and much furniture which belonged to his hero, Thomas Wentworth, 'The Great Earl' of Strafford, the Strong Man of Charles I's reign who was beheaded on 12 May 1641.

Arthur E. Simmonds.
East Anglian in exile

They have put out the sun in this place,
And I cannot live here.
Not here, where drizzle falls out of grey skies
Seeding soot onto unfertile cobbles.
Not here, where every wall
Which might let little things live in its crannies
Is dead and dark,
Only standing to protect, protect fiercely
As a corpse can, some dirty alley.

I know a place
Where walls are warm and welcoming
To those who lean and leaves that grow
And tiny running creatures.
Where the sun is proud and free,
Not the condemned prisoner these have made him.

A place where rain drives down to eager roots.
Drinking is there and cleansing,
Men can breathe deep, stretch wide, live,
Live, live, live! Oh Hell, this is a place,
Of dirty shallow narrow death
And I cannot live here.

What will I do then? Because here I have work,
Here I have a house, here I have a wife,
Here, God forgive me,
I have brought my children.
Here where the slinking walls, expectant
Drip and drool into the stinking
Shrinking, sour old virgin filthy alleys.
Here where the great mocking hooters crash
Across the town's disease, across the erupted
Houses, paintless pubs, dog-dirtied shop fronts.

I am here, and all mine are here,
In the place where they have put out the sun
And shut out the world
And thrown the muck of their wrong, wrong,
Wrong ideas all over the stars.
But I cannot live here because I have been
In a place where the moon softens the stubble
By night, and the winter trees fight the skies
With great shouts of war.
Because I have stood
Beside potato clamps higher and more permanent
Than the shipyard cranes and the floodlights.

Because I have dirtied my shoes
In the brown rivulet running out of a manure heap,
A streamlet cleaner than the river here,
The damned great slopping river
With the rust all up its sides.

I am here, and I cannot stay here,
And it is not what I will do, but what I must.
One day I will walk away, away down the road
Where the darkborn people drop their trash,
Too tired to carry it even to the gutter,
Away down the unswept road, past the black house
Behind the bent broken railings.
Walk away and leave it.
Miles and miles and all the miles I need,
All the way home.

Till my feet tread fallen leaves again
Under oak trees and by strong hedges.
Till my hands trail in standing corn,
Till grass bends and springs back at my passage.
Miles and miles and all the miles
Years and years and all the years
All the way home.

Because they have put out the sun in this place
And I cannot live here.

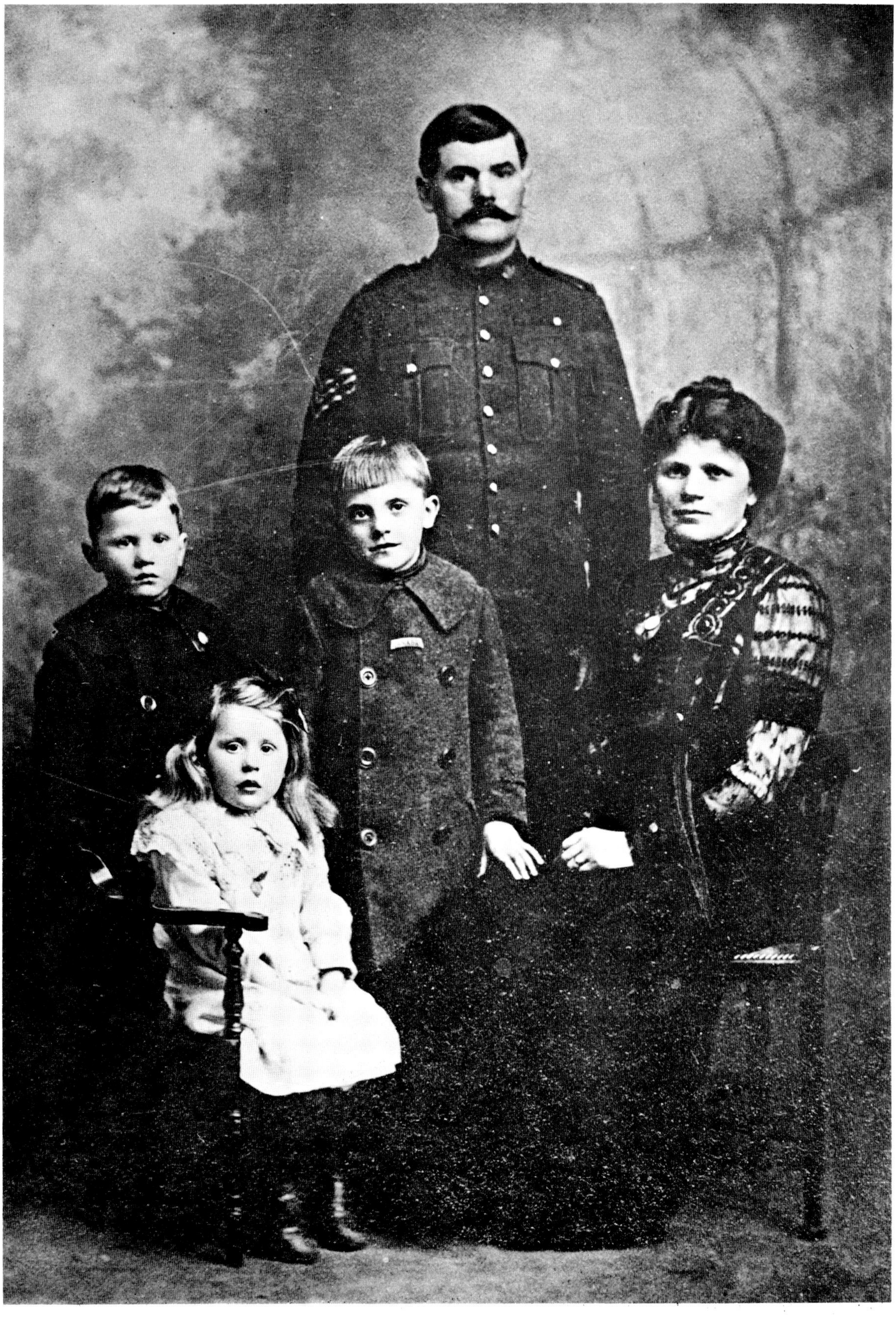

Spike Mays
An East Anglian Childhood

ON 5th August 1907 I was born at Glemsford, Suffolk. A place of lucid light, barely a couple of willow tits' flights from where Constable painted his masterpieces. Born at Barnadiston, Suffolk, John Mays became my father — after soldiering far and wide in the Suffolks. Not long after he had shaken India's dust from his infantry ammunition boots on *HMT Plassey,* he rejoined his parents at Willow Hall, Great Thurlow, Suffolk. Soon, he had met and married Elizabeth Amy Ford — a mighty pretty East Anglian who was born in Bartlow Hamlet, Ashdon, Essex — and made her my mother. If she had three legs she could have walked about six rods and put down a leg in each of three counties; Suffolk, Essex and Cambridgeshire. Before graduating by dead girls' shoes to the envied position of cook in one of Knightsbridge's 'best' houses, she had been scullery maid, housemaid, chambermaid and in-between maid for some of East Anglia's elite.

By the time I had got round to the tricks of remembering, they had increased the family by two. Brother Leslie Gordon (Fon) — only 11 months my junior — and baby sister Audrey Phyllis (Poppy). Although christened Cedric Wesley, following father's overdoses of *Ivanhoe* and chapel hymns, I was abbreviated to 'Ced', and was far too busy to bother about a brother and sister. Things of greater consequence and fascinating interest abounded in the great outdoors near to where we lived in a bungalow. Mother christened it *The Kuldysack*. Apart from a rusty-hinged five barred gate at the end of a flower-banked lane, deep rutted by the iron shod wheels of wagons and hay-wains, there was nothing but nature's majesty. Towering trees, the highest and bushiest of hedges and battalions of song birds. Just for us.

I was jealous of brother Leslie's cascading curls. Parsons picked him up and kissed him. Scruffy tramps and down-at-heel journeymen on their way to the Unions' dosshouses chucked him under his fat chin, made gurgles and clucks and said how pretty he was. Even when I was all tarted up in my best frilly frock, wide scarlet ribbon sash, and even held out my ginger Teddy Bear for inspection, no one noticed or cared. I felt I was unwanted and un-loved because of my straight, stringy mane.

One day I sat lovely Leslie on our three-legged stool and got to work on him with mother's scissors. He squealed like a stuck porker as his curls hit the coconut matting. Mother tore in from the kitchen floury and furious. Just in time to stop me hammering into Leslie's shorn head a nine-inch wire nail. At once I became notorious, and was introduced to strangers as a potential murderer.

The King did not overpay father for being a postman. He had to do another job. Weekdays he would whip off his stiff shako with its shiny peak, his beautiful jacket and red striped trousers. Then, dressed in clothes looking like a Baptist jumble sale, he would rush off to work on a broken-down farm. I liked Sundays. He used to take me to his allotment and tell me about birds, their plumage, flight, calls, songs and habits, as he dug, sweated, planted and hoed to grow us food.

Left: When father came back from Canada.

'If we don't pull up they owd weeds, we'll starve.'

One Sunday I went to the allotment without telling mother. Father had gone to the Harvest Festival, and was bellowing thanks to God at the top of his choirman's voice for all things being safely gathered in. My parents did not thank me for 'gathering in' from their beds every juicy carrot and bold Spanish onion. Instead, I got a brace of good hidings. They didn't understand. 'I were only weedin',' I told them. My backside stung for a week.

Doctors said I was puny, undernourished. Ought to be fed on port wine, full cream and Benger's Food. They did not say who should pay. Only that I should not go to school until I was seven. I beat them, and went when I was six in 1913.

It was a poor time for Suffolk. Unemployment was rife, land was deserted and skilled farm labourers were leaving the fertile fields of East Anglia for distant Canada. Pamphletic promises were made about vast wheatlands, eternal work, high wages, and the finest of homes for the families who could follow with fares paid. Mother was almost unconsolable when father left us, hoping and praying to improve our lot. He failed to find work in Canada. Mother's grief was pitiful when we had to leave The Kuldysack and go to live in that awful cottage at Helions Bumpstead, Essex. It was there she had to sell her wedding gift pictures as part payment to some Good Samaritan who means-tested her and trickled out coins from Parish Relief. She could only work in the fields in the seasons, and took us with her for leazing, gleaning and stone-picking. Ninepence for a bushel of gleaned beans. Perhaps two day's work, with her poor fingers already shredded and bloodied by bayonet-like, scythe-cut beanstalks.

Her first-aid kit was her patched petticoat. From it she tore narrow strips to bandage her fingers against stalks and thistle pricks, and never once complained. I used to be glad to see Uncle 'Wag' come along. Now and again (screwmatics permittin') he would hobble from Wethersfield to give mother a florin from his labourer's pittance. And then we had meat for Sunday dinner. A buck rabbit was only sixpence, and we could sell the pelt to old Germany, the rag and bone man, for twopence, or two paper windmills. Our staple diet was stale bread (one farthing cheaper per quartan than fresh bread), skimmed milk and potatoes. But mother made us say grace before and after. If the food put us down in the dumps she would sing funny verses to prove there were people far worse off than us:

Poor little Joe, out in the snow,
Nowhere to shelter, and nowhere to go;
No mother to guide him, in the grave she lay low,
Cast out in this wide world was poor little Joe.

This always cheered Fon and Poppy, but it made me weep like a land drain. Her fortitude faltered when the black bordered letter came. She gasped as she read, then misty-eyed she croaked to us:

'Auntie Harriett has died. We're going to Ashdon. Granny Ford wants me for the funeral.'

Nine miles was a tidy march on empty bellies. Mother dipped fingers of stale bread into a cup of watered vinegar...'To give it a mite o' taste'. It made me spew into the fireplace, but I had two goes to please her, and managed to keep some down. Sleeping Poppy was put in her pram. Fon stood on the back axle. Old enough to walk, his legs were rickety bent, he was not strong enough. His curls cascaded over the pushing handle and mother's right hand as she took my right hand in her left and pushed off to Reuben's Corner, Ashdon. The half-living marching to see the dead. At Shudy Camps we sheltered from a thunderstorm under the eaves of a reed-thatched barn. I stole a swede from a farmer's field. We bit chunks off it and fed them to our flock like old starlings feeding fledglings. It was sweet after the sour of vinegary bread and gave mother heart to push the pram up long, steep Whiting's Mere Hill. Presently, we were in Granny Ford's. Next day folk came miles — for the funeral. I thought they had come to drink Granny's belly-warming home made wine, and eat up all her lovely 'vittels'.

I had only seen death in birds, and small mammals of our fields and hedges. And there was pretty Auntie Harriett, silent, still and strangely stiff in her yellow box of brass-bound elm. I pressed my finger into the pale of her death-waxed cheek. A dent went in, and did not come out. I thought I had spoiled her face for heaven, and was shocked into screaming nightmares. The ill-wind of her death was good to us. Relations who had not cared enough about our plight to come and say hello came in droves to say goodbye to the dead. Some gave money to mother, others sent parcels of cast-off clothes.

Kaiser Bill's ill wind blew us more good, and for longer. Soon after the Great War began — on the eve of the seventh anniversary of my birthday — Helions Bumpstead seemed to get itself transformed from discontent to defiance and delight. Most of the young men had gone to a secret place called The Front. Because no one told us boys where it was, and no one seemed to come back from there, we thought it must be farther away than Canada. Our old men were jubilant. They congregated in and out of the Marquis of Granby and other pubs, waving flags, singing 'Come and join Lord Kitchener's Army', and 'Britons never shall be Slaves'. And they had been slaves of the farmers all their lives. If the village had gone daft, it was far more cheery, and people spoke to us.

Best of all was father's envelope from Montreal. Funny-stamped, blue-lined and money-fat, it bulged with a brooch for mother and bronze badges for us children; maple leaves, beavers, crossed pickaxes and shovels over a scroll, '1st Canadian Pioneers'. Because of wicked Kaiser Bill, the Canadians had found father a job at last. Soon he would be home with us. Coming across the U-boated Atlantic with the '2nd Expeditionary Force'.

We pinned the badges on our threadbare jerseys; sang bits of 'O, Canada, *we* stand on guard for thee' and 'The Maple Leaf *our* emblem dear'... But it was just boasting and showing off to the Bumpstead boys who had ordinary East Anglian badges. We were soon sorry. Two of our best mates who wore the castle cap badge of the Suffolks soldered on safety pins had a War Office telegram. Their father would not be coming home from The Front. My father came marching home. In brown knee boots, just as I was going through the school gate opposite the church. Button-bright and Sam Browne-belted, he picked me up, kissed and scratched my face with his hedgehog-prickle moustache, then took me to Headmaster Shaw. Standing in the porch he had seen our reunion, and knew what a rough time we had endured while father was away.

'Off home with your father, boy. No school for you this week. God bless you all.'

I had missed him terribly, but never thought his return would bring such changes and happiness. Through mother's care and courage we had been

33

conditioned into the blind acceptance of our lot — the changelessness of the unquestioning poor — aided and abetted by the frequent recital of snatches from her favourite hymn...'O, Thou, who changest not, abide with me'.

Shortly we moved to Ashdon, to the cottage next door to Granny Ford's where mother was born. It was in one of those wonderful country places, a blessed hamlet. No church, no chapel, no shops. Just picturesque clusterings of clay and wattle and timbered cottages thatched with skill in straw and reed. There was but one community centre, the Bonnett Inn, where my maternal grandfather Reuben Ford had his luncheon pint for over 50 years, and his stool still stands in Reuben's Corner.

For the first fortnight of father's leave we became pony-trap travellers, and learned more of the beauty and delights of East Anglia by stopping at old pubs and nice-smelling shops for ginger pop in fat brown bottles with wired on corks and no marbles, and huge wagonwheel biscuits tasting of ginger, cinnamon and sprinkled with little bits of candied peel. The villages were unspoiled and each end or hamlet was another Constable masterpiece. Not a motor was on the road, but there was lots of useful horse-dung, and towering hedges filled with birdsong, the background music to the clip-clop of our pony's steel-tipped toes.

I shall never forget that wonderful fortnight. It was so much more satisfying than the train travels when we camp-followed father to Hounslow, Folkestone, Shoreham, Hastings and dirty bits of noisy London. Boys used to tease me in all those strange playgrounds about my Suffolk accent, and pinch in class and punch in the porches. I was unhappy with these English *foreigners* and wished to be back in fields and meadows.

Canadians crammed Hounslow Heath with sports, gymkhanas and galas. They gave prizes to all the children competitors, and gave me candies, chiclets and sticks of rainbow-coloured chewing gum tasting faintly of mint and monotony. At night our noses would be window pressed. From the Bell Inn a tram ran to Hounslow Heath. The only one in the world with a real searchlight. We used to watch it sweeping the sky for Zeppelins and Gothas. But it didn't pick out one while we were living in that house next to St. Paul's Church.

I learned a riddle from a Hounslow boy, and got a first-class clip of the ear when I tried it on mother....

'How did Captain Robinson, Victoria Cross, escape when the Germans shot him down?'

'How do you expect me to know that?'

'Have a guess, then.'

'No..You say.'

'He greased his arse and slid down a searchlight.'

Mother loved Folkestone. She walked the Leas with the wind fluffing her auburn hair, and I seemed to see the wind, as if it was really visibly present in blowing away from her eyes that pain of long separation, and bringing back the lost roses to her cheeks, to make her lovely and lively again. But I hated Folkestone and its barracky red brick houses.

It was also because I used to sneak harbourwards from bed to watch the wounded come home to England. Coughing from the cruelties of mustard gas like broken cart horses only fit for the knacker's yard; bloodied, bandaged, blinded and propped on crutches and hooked ash sticks as nurses and orderlies led them from ghost-white red-crossed ships to engine-purring ambulances of the dark dreadful nights. There was no one else. Only sentries in boxes with bayonets fixed; some half asleep, others awake and puffing stealthily at cigarettes. And myself, crouching, scared stiff behind that wall pillar, but unable to repel the attraction. Mornings were different. The red town was bee-hivey with activity, people, bands, flags and song. It seemed to me such a shame that so few met them on their broken-bodied return — after all that palaver to send them to The Front. My favourite uncle, Bert Whistler, did not return. Filled with German machine gun bullets he was buried soon after he was commissioned in the South Staffordshire Regiment. He was always smiling, smart and kind, and taught me to tie the Staffordshire knot.

We came back to the peace of Brick and Stone Villa when father went to The Front and started to get wounded five times, and to stay there for the remainder of the war and for many years afterwards. There were only four children of school age in our hamlet...Fon and me, and two girls. Dolly and Miller Cooper used to kick our front door...'It's twenty ter nine. Hurry up, Ced!'

When the sun shone and dew had dried, we shunned the flint-faced road which led for a mile to school and took to the field paths and meads. I used to loiter at Mill Pond, hoping to see a moorhen or kingfisher, or net frog spawn and tadpoles for my string-handled jam jar. Perhaps cut bits of willow for making decoy whistles, and do all manner of really useful things. But Dolly would tug my jersey, or my ear...'Drat you, Ced..The bell's gone..Bugger it, we're late ag'in!' And we joined hands and raced across lush grass, golden with buttercups and the paler pagles; making rabbits show their white tails before skeltering into their burrows. Not a book, pen or pencil lurked in my school satchel. Just snares, a mole trap, two peashooters, bits of binder string from the big reel of the Massey Harris, a whalebone stolen from Granny Ford's stiff stays to make another peashooter, and a bag of glass ailly marbles. Baked hard in the 'bakus' and two years old — the right age to do the most mischief to the conkers of other boys — was my prize conker, strung on window sash cord. It was already a 32-er, and was wrapped with my dripping sandwiches for safety. If I was caught with 'an owd bakey' I would be sent to Coventry and made to pay the cheat's forfeit, six glass aillies.

Like most other boys I made my own toys from wood cut from copses or scrounged from shopkeepers. Elder and oak for peashooters and pop-guns; willow for whistles, beech and wych elm for spinning tops (hobnails from Uncle Will's snob's shop for the steel tips). From Vic Eason, general storekeeper cum postmaster, small bundles of packing case wood for bird-scaring rattles, sledges, and bull roarers. The latter a piece of wood cut into an oval with sharply serrated edges, attached to a cord. When swung round the swinger's head it gave off a deafening roar. Hazel was used to make straight arrows, but young elm was best for long bows and cross bows.

When not too busy shoeing Shire horses, or twisted by the torture of his rupture, blacksmith Bill Smith made iron hoops and trundlers (hoop guides) for sixpence. Sometimes on the 'strap'.

'If you're hard up, boy, pay a penny a week, or pump me bellers. Take yer pick'.

I pumped the bellows, and enjoyed watching sparks dart as Bill thundered like Thor at glowing metal to make horse shoes, and clouds of steam and bubbles in his trough as the shoes were dipped and sizzled. But I used to cough when the yellow smoke from burning hooves tickled my throat and made my eyes water. Fon and I were the only ones with steel runners on our sledge. Bill put them on bits from the soapbox wood for nothing, and gave us three shiny horse shoe nails to bore holes in our conkers. Just because we led two Suffolk Punches to Overhall Farm in a hailstorm. We also made flails, from ash sticks and bits of leather. Father suggested it after we had grumbled about threshing our gleanings with ordinary sticks. In no time at all we could swing the flail 'figure-of-eight'. Then threshing was fun, not work any more.

In the summer holiday when roses blazed in cottage gardens — long after Ted Allen brought mother his first chip basket ('fer a taster, Liz') as he did each year before nailing the notice on his gate 'STRAW BERRYS FOR SALE' — brother Fon and me were busy in the fields and woods. I led the wagon horses at haytime and harvest, and hollered louder than boys on other farms..'Howd ye foight' and 'Whoah, there!' Life was healthy in clear air over golden sun-drenched stubbles. I felt fitter and stronger than puny Jack Dempsey, Joe Beckett, Georges Carpentier and those other boxers and athletes Tom Webster caricatured in the *Daily Mail,* and I was in secret training for the Championship of the World. I had three live punchbags. The bulg-

Grandad Reuben Ford at Walt's cottage.

ing muscles over horses' forelegs. Mine were at the top of the near-fore of my three horses, Jockey, Boxer and Punch. I clenched my fist and got my weight behind each knockout blow as I lashed out when sheaves were pitched to the loader at each shock. But the hairy giants never fell for the count. Sometimes — just as if a gnat had landed — the muscle gave a bit of a twitch.

When grain and hay had been carted, and we had sung Harvest Home in church, and in the Bonnett Inn for the Horky (the harvester's own ceremony), fork-sticked and basketed I scoured hedges for blackberries, crab apples, the princely quince, black and white damsons and sultry sloes; and then the emerald meadows for piss-the-bed dandelions, cowslips and bits of bitter sorrel, for the jam and wine making. And when the days shortened I poached.

Rabbits, hares, pheasants and partridges fell to my coppery snares — left in glittering coils by men of the GPO, who had tried by telegraph to connect us to civilisation. Gentlemen came, in motors, all dressed in heavy overcoats, to give me sixpence for an untorn moleskin. But before they came I had tracked down the blind furriness by counting his mountains and putting my trap between his last earthy Everest and drinking place. It took a week of cunning before I placed his pelt on a board; pinned with spikes of blackthorn, facing the sun — after I had fed the flesh to my fangy ferret.

In all my loneliness I was never alone or bored in fields and woods. But in winter, or when the rains came, I read books and comics. And in the *Magnet* and the *Gem* I read about strange people who seemed to know little of life and appeared to resemble the local grammar school boys. All books, papers and pencils. Sometimes I envied them, and then I counted my blessings. I was 10 when I had my own garden. After seeing peaches on the sun-kissed mellowed walls of the library gardens, and spiky-leaved plants and flowery ferns in the greenhouse. I told Bill I wished I was a gardener, like him. He whisked me to his potting shed, chock full of the smells of peat, herbs and earthy flower pots. In little envelopes stuck on sticks he put in seeds, and gave them all to me...

'Mark this...Make yer own garden, boy!'

Never was a plot better tilled. Not a midge could fly sideways through the mesh of black cotton I criss-crossed over my precious seeds. At night I knelt and prayed for them. For countless ages nothing happened. I lost hope and interest until mother pointed them out. 'They're a good half inch, but you can pull that one out fer a start...It's a weed.'

'Can't be,' said I. 'They're from Walton's Park, the head gardener's seeds.'

'God is the head gardener. He makes weed seeds, too. Go, now...Ask YOUR head gardener.'

Bill said mother was right. When I asked how to tell weeds from flowers, all half-an-inch high, he jabbed me with his potato dib:

'Easy, boy. Pull the lot up. Anything growin' arter that's bound to be weeds'.

Ashdon Elementary School was hardly worthwhile in terms of Education, but its pupils were lively and intelligent and deserved a better fate. Our teachers had the most valuable human qualities, but were compelled to cram our minds with inconsequentials; dead and alive monarchs of the realm in terms of history; and from the 'big room's' map of the world bright pink blobs were pointed to us by an untipped billiard cue as we were enjoined to be Patriotic, cherish the British Empire, and make the Land of Hope and Glory — and Mother of the Free — wider and mightier still; with the help of God and his local servant the Reverend Hartley (C. of E.), former Chaplain of the Royal Navy, who put us in our inferior places once a week as we sung for him his favourite hymn:

The rich man in his castle, the poor man at his gate;
God made them high or lowly, and ordered their estate.

We chanted tables up to 12 times 12, learned the three Rs and patriotic passages from Shakespeare and Kipling.

My education began in that school when headmaster William Tuck returned from his house next door with tears in his eyes, and a tin kettle in his hands from which he poured warm water to wash the feet of a shoeless child. He wept when I took him a basket of blackberries and mushrooms. Because he had no pence he gave me a book, *Tales from Shakespeare,* and stuck in its front an ornate label bearing the three scimitars of Essex in red and gold, and 'Prize Awarded to Cedric Mays'. When I was 12 he recommended me for a scholarship to a grammar school. I passed the examination, but could not go. My parents could not afford the fare and the 'uniform'. This was a bitter blow for my father: 'I hoped you'd be lifted outer the rut, son. But you'll hev to go to work to help put food in the bellies of your brother and sister.'

I adored Mabel Eason (née Smith), the charming daughter of our blacksmith, and thought her to be an East Anglian angel who worked miracles at a moment's notice. When I was leaky-booted, sockless and chilblained, she washed my feet in warm water. She taught in day school and Sunday School, played the piano for both, plus the organ for All Saints (Matins and Evensong), and two nights a week at choir practice when she taught us boys fine music from the anthems of Handel and Bach. I used to walk two miles from our hamlet to Church End four times on ordinary Sundays, and five times on Holy Communion Sundays, and the church was nearly always filled. My Sunday School attendance book bristled with cloud-puffing seraphs. On *early* attenddance I received to stick into it a biblical stamp bright with haloed cherub trumpeters, all blowing jets of pink wind. A filled book qualified me for free attendance at the Sunday School Treat (Parson's bun struggle) where, in the Rectory meadow, we played games, said grace twice, ate jellies, blancmanges, cakes and buns, then raced in sacks, with eggs and spoons, under tarpaulins, sometimes with one leg tied to a leg of another boy, for money. I once won first prize for the sack race, only because I was slow and all the others fell over, and went home delighted with a whole silver 'thrupenny joey'.

Church and Sunday School made a deep impression on me, particularly at Harvest Festival when our church was decorated with all the good things of the earth that were grown in our fields, but my real education began in the back yard of a pub, the Rose and Crown Inn. At school dinner break I used to go to the former Cromwellian coachouse which had been converted into a builder's workshop, where Christopher Ketteridge — six years my senior and apprenticed to his father York as a bricklayer — would be mixing cement. Chris was a fine scholar who had won scholarships but could not take them up. He used to draw murals and write poetry on the white plaster panels between the oak timbered studwork. No sooner did father York's eye light upon them than they would disappear under two deft swipes of his three-pronged distemper brush. One poem earned his respect and stayed. It appeared to be written in Latin. Chris and I used to recite it but I did not understand a word for weeks:

> *Sedito sali cum sedi anita longa me. Fors uper*
> *abit o meta pio vel summamante. Foro midea miartis*
> *ures O cantu caref orme? No tature nota bene jo*
> *no dux nopes ome. O cari cantat allino tos super*
> *longae. O misere mi salis dum no donna mor tome.*
> *O mari aggi molle cum anita mihite.*

One day Chris told me how he had found it printed in a copy of *John o' London's Weekly,* given to him in a bundle of papers by the matron of the

Waifs and Strays Home (now more politely known as the Orphanage) in Rectory Lane. We have laughed about the simple interpretation for as long as we have been firm friends — 53 years.

>*Said I to Sally, come, said I, and eat along of me.*
>*For supper a bit of meat, a pie of veal, some ham and tea.*
>*For O, my dear, my heart is yours, O can't you care for me?*
>*No tater, not a bean, Joe. No ducks, no peas, O me.*
>*O care I can't at all, I know, to sup along of he;*
>*O misery, my Sally's dumb, no donna more to me.*
>*O Mary, Aggie, Molly, come and eat of my high tea.*

Chris lived with his parents in the nearest mill cottage to Bragg's Mill, an old post mill standing as a fine and sturdy landmark high above the village. We made it our private university. By its grindstones, night after night when most of the villagers were sleeping, from books on Pelmanism, and others by the Frenchman Monsieur Coué on Auto Suggestion, Chris subjected me to the perils of Intelligence. High on the list were Observation, Concatenation and Recollection. I was sworn on my Boy Scout's honour to state loudly on waking, 'In every way, and on every day, I am gradually getting better and better'. And I did, and I was; for I began to take real notice of folk, creatures, birds, flowers, crops, fields, woods and footpaths, even to counting the nails in farmhands' clodhoppers and in their gates and wooden fences. It was time-absorbing, revealing and worthwhile. Each night I would be tested by my bricklayer professor before we took out our books in the candle-lit mill loft.

We read Rider Haggard, Edgar Wallace; then sat on the mill's sails reading chunks from Macbeth with owls hooting all around and odd dogs wailing to get the effects right. We invented our own games and pastimes, from making the first cats' whisker wireless set in the hamlet, to creating a circus game which we played with great dexterity in Mill Meadow, using rubber quoit rings and hazel sticks; but we both worked hard during daylight, even though I was still at school. Chris with his trowel and bricks, building permanent memorials to his talent, whilst I had been taken on as a bootboy at Walton's Park, where everyone treated me with kindness, respect, and taught me many useful things about life. I finished cleaning boots and knives, and grooming ponies, and collecting drinking water and fire kindling in the dog cart when I was 14 and a bit, then went to work at Place Farm where Mr. Bidwell, the kindly tenant farmer, let me work as often as possible with my father, whom he had taken on as a labourer because, as a war wounded soldier, he could find no other work. We were still wretchedly poor, but reasonably content. My father taught me to sharpen scythes, sickles, shears and other edged tools, and how to use them.

I felt amply compensated for low wages by working outdoors, in spring and summer, and not only during harvest time, and my heart used to sing when I was in Langley Wood with my father and Pipper Free; cutting down trees, clearing the glades of bushgrowth with saws, axes, bill-hooks, beetles and wedges. My horse-leading dreams of becoming a boxing champion were renounced, for I had become the world's finest lumberjack. As a tree fell to our axes, cracking its limbs and swishing its brushwood to make blue jays and harsh magpies shriek protests, I would holler 'TIMBER!' louder than any woodfelling French Canadian, then collect the sweet smelling chips, the fellers' perks, for firewood.

Artists infiltrated into fields and woods to paint and sketch us in spring and summer. No one bothered in winter, not even 'folk singers' who compose swede-bashing madrigals for the BBC. But my friend Poddy Coote and I kept going in winter's worst days by singing hymns and psalms, clad in our improvised duffel coats, one sack apiece slit down one side and put over the head. Cold and bleak were the winds and fields as I 'lifted' mangolds and sugar beet, with ice in their leaves. Prickly, itchy and humiliating were those barley and rye spikes that raped my stockings and jersey and took root in them for days after I had 'took chaff' from the threshing machine, or mixed the cattle bait.

I might still have been a farm labourer if I had not found a sweetheart while still at school. We got on like houses afire until those winters of farmworking, walking all the woodlands and field paths from the time we were in Standard VII. She was never out of my mind. Trees still stand bearing the scars of bleeding hearts and cupid's arrows I cut over our initials in their young bark when we were young and so much in love.

But winter, too much of it, and wages, too little of them, took me from her. Brother Fon went first. He used to walk five miles to and from Saffron Walden, six days a week for 10 shillings a week, before joining the Grenadier Guards as a drummer boy. A month later I followed, and left the beauty and poverty of East Anglia for Canterbury, the city of Britain's cavalrymen, and became a bandboy on 17th March, 1924, in the Royal Dragoons.

Only one month ago, 47 years since I left Bartlow Hamlet, I went to Haverhill, Suffolk to see brother Fon. Fifty years earlier we had both gone to Haverhill Gala, where women were gay with flower-bedecked hats the size of beehives; all bustly of bottom and leg-of-mutton sleeved. They had travelled miles by road, in pony traps, wagonettes and dog carts. All candy-striped and shiny in the strong light, huge balloons with men and women in their baskets were straining on ropes, ready to take off. There were hurdy-gurdies, swings, tinkers, clowns, coconut shies, hokey-pokey stalls, horses and ponies for the judging; long grass, high hedges and higher spirits. There was music and laughter. Even after we left it seven miles behind on our way home I heard the roundabouts singing in the wind. I shall never forget the tune, and certainly not the words. For when I sang the choirboy's version to her, mother told me to moderate my language as she landed me a first-class clout of the ear. I still like the words:

Oh, oh, oh, my sweet Hortense,
Got hairs on her belly like a barb wire fence.

So in March 1971 I tried to recapture the beauty and vitality of my East Anglia, and walked nine miles to retrace mother's steps before the Kaiser's War when she pushed the pram to Auntie Harriett's funeral. The barn under which we had sheltered looked mothy and slattern of thatch. Shudy Camps Church was locked, bolted and barred. As if the stench of dung from the new battery pig farm was trying forcibly to enter where humans had ceased to go. But in a copse near the road junction was an unusual shrub. Half a century ago Cousin Charles Ford amused himself while waiting each morning for a tumbril cart to take him to work by trimming blackthorn into the shape of a pheasant. Just a few twigs a day with his shutknife, over all the years. I was delighted to see that it had escaped the teeth of those rapacious chain saws which have hacked all those life-bearing hedges to ground-level nothingness.

Fields are exposed to that keen wind from the Urals. There are no more Suffolk Punches, just tarpaulin draped tractors. There were no pony traps. I counted 85 motors whose drivers neither waved nor offered me a lift; not that I needed the latter. Two rabbits had been ground into the road by whirling wheels, and one thrush. Only one pair of human feet other than mine were on the road, although I met three people not in motor cars. At Nosterfield Farm there were two young girls. One seated on a pony, the other on a bicycle with her hand in the mane for towing. I told the young equestrian to press her knees to the saddle, her toes up, her heels down, and her legs behind the girth and ease and feel the reins. She told me her pony's name, said I knew about horses, and was my tie the Pony Club tie. I said it was, in a way. It was The Blues and Royals tie....'Have they a club in Saffron Walden?'
The feet almost on the ground belonged to the new landlord of the old Bonnett Inn, who did not know where I could get a cup of tea on a Sunday afternoon. I was pleased to see him being hurled on an airborne walk by his great dog.

I walked past Brick and Stone Villa with a lumpy throat. Granny Ford's and OURS had been knocked into one cottage with an altered name, BRICK AND FLINT COTTAGE. Where father had his wonderful garden there is now an ultra modern bungalow, with all mod. cons. and a garage. Where towered the trees of the Golden Noble and William pear, there is concrete.

I walked another mile to the school to knock on Mrs. Smith's door in Collier Row. She took the cottage next door when Granny Ford died, and was a great friend of mother's. I asked if I walked up Church Hill would I be in time for Evensong. I did not say that I would like to see the grave where John and Elizabeth are laid.

'Oh, Ced, boy...Don't hev it no more. Nobody turns up. Hev arternoon service instead. Parson might soon knock that on the head. On'y three turned up last week.'

And then I went to the back yard of the Rose and Crown, where Chris used to mix cement. I had a drink with the ex-Grenadier landlord before I looked out of the front window. There was a motor car at almost every house; but not a soul in sight. The blinds were down. As if from the death of my village. But the same flickerings of light appeared on all the blinds at the same time. I looked to the stars, almost obscured by TV aerials....When I was a child I understood as a child. I am so glad that I have not yet put away my East Anglian childish things.

Spike Mays was born in Suffolk in 1907, and brought up in Ashdon, Essex, which he describes in the first volume of his autobiography, Reuben's Corner. *At 16 he enlisted in the Royal Dragoons as a band boy and his second book,* Fall Out The Officers, *deals with that period of his life. At the age of 44 he won a scholarship to Newbattle Abbey College, and later went on to Edinburgh University. He is particularly elated by Maurice Wiggin's review of* Reuben's Corner *in The Sunday Times: '... After due reflection, I want to say that in my opinion this is a better book than the celebrated* Cider with Rosie.'

41

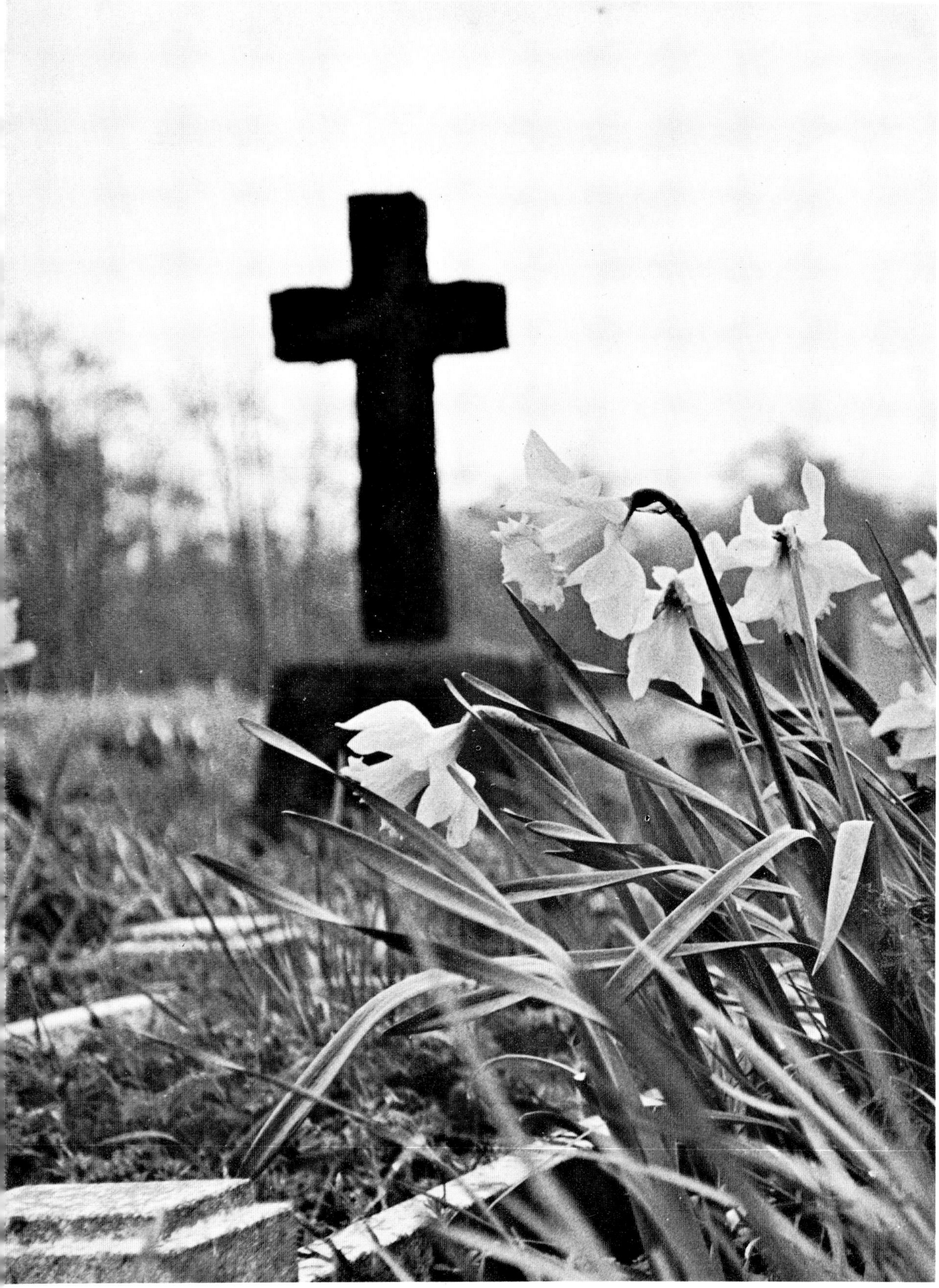

Norah Lofts
Where My Heart Lies

UNDER the merciful, drug-induced haze something of the mind remains, running back into the past, as do the minds of the very old. Because there is no future. Because there is no future for the very old; no future for me who do not even know how old I am, except that I am young and must die tomorrow, for crimes I did not commit.

A merciful death they say; the King is merciful; Death is merciful. Tomorrow the sword. One flashing stroke. No pain they say. A headsman, specially skilled, is being brought from France to end what should never have been begun. No! No! There were happy days, too. Think of the happy days, the young days, the free days under the arching skies, in the crystalline air of East Anglia.

Blickling in Norfolk is where the memories begin. Mary, my sister, George, my brother and often Thomas Wyatt my cousin, left in the charge of a governess whom we called Simonette. For Mary and George and me she was mother, too, ours being dead; and father, since ours was seldom at Blickling. He had another estate, Hever in Kent, only 30 miles from London and that suited him, assiduous courtier that he was. Simonette ruled our lives. In many ways she was unorthodox. She did not believe that our ponies would throw us and break our necks, or fear that we should lose our way and starve to death like the Babes in the Wood, or think that contact with common people would make us verminous and foul-mouthed. Mornings were for lessons and we were expected to present ourselves at the supper table, washed, brushed and not smelling of anything — Simonette had a sensitive nose. Between times we were quite free to ride and walk, to wander, stop and stare and share, in quite an unusual way, in the life of the countryside.

Part of the charm of both Norfolk and Suffolk is the variety of landscape, of scenery. Blickling lay on good ploughland, with oaks and elms standing in clumps; but within a day's ride, almost within a day's walk, there were woods so dense, so untouched save at the fringes by charcoal burners, that the red deer had no fear of man; and areas of soil so poor that only sheep could live on the sparse, thyme-scented grass, and a few places where the soil was so stiff and stubborn that double teams of oxen were needed to draw a furrow. We knew them all. Later — and again thanks to Simonette — we knew another region, the coast.

Blickling, and all the other manors that we knew, consisted of three great open fields, divided into long strips by baulks of land left unploughed. Every year one field grew wheat, the other barley or oats; and one lay fallow, resting. The resting field was always prettiest, a carpet of wild flowers in summer. Each manor also had a vast stretch of common land which served as pasture for the oxen, the cows and the goats, a few donkeys, an occasional horse.

There was a day in the year, in the early spring, not noted in any calendar except the country mind, called Plough Monday. It was a sight to see; all the ploughs out, unhurried, moving at a steady pace, almost keeping time and

Left: Gissing, Norfolk.

the furrows lengthening, tilting over, richly brown and shining; and then, as the sun lowered and paled, taking on a purple tinge, like amethysts, like the meadow orchis.

After the ploughing, the sowing. That again as orderly and well timed as the ploughing; each man, on his own furrows, with a basket hanging at about waist level; hand in, hand out, scatter but move as you scatter, that was the secret. Once Thomas (or was it George?) made an irreverent remark — 'You know, that fellow in the parable must have been pretty blind!' We all laughed. It took little to amuse us then.

Best of all — though there was sadness in it because it meant the end of summer — was the harvest. In this we could share. Everybody turned out to help with the harvest. The men moved ahead, cutting the brittle stems and throwing the severed corn backwards; women, children and old men and runabout creatures like 'they young Bullens' as we were known, followed and made the cut corn into sheaves by binding an armful with the flexible strands of honeysuckle or the creeping plant known as Old Man's Beard, or with plaited rushes. Six such sheaves, lodged together, ears of corn upward, made a 'shock'. Behind the sheaf-binders and shock-makers came the gleaners, the even younger children, the older men and women, hawk-eyed in the stubble for a single ear which might have been dropped.

For our casual and purely voluntary labours in the harvest field we were very well rewarded with mugs of home-made ale and a kind of bun, called a Fourses-Cake, because it was served at about four o'clock in the afternoon. To describe, to remember, the taste of Fourses-Cake is impossible, meaningless. A thing made of dough, very slightly sweetened and spiced and in rare cases enriched by a currant or two. Out of its context, nothing, but on a hot afternoon in the shade of a tree that marked the field's boundary, between gulps of ale, it was as good as anything I have ever tasted — and I have lived in two courts, that of France and of England.

One summer we missed the harvest because Simonette thought it was time for us to see the sea. Perhaps she longed for it herself — she was a Breton, born and reared at Quimper. So that year with servants and baggage — and with Thomas, I remember that because of the songs — we all went to Brancaster and lodged in a very curious, tumble-down place, part inn, part pilgrim hostel, loosely connected with the religious house at Walsingham.

On our way to Brancaster we visited the shrine of Our Lady of Walsingham which was as beautiful as the legend attached to it. It was said that when, 500 or more years ago, the Infidel ran over the Holy Land and destroyed Our Lady's little house in Nazareth, She appeared to a wealthy woman in Walsingham and requested her to build a replica, saying that She Herself would provide the specifications. Of course, by the time we saw it, it had been added to and changed. The shrine was heaped with gifts given by the pious or by the fortunate people who had experienced miraculous cures on the holy spot.

Twelve? 13? My date of birth was uncertain, but I was old enough to be aware of my physical blemishes, the rudimentary extra little finger on my left hand, the mole, large as a strawberry, on my neck. Would any man wish to marry a woman so marred? I prayed — Holy Mary, Mother of God....half-hoping that the ugly things would drop off on to the black marble floor. No miracle for me, however. My ill too trivial, the Blessed Virgin aware of greater need, the sick, the lame, the blind.

Like all pilgrims we had left our shoes in the little Slipper Chapel and gone barefoot to the shrine. No hardship in summer with the dust velvet-soft underfoot and between our toes.

Then there was Brancaster, pale brown sand stretching as far as eye could reach, to left and right, and at low tide, to seaward. At low tide there were pools left in the sand; we jumped or waded through them to the next uncovered stretch. We played at being explorers, Christopher Columbus, Vasco de Gama; we pretended to hunt for treasure and found it, in the form of cockles, to be taken home and eaten, fresh boiled for supper, and in pretty shells. Once I found a piece of amber. Then we would come home, singing one of the songs which Thomas made easily. In the seemingly endless space our voices sounded thin and sweet, less than the sea-gulls' cries.

The memory of Thomas' songs brings another. Not long since, the King, a maker of good songs, made one which runs:
> *Oh western wind, when wilt thou blow,*
> *That the small rain down may rain?*
> *Christ, that my love were in my arms*
> *And I in my bed again!*

Christ, that I were back in Brancaster, ignorant of the love that concerns itself with bed, knowing only the fondness that lasts better and does not seek to destroy, the fondness I felt for George and Mary and Thomas and Simonette.

I must not think of George — he went to the block yesterday with four others, all accused of treason in that they had had carnal knowledge of me, Henry's queen. It was his wife who accused him, jealous because with him, too, fondness had lasted......

A thought like that, a thought of the morrow, can jerk me out of the dreams and the memories. I rear up, I scream, I say things which, in full possession of my mind, I should not say. Those with me, locked into this stone cell which for me has but one exit, murmur, soothing, saying 'drink this!' I drink and sink back. I think — For the innocent, however faulty, but innocent of that for which they were accused, for which they suffered on this earth, Purgatory should be brief. We sojourn there, and then — Paradise. Paradise cannot be measured in time or in distance, there everything will be one, the wood behind Blickling, where that rare flower, the oxslip, grows, the field under plough, the harvest field, the Shrine at Walsingham and the beach at Brancaster, all one...Less absurd than it may sound. What colour is a diamond? No colour, but holding within it the possibility, no, more, the existence of all colours. So, I think, will Paradise hold, simultaneously, all the good experiences unmindful of time or space...

Norfolk. Suffolk. Must I remember what intervened?

Echoing back, faint as the voices of the children on the sand banks, Mary, the King's sister, furious, weeping, saying that the King of France was an old man, that she did not wish to marry an old man with broken teeth and foul breath. Protest availed her nothing. France and England must be either hand-clasped in friendship or at one another's throats. So Mary Tudor must marry Louis XII of France, and must take four English girls with her, for company. I was one.

Then in a few months the old king of France dead and Mary married to the handsome swaggering man she loved, Charles Brandon, Duke of Suffolk. But I stayed on with the new Queen, Claude.

Must I, even in memory, try to vindicate myself? Queen Claude was the most pious woman in the world; we, her ladies, lived like nuns. Does one emerge from such influence promiscuous, lascivious, incestuous, false, as I am said to be? Would Katharine, Queen of England, second only to Claude in piety and correctitude, have taken me into her service years later when, because war threatened, I came home? These are questions that have never been asked and it is too late now. Tried unfairly and condemned. Tomorrow to die...

Think of other things.

Of love? Though it ended badly. Perhaps between the happy, carefree days in Norfolk and the healing days in Suffolk, Harry Percy should be remembered, for our days were happy, too, the few there were. We were in love, the kind of love that is content with a stolen glance, a pressure of the hand in the dance, a kiss, almost chaste behind a screen. But Harry's father, Earl of Northumberland, came roaring down from the north and was closetted with Wolsey, that great red cardinal and together they concocted a tale. Harry was troth-plighted, they said; a thing as binding as marriage, to another girl.

The kind of love there was between Harry and me comes but once in a lifetime; and only once, thank God, comes the kind of heart-break that I took home to Hever, misery eating me thin, resentment gnawing me hollow. 'A graveyard cough', said my kind little stepmother. Bed and hot possets of honey and horehound, good for the body maybe but useless to the screaming mind. Kind, she was kind, endlessly kind, but no company, a woman of humble origin, devoted to, yet frightened of my father, and presently even more frightened of the King.

And yet she saved me; out of her kindness and her fright, torn between her sense of what was right and proper and her fear of offending, she saved me.

I do not wish to remember, I will *not* remember Henry Tudor, King of England who loved me so much that he broke with the Pope in order to marry me, who loved me so little that, frustrated in his desire for a son, caught by a pretty face, he willed me to death on a charge that will make my name a hissing and a byword forever. I do not wish, and yet I must, if I am to think of Suffolk.

He began coming to Hever, making his object plain. Me for his mistress. I, now said to be the ultimate in unchastity, refused this dazzling offer. Ah, I know that now they say — cunning, crafty, her eye on the crown from the first! Quite untrue; how could I have known then that a firm 'No' would not rebuff him permanently? As for crowns; heaped on top of one another as high as St. Paul's they would have meant nothing to me then, with my graveyard cough and my broken heart.

Father said angrily: 'If you wish to live like a nun go live in a convent.' What did I care, all places the same to me? But my little stepmother, wanting me away and the strain ended, did not wish me into a convent. Could I not go, she suggested meekly, to my aunt Calthorpe at Erwarton, for the good of my health? To me, privately, she said: 'His Grace will not be able to ride to Erwarton as the mood takes him.'

Nobody rides into Suffolk as the mood takes him. The roads deter. The upkeep of the roads is supposed to be shouldered mainly by the inhabitants of the places connected by a certain stretch. In sparsely inhabited country like Suffolk this is a heavy burden, evaded whenever possible. Where there is much traffic some expense can be recuperated by dues from travellers, of whom Suffolk has few. No great city like Norwich, the second largest in England, no great port like Lynn. It is significant that the best, indeed the only good road in Suffolk is the stretch between St. Edmundsbury, a centre of pilgrimage and a place just a day's journey away, Sudbury, to the south.

Little more than twice as far from London as was Hever, Suffolk was remote, almost another world; and Erwarton, lying on a spit of land between two river mouths, in heavily wooded country, seemed like the end of the world.

So it seemed, so it might have been, but for my aunt. She is not bound for Hell, but if she were I swear that she would set about re-organising it, telling the Devil the fires were not fierce enough, the imps with the prongs idle good-for-nothings, the worm that dieth not insufficiently attentive to its duty. In Paradise where everything is perfect....Oh dear, would my aunt Calthorpe be happy with nobody, nothing to criticise, in the timelessness, the one-ness that I imagine Heaven to be? Perhaps for her it will be an endless day in which she can attend to her diverse and scattered interests, her enclosed sheep run at Fressingfield, her open one, in the Breckland, north of Bury St. Edmunds, her weavers in Lavenham and in Kersey, some protegee making clay pots in Wattisfield, a grown-up godchild to be married from Framlingham castle and a very small one to be christened at Orford.

In bad weather she could not ride often or far, but she made up for that by her activity as soon as the roads were passable. And I went with her. She never referred directly to the reason for my being with her, but she made remarks intended to be noticed — Busyness the best cure for misery; virtue a woman's best jewel; the only prosperity worth having being the result of tending to one's affairs. She tended hers with a will; we rode many miles through the gently rolling countryside, often being away from Erwarton for several days on end. Failing the hospitality of a friend we stayed at hostelries, the best of them run, or at least controlled, by the religious orders.

In me began the healing both of mind and body and a visit to my one-time mistress helped, teaching me something that most women learn not at all, or only by hard experience. Mary Tudor had risked all in order to marry her true love; now, lonely and neglected, she lived at Westhorpe — was it chosen for its inaccessibility? — while her husband disported himself at court. The question must be asked, though it cannot be answered. Allowed to marry should Harry and I have known so short a joy? Mary was still beautiful, but her ailing, dispirited air, her over-passionate devotion to several undisciplined little dogs told their own tale.

Was Sir Thomas More thinking of Suffolk when he fulminated so bitterly against enclosures and wrote that she had eaten men? In many places where we stayed, places we rode past, the great fields, the arable acres which had employed many men, at differing tasks during the whole year's cycle, were now enclosed sheepruns, hundreds of sheep, tended by a shepherd, sometimes a boy, always a dog. The unemployed, the dispossessed roamed the roads, called 'sturdy beggars' to distinguish them from the infirm.

As a guard against them, wherever she rode my aunt was attended by two men-servants, dressed identically in good tawny Lindsey cloth and armed with clubs. The practice of putting one's servants into livery had been expressly forbidden by the old King. The law had been aimed at the great lords and their armies of retainers, but it applied to all. When I remarked upon this to my aunt, she laughed and said: 'Tosh. Edman and Edred are twins; they have been dressed alike since the day they were born.' Then I laughed too. How long since I had laughed? 'Even to the Calthorpe badge?' I asked. She said: 'Look again.' I did so. The embroidered devices on their breasts were their names, Edman and Edred, but so cunningly worked by some skilled needlewoman with her tongue in cheek, that at five paces they looked like the Calthorpe arms. 'They must be able to tell their own tunics apart,' my aunt said.

Too simple a joke to be remembered? But part of that — yes, that happy time. I remember wishing that I could stay at Erwarton forever, with the Stour running silver on bright days, leadenly on dull ones, and the clean fresh scent of the nearby sea borne in the easterly wind.

Did I speak then? Emma! Margaret! Did I speak? Did I say 'Bury my heart at Erwarton'? I trust not. Poor dear faithful women. It would confuse them the more, for I seem to remember saying... Oh when, when? I was more clear in my mind then. I remember saying that I wished to be buried at Blickling or at Salle, where my grandparents lie..,. So if I said what I thought I heard myself saying, they will be confused. And they will weep, being so powerless, knowing that I must lie with the condemned.

It does not matter where they bury me, or how. I know, and I believe, that when the trumpets sound on the Resurrection morning, the dead will rise and stand with the living to be judged. With God nothing is impossible and men who have been hung, drawn and quartered, men eaten by wolves, men lost in the depths of the sea, will be no worse off than those laid to rest with all the pomp and ceremony of sable-hued funerals.

But the Tower is cold and stony and stained with blood, and London is the place where the mob cried in the streets, 'We want no Nan Bullen', the place where, though I wore the crown, I knew no happiness. I do not wish to lie here.

The clock! Twelve strokes. Tomorrow is today; today is yesterday. There lies the clue to eternity, could we but grasp it, but we cannot. Timelessness is not for us, creatures of time, slaves to clock and calendar. Today my mutilated body will be shovelled under in St. Peter's church in the Tower precincts; and I, no, merely the body waiting resurrection. Me, my spirit, the distinct thing that made me Anne Boleyn and nobody else... where? Dear God, knowing how wronged I have been, I beg, as a prelude to Purgatory, Norfolk, Suffolk, one last glimpse of a lovely land.....

*** It is just possible that Anne's attendants managed better than she believed possible. In Salle church there is a plain black marble slab under which she is said to lie. When I saw it I was prepared to root it up with my fingernails if necessary. Her body was supposed to have been placed in an arrow-box, rather short and narrow for a coffin and it is possible that the deposition of the body could have given some proof of identity — the

vulgar line — With her head tucked under her arm. But the patron of the church was, I was told, averse to any investigation. And God forbid that I at a time when patrons are rare should offend. In Erwarton, in the last century a metal, heart-shaped casket was found. N.L.

Norah Lofts is Norfolk born and Suffolk bred — real 'grass roots' farming stock. She still considers farming to be the only real occupation and 'grieves to see the loss of agricultural land for any other purpose — however worthy'. She has written over 30 books: I met a Gypsy, The Devils Own *and* The King's Pleasure; *and a Novel about that beautiful and mysterious six-fingered witch, Anne Boleyn,* The Concubine. Jassy *has never been out of print in 27 years, while other publications 'lie down quietly and wait for Corgi Books to resurrect them'. Nora Lofts now lives at Northgate House in Bury St. Edmunds.*

On Nacton shore.

gallop through the Chase.

Nacton Creek.

Emma caught a Bluetit.

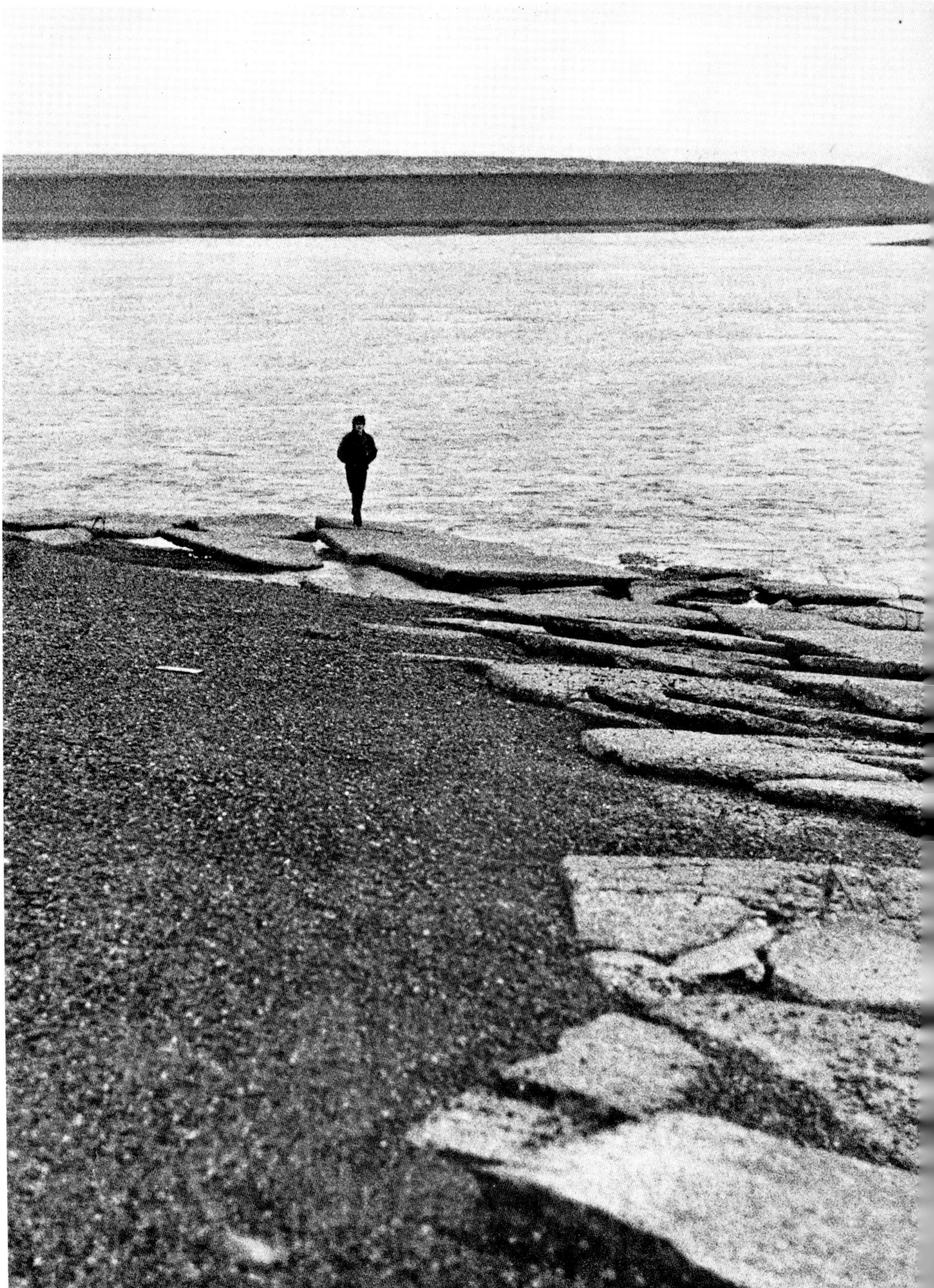

Hammond Innes
A Traveller Returns

SUFFOLK! How many times have I returned to Suffolk since we first settled here in 1947? From the Andes, from Africa and Arabia, from the Labrador, the Pilbara, the Maldives, from sailing voyages and long exhausting journeys. Always with a book in mind and a grateful feeling that now I can unwind.

Travel is exhausting and a traveller without roots is a migrant whose life is meaningless. But given roots, then the traveller returned is a man refreshed with new experience, his horizons broadened, his mind sharpened. But why should Suffolk be a better haven for a writer than other counties, or other countries, for that matter?

I will try to explain, because if I weren't sure of this I wouldn't have stayed here all these years.

First, there is the proximity to London. This is vital. London is without question the most exciting, fascinating, exhilarating city in the world. Maugham always said, London for conversation, and it is still true, a place of ideas, of contacts, of world-wide experience, never insular, always outward looking. The best place in the world for a writer to re-charge his batteries after a bout of work. And because of its mercantile background and the ramifications of the City, it is like a door opening on the rest of the world, the open sesame to every variety of background and experience.

I can leave my Suffolk home after dinner and in two hours I can be in my London studio, having driven along the Embankment, past the Houses of Parliament and Buckingham Palace, past Hyde Park and Kensington Gardens, to an area that still belongs to the great days of English architecture. It is true that on the return journey my wife and I have to get up at 5.30 in the morning and leave at six. But this is not all that different from being roused at four in a lumpy sea to take the early morning watch. And it is worth it for the sake of a fast run and a clear day's work, and London at six in the morning is often very beautiful.

At Colchester we leave the A.12 and drive by ever smaller, less frequented roads 13 miles into the quiet of the Suffolk countryside, through Nayland, first of the old timbered villages, and Stoke-by-Nayland with its great church. I cannot count the number of times I have driven this route, but it never palls. From Polstead on it is pure Suffolk and, returning from abroad, the sense of peace sweeps over one, the wide skies, the softness of the green, the patchwork of the fields, brown from the plough in winter, golden with corn in summer.

In the last mile there are two wych elms. The first of these is of such perfection of shape it is almost breathtaking and I am remembering the times I have seen it in moonlight or in winter with its bare branches black against the diamond brilliance of the stars. And then, around a bend, the tower of the old wool church stands against the sky. A moment later and we are back centuries in time, the steep hill falling to the watersplash and flanked by old timbered dwellings.

55

Left: Shingle Street, Suffolk.

Chasing the sun is one of the mirages of our time, sedulously fostered by the travel industry and the media. So many countries have sunshine — hard, arid, blazing sun, their land burned up and brown. But there is hardly a country in the world so soft, so pleasant and so green as Britain, with such a magical quality of light, ever-changing, never monotonous. And in East Anglia the magic is intensified, for we are on the outskirts of the Atlantic weather pattern, on the threshold of Europe's harder climate. Thus, we have the best of both worlds — more sun, less rain; and the autumn, that loveliest of all seasons of the year, seems unending.

As I write this I am mentally deep in Australia, halfway through a novel that is in part backgrounded on the nickel boom. We were in the Red Centre, in Kalgoorlie and the Iron Ore country of the North-West. We stayed at the Ironclad in Marble Bar, the hottest place on earth, which once recorded temperatures over 100°F for 167 consecutive days, at the Conglomerate at Nullagine, and travelled deep into the outback using four-wheel drives on tracks treacherous with bulldust; heat and flies and the air burned dry under blazing skies, the land all dead, nothing growing but the mulga and the spinifex, rock and gravel and dust all red in the sun.

It has a certain terrible beauty, but now it is all in my mind, for as I think out the lines I write the garden here is a blaze of crocuses and snowdrops, the last of the aconites. The daffodils will burst into flower at any moment. And when I look up from my writing, sitting here in the big thatched study that was once a maltings, I look out through the windows to a tumble of old red roofs above the watersplash, cottages that were built here long before the *Mayflower* sailed for America or Cromwell bedevilled the country with his Puritanism. And when I am stuck, as I so frequently am, I can think it through walking in a little valley of unbelievable beauty.

This valley has been formed by the stream that runs the length of our garden and where I go out from the garden there is a small field where one of the villagers keeps a donkey. It is a period piece of tumbledown chicken coops and in the night I hear the geese warning off marauders, and then the owls in our willows cease to hoot and there is a breathless stillness as death passes silently on four feet. Dawn breaks, and to the dawn chorus is added a familiar voice, the braying of that old moke.

The valley is in gently rolling country, a mixture of down and meadow, the grass kept smooth as a lawn in winter by the farmer's cows. The bottom meadow was once all marsh, but in recent years the Catchment Board have confined the stream in a narrow cut and planted bat willows along the whole straight run. Now the water is crystal clear, running fast over a bare flint bed, and there is watercress.

Higher up the valley there are old solitary oaks of huge girth and, in a meadow that has never seen the plough, cattle stand in summertime knee-deep in wild flowers and the stream is bright with the yellow of kingcups. Higher up still, the stream is barely a yard across, winding back and forth between sheep-cropped banks. Here I can sit and think, the murmur of water and the sound of animals all about me, everything so still and peaceful that one feels in contact with the old England. The only modern intrusion is the roar of jets from a neighbouring fighter station, a comforting sound in an uncomfortable world to one who was on fighter stations all through the Battle of Britain. And the contrails in the sky are often very beautiful.

Some of the best lines in all my books have been worked out, thought out, spoken aloud in that enchanted valley. Walking homeward with my Alsatian, there is the church at the end of the valley. No sign of the village, just the great tower standing like a signpost pointing heavenwards. And the larks singing. Winter and summer the larks soar skywards. And there are mallards in the stream, often a heron, occasionally a kingfisher. And in the autumn there are mushrooms.

I sometimes think that most of what is good in my books, most of what is real and solid and basic in my writing, I owe to that valley.

There are times, however, when this is not enough. I feel hemmed in and stale. Then I drive six miles to the Great Wood and walk our forestry plantations. This large area of woodland now has almost every variety of tree that will grow in the Eastern Counties, from the softwood evergreen of spruce,

Hammond Innes at the helm of Mary Deare.

pine, cypress and cedar, to oak and ash and beech and chestnut. There are deer in the wood, wild duck and woodcock, a rare orchid and a rarer moth. And in springtime it is full of primroses. In late May or June we go there in the evenings. A bottle of wine and a picnic supper watching the sun go down and listening to the nightingales — what more could anyone ask of life? And then to walk through the stillness of the trees as dusk gathers and the birds settle in silence for the night.

It is sometimes difficult to realise that all this of the old Suffolk villages and countryside that I have described is only a few miles from the sea. And though nobody could claim the East Coast to be particularly beautiful, it has an atmosphere — a quality of light, of old buildings seen against the wide skies — not to be found anywhere else in England. And off-shore the Thames banks thrust long hazardous fingers. Here the tides run uncertainly and the buoys are difficult to locate and identify even in good visibility. Returning from voyages on the rocky coasts of Scandinavia or Biscay the approach of these banks signals an immediate concentration of one's navigational faculties.

When I was learning to navigate, just after the War, you could count 19 wrecks above and below the water between Harwich and the Sunk. The wrecks are mostly gone now, but the flak towers remain and there are drilling rigs and platforms further north. Few areas of the world provide a better schooling for the navigator and those that have apprenticed themselves on the East Coast sail other shores with reasonable confidence.

Returning from rocks to banks is like sailing out of sunshine into fog, the hazards concealed and nothing fixed. From Dover Straits to Harwich you can reckon to burn up more nervous energy at the chart table than anywhere else on the coasts of Europe. And then, suddenly, you are inside, the flat coast's sheltering arms around you, the peace of an estuary opening up ahead.

And that evening, whether behind Mersea Island or in the Orwell or the Deben, you swing to the tide close against gleaming mud banks. No warps to tend, no boats jostling you, no music blaring from a café — just the gurgle of tidewater at the bows, the piping of curlews on the mud, and beyond the mud, the deep satisfying stillness of the countryside. Returned, you are instantly refreshed, and this is something extra; for in the voyaging, as in travelling, you had been seeking refreshment of the mind.

Hammond Innes is a Scot who has lived in Suffolk since 1947. During that time he has written 15 novels, all world best-sellers, two books on his travels — Harvest of Journeys and Sea and Islands — and a history of the Spanish conquests of Mexico and Peru, The Conquistadors. His novels have all been translated into at least a dozen foreign languages and most of them have had a world sale of over two million each. The Conquistadors has been the Book of the Month Choice in America and his latest novel, Levkas Man, is still high on the list of best-sellers both here and in America. The wide range of his travels is well-known, his fascination in the effect of terrain upon racial characteristics being reflected in his novels. His other interests are sailing and forestry.

Allan Jobson
The Victorians

VICTORIANISM is in the ascendency. Articles that were ridiculed and despised a short time ago and could hardly have been given away, are now being sought after, greatly prized and priced accordingly. If you have something which appeared in the catalogue of the Great Exhibition of 1851, you would be advised to cash in on it, that is if you are hard up. The Dealers are making the market.

Why all this? Is it not because these trifles, in many cases more than trifles, reflect a great age, indeed a rounded and complete period of time. There is not the shadow of a doubt as to what is meant when one speaks of the Victorian age. Unlike others, such as the Elizabethan and that of Queen Anne or the Regency, it refers exclusively to the reign of 'Victoria Regina Ind Imp'. It stands out more clearly than any of its predecessors, or successors. If one could put back the clock, for me it would be to that of the great Mother Queen. When centuries hence and we are all gone, what will the historians of those days have to say about it? They will cavil in their great wisdom derived from the red-bricked depositories and hindsight, but they will probably see it as the flower of England's civilisation; or, maybe, they will say it was a sweat-laden age. It certainly was, but sweating to a purpose. When Stracheys have strachied all they can, its greatness remains. It was not necessary in those days to be with it; IT WAS, and that was that.

Both my father and mother were Victorians, my father coming of a Lincoln line, but in the case of my mother, even more than that, a Suffolk Victorian. She was born about 1852, when the Queen was a sparkling young woman, into a pure-bred Suffolk family. One couldn't be more Suffolk than that. Her father was born in 1829, of a family that populated the village of Middleton-cum-Fordley in the 19th century; so all in all we were very Victorian, including myself who was born in 1889 and therefore 11 years old when the old Queen died.

Now we hear a lot today about the terrible hardships and privations of that period: closed villages, feudal overlords, grasping farmers, and the like, but I never heard my mother or grandfather once complain of the life they had 'endured'. My grandfather lived and died in the same village into which he had been born. It is true my mother left home as soon as she could, of necessity. I like to think of her standing on her own feet, being seen off by her florid-faced father with tears in his eyes, waiting for the funny old puffing engine coming round the curve at Bramfield, that was to take her to Shoreditch, the then London terminus. She loved her early days in that lovely countryside, its fields, its flowers, its folk, but she never wanted to go back, save to see and hear of her own people. If it was as awful as we have been led to believe by modern writers, it would surely have left a nasty taste in her memory. It may well have been hag-ridden, but one great relief lay in the fact it was not sex-ridden. And there was no student (sic) problem.

To my mind Victorian Suffolk conjures up one of the loveliest pictures possible, the sort of scape that made Constable an artist. It was a scene that really did not disappear until the mad suicide of the First Great War. The gritty roads were lined with green verges, wide enough to provide grazing for a bullock or two. The fences (hedges) were of great height and covered over with wild flowers. I can just remember them. Footpaths, with stiles, ran through the cornfields, and larks were forever ascending from their stony nests, into the Suffolk sky, until they became a 'sightless song', while graceful sorrel horses drew the plough and the wheelwrights' wagons.

The distant scene always intrigued me as a child, fringed as it was by elms of fantastic shapes, dotted by thatched cottages and farmhouses, with here and there a windmill at work. But more than that, overall was a peace that could be felt, and a perfume that pervaded everywhere and everything.

Then of course, the people spoke the language, naturally since they knew no other. Not something drummed up for the flickering screen, but as a means of communication. How my mother loved it and laughed as she recounted it. 'Dew yew wrop yarself up-thass whooly some cowd out abroad es' morni'n.' Or the sick man's reply to an enquiry: 'Well, sir, I fare sew quare, I dunno how ter fare.'

It is hardly necessary to write of how they worked and how proud they were of their husbandry. Farm labouring was a skilled job. My grandfather could thatch, make mats, thrash with a flail, sit up all night with a cow; besides reap and sow, plough and mow, set up a corn stack and drive a team. How the stackyard shone as it slowly filled up with the gold of the fields and the glory of the year.

I cannot say much in extenuation of the tenant farmers. They were in the main a grasping greedy lot. It was they who resented the abolition of the Corn Laws, as later on they scorned compulsory education of 1870. Here is an epitaph to one, which I came across recently. 'In the stackyard at Mr. W. Meen's farm, Stradbroke, there is a stack of wheat which has a remarkable history. It was built in 1873, and the owner made a vow that he would never thrash it until it realised 25s. a sack, a price which has never been offered. The stack stands on an iron support, two feet from the ground, and is in an excellent state of preservation, being free from mice and rats. Recently (1925) some of the ears of wheat were pulled out, and the grains were found to be quite bright, though reddened with age. It is estimated that the stack contains 250 bushels.'

The curious fact remains that in that age of penury a thrifty man like my grandfather, whose wages could only have been reckoned in shillings a week, left behind a few hundred pounds which he had amassed by his own enterprise and initiative. He grew seed on his allotment and his garden and sold it, obtained an old dickey by some means or other, by which his 'gals' peddled sea-borne coal from door to door. And he was a contributor to sundry charities all his life. Frugality was the great key note to life in those days.

What of the gentry and the landed proprietors? In my mother's village they were the Doughtys of Theberton Hall, the Rev. E. Hollond of Benhall and Lord Huntingfield, altogether a very enlightened lot. It is true Lord Huntingfield's name was used as a bit of a bogey to depredatory youth, as that of Napoleon to an earlier generation. 'Yew better mind yarself lest Lord Huntingfield come riding by!' But my mother when a young girl knew his habits, would waylay him and open a gate for him to come trotting through.

More than likely he would stop and give her a penny, which without hesitation would go into her missionary box, and not into her pocket if she had one.

As for the Doughtys, one could not speak too highly. True, Squire Doughty required due recognition by a doffed cap or a curtsy, but little Mrs. Doughty was a gracious lady, as were her daughters, always willing and anxious to give a helping hand to anyone in trouble, or bestow clothing where it would be welcomed. Then, one must not forget it was a brother of that squire, Charles Montagu Doughty, who taking his life in his hand and living as a native, wrote that almost epic travel book — *Arabia Deserta*. I would not say a lot about his poetical works, although some have hailed them with joy, while others fail to understand or appreciate. Moreover, it was his gifted daughter, Dorothy Doughty, who modelled and coloured those beautiful little birds for the Royal Worcester Porcelain Company, that went to America to obtain dollars in the Second World War.

If other villages were as fortunate in their squirearchy, then they did well. I should think in the main it was so. But we must realise it is largely through their efforts that villages have remained as they are in much of their beauty, closed villages especially. There was one at Dunwich, a neighbouring hamlet where grandmother had a sister.

I know the lady at the Hall could be a matriarch, before whom sons grown to manhood would quail, like the celebrated Lady Carlisle, a champion of Liberalism and teetotalism, of whom it was written: 'If ever her name was mentioned I used to see a platoon of footmen in livery carrying bottles across the lawn and reeling from the fumes while a teetotaller Countess poured out the contents into the lake till it blushed with the priceless Montrachet and Chambertin.' Needless to say this tale was apocryphal. But taken all in all it was a gracious age, with gracious squiresses and gracious daughters. If you have any doubts on this score, go and study a collection of dresses such as those on exhibit at the Victoria and Albert Museum. I was there quite recently and the most wonderful creation that caught my eye was that of a Court dress worn by a Marchioness of Bristol, given by her daughter. Moreover, the sons also were worthy of the term gentlemen and, if they misbehaved themselves, joined the old Queen's Army and became gentlemen rankers, a phenomenon of Victorian times.

One must also mention the wonderful gardens that existed, such as Glemham Hall in the time of the Earl of Guildford, Seckford Hall, Hengrave, Sudbourn, Melford; and above all Shrubland Park, the finest site of anywhere in Suffolk, with an Italianate garden laid out by Sir Charles Barry. Happily this still survives. Capability Brown was responsible for some of these, with his rolling lawns, artificial lakes and clumps of trees; altogether a most difficult work of art, allowing for nature to complete the scheme by growth and settlement.

Sport also might be said to have reached its apotheosis in those years, with Sudbourn as the most wonderful venue of all. In order to press the point I append a short poem 'To an old Cock Partridge', culled from an early number of *Country Life:*

> No doubt I often failed to bring you down
> With either barrel as you hurtled by,
> Flushed from the swedes, a patch of whirring brown

> *Against the autumn sky.*
> *No doubt I murmured certain words, but now*
> *Vanished is all regret, and I rejoice,*
> *When in the dusk of March across the plough*
> > *Of Galleous comes your voice.*
> *Is it Love's note to call your mate to rest?*
> *Is it a fighting challenge that you fling?*
> *I know not; but to me it is best*
> > *Of all the sounds of Spring.*
> *I love the thrush, who wakes the world at dawn,*
> *The ring-dove cooing in the coppice park,*
> *The blackbird in the chestnut on the lawn,*
> > *The Heaven-adoring lark.*
> *But somehow more than these, tho' these be good,*
> *The glamour of the Country you impart,*
> *And to us revellers in field and wood*
> > *Disclose her very heart.*   R.S.T.C.

Turning to culture and the Church, the whole of Suffolk was then under the diocese of Norwich, which at one time had acquired the title of the Dead See; that of St. Edmundsbury and Ipswich was not created until 1914. When pursuing certain researches I have been amazed at the wealth of many Suffolk village livings, a large number being valued at four, five and six hundred pounds, even up to nine hundred and a thousand a year; together with a large parsonage and glebe land, which latter was often farmed by the incumbent. Like centuries before it was a period of long tenures, although the supposed case at Orford of Francis Mason, who died in 1621, in the 110th year of his age and the 80th of his service as a Rector, has been discounted as a misreading. It is hardly to be wondered that they held on like grim death, because if those amounts are translated into modern values they would be only equalled by Cabinet Ministers.

Clergy in Suffolk were predominantly Cantab and many of them were great scholars, and some were christians as well as churchmen. In many cases they built the schools, although they saw to it that both master or mistress was a practising member of their church and a communicant. A tale is told of one who interrupted his discourse to catch a rare insect he saw creeping up the wall. Such was the Rev. Professor J.S. Henslow, rector of Hitcham, mentor of Darwin. He was one of the leaders in providing allotments for the farm labourers and horticultural shows for the produce. The farmers opposed the idea because they suggested their men would save their strength, give short time, and even steal the corn. Some of the parsons on the other hand said the people must be kept down with a rod of iron. Some were looked upon as a bit queer, such as the rector written of by Charles Linnell in his *Some East Anglian Clergy*, who had been everywhere on his *philosopher* (penny-farthing). But then some of the parishioners were equally individual, as the old girl who had been confirmed by three successive bishops, Dr. Pelham, Dr. Sheepshank and Dr. Pollock, and felt ever so much better for it. There was also the sainted Dr. Bowers, Bishop Suffragan of Thetford, sometimes called the Bishop of the Great Eastern, so well was he known on every part of the system. All in all, many of the Suffolk clergy would have been worthy of Samuel Wesley's epitaph for a country clergyman:

> *Minding no business but his own,*
> *For party never heard to strive,*
> *His flock not only mourn him gone*
> *But even loved him when alive.*

I must say I rather like that last line.

I do not think my grandfather was much of a scholar, but what refinement was his came through Methodism. One who was conversant with King James's Bible and Wesley's hymns could hardly have been counted illiterate. I don't know if he could write, but grandmother could and a good letter at that. He lived in an age of local pride, when there was a suit of clothes for Sunday wear, and a great fear lest circumstances beyond their control should take them to the Workhouse. They were places to be dreaded, the local one in my grandfather's case being at Bulcamp. 'Every grown up pauper shall every day wash his face and hands and comb his hair'.

Societies for study and research in local history began and developed apace in these years. I possess the first three volumes of the *Proceedings of the Bury and West Suffolk Archaeological Institute* established March 1849, for the *Collection and Publication of information on the Ancient Arts and Monuments of the Western Division of Suffolk and Archdeanery of Sudbury.* These were owned by A.P. Dunlap of Bardwell Rectory.

Then appeared *The East Anglian or Notes and Queries on subjects connected with the counties of Suffolk, Cambridge, Essex and Norfolk.* The first number is dated October 1858, the price being threepence. They were edited by Samuel Tymms, F.S.A. These were followed by a new series, commencing 1885, edited by C.H. White, curate of St. Margaret's, Ipswich. *The Proceedings of the Suffolk Archaeological Society* produced its centenary number in 1948, but whether it claims its origin from the Bury and West Suffolk volumes mentioned above is not clear.

But what of the scholars produced by the famous Bury Grammar School under its headmaster Benjamin Heath Malkin? Amongst these were John William Kemble, Philologist and historian; Edward FitzGerald of *Rubaiyat* fame, James Spedding, editor of Bacon's works; and William Bodham Donne who became manager of the London Library. A later scholar Dr. M.R. James, was Provost of Eton. That surely was not a bad contribution to make to the culture of England as well as the home county.

Then, of course, the first accredited woman doctor in England came out of Aldeburgh, as also the first woman mayor in the same person, Elizabeth Garrett Anderson. But it also produced her sister, Mrs. Fawcett, wife of the blind Postmaster General, and a leading non-militant suffragette. As also Edward Clodd, who was one of the founders of the Folk Law Society, *Suffolk Folk Lore* having been collected and edited by Lady Camilla Gurdon, who died 1894.

I was greatly intrigued to discover that it was a native of Ipswich who attended the Ipswich School, Sir John Cordy Burrows, F.R.C.S. (1813-1876), who was a prime mover in persuading the fathers of Brighton to purchase the Royal Pavilion for the town. He was apprenticed to a doctor at Framlingham, completing his medical education at Guy's and St. Thomas's Hospitals. At the age of 25 he settled at Brighton, becoming an active member of the Literary and Scientific Institute and mayor. When he died it is said the numbers attending his funeral were as great as those who had followed the

Rev. F.W. Robertson.

When we next visit Brighton and the Pavilion, which both my wife and I so much love, we shall feel an added interest in that its courts are open, partly as the result of the activities of a Suffolk Victorian, whose statue is in the grounds.

It was in Victorian times that agriculture in Suffolk grew to its zenith. One old practitioner put it down to the introduction of Ransome's Iron Patent Plough, outmoding the old wooden plough. Machinery and steam power had done much to revolutionise work, while the rise of agricultural societies and exhibitions with prizes, had evoked competition. But he had little good to say about the farmers who appeared to be blind to progress. Moreover, it was in 1849 that Raynbird's *The Agriculture of Suffolk* was published.

Then came Agricultural Unionism and the Strike and Lock-Out of 1874. Unionism soon took hold in Suffolk owing to the low standard of living then obtaining. A letter from the Bishop of Manchester to the *Times* in support of the men brought a very spirited reply from Lady Stradbroke, who suggested that nothing was wrong with the agricultural labourer in Suffolk. Sir Edward Kerrison suggested a scheme of arbitration on wages to help solve the matter. The strike and lock-out by the farmers continued throughout the spring and summer of 1874. The strike failed and there was little support for the unions in the depressed years that followed. Needless to say a number of families managed to emigrate to Australia, New Zealand and Canada.

An article appeared in the *Eastern Counties Magazine* (1900) on the decline in the rural population at the end of Victoria's reign. The writer makes a distinction between the coastal regions, because of the opportunity of some of the land workers to take up fishing for part of the year, as also to take in visitors. But the rather curious reasons for the decline are given as the coming of the railways, the penny post, putting down arable land to grass, the migration of skilled labour to the towns, and the low wages paid to the farm labourer.

Many of the villages still retain their old family associations, and are mighty proud of the fact. However, one must confess it is a losing fight. New people occupy the cottages, the old rectories, and the farms. Before very long it may well be that many villages will die, killed by modern local governments; as sure a demise as that by the Black Death of long ago. But the memory will remain, and not least, tinged with splendid achievements, the Victorian years.

So far we have dealt with the villages and the countryside. We might look in at the two chief towns of Ipswich and Bury, both of which flourished exceedingly during the years of Victoria's reign. The first mayor of Ipswich, B. Brame, took office in 1836, only a year before the Accession. The population in 1831 was 20,200 and in 1901, 66,630.

In 1846 the Eastern Union Railway, a 5ft. gauge line between Ipswich and Colchester was opened, and another service between Ipswich and Norwich was initiated in 1849. The Eastern Union Railway and the East Suffolk Railway were subsequently worked by the Great Eastern Railway. The original Ipswich station was at Croft Street, Stoke, on the south side of the tunnel, and looked almost as important as a wayside station. After the opening of the tunnel, 14 years later, it was moved to its present site and opened on July 1, 1860.

The Ipswich Express, a four page paper, was started at Colchester in 1839, published by John Bawtree Harvey of Colchester and Stephen Piper of Ipswich. *The Suffolk Mercury* was transferred from Lowestoft to Ipswich in 1860, and the *East Anglian Daily Times* appeared for the first time in 1874.

Joseph Fison and Co., as a firm, was founded in Ipswich in 1847. In 1843 Edward Packard made history by discoveries relating to the manufacture of superphosphates. His researches were carried on independently of those of Sir Joseph Lawes, and the results were announced at the same time. The firm of Edward Packard and Co. was established in Ipswich in 1849. This put Suffolk in the van for scientific farming.

Ransomes, Sims and Jefferies moved from Foundry Road to Orwell Works in 1849 and their ploughs became famous the world over. Then E.R. and F. Turner was founded in 1847. Their first portable engine was exhibited at the Royal Agricultural Show, Norwich, in 1849.

The story of R. and W. Paul is fascinating. It begins with a small country grain and barge-owning business conducted by Mr. Robert Paul about the middle of the century. This became the inheritance of Robert and William, when youths of 18 and 15, and later they carried on under the name of R. and W. Paul. As a result of their energy and enterprise the small country business, with few connections and no foreign trade, developed into a grain and manufacturing business, of cattle and poultry foods, importing from all parts of the world; and also maltsters.

Cranfield Brothers commenced in 1884 and by 1903 had outgrown their old mill, which was replaced by a new one in 1911.

About 1892, Christchurch Park came into the market and was all but lost to the community by certain dissidents. However, second thoughts prevailed and it became the property of the Corporation. Its significance and value to the town was confirmed when the mansion was bought by Felix Thornley Cobbold and presented to the Borough.

Turning to Bury St. Edmunds, the first number of the *Bury Free Press and West Suffolk Observer,* appeared on Saturday, July 14, 1855. The paper then had a staff of five, one being a boy. The town's few surviving Waterloo veterans were entertained to dinner at the White Horse, in 1858. Practical sympathy was felt for those veterans who got safely back from the Crimea. In May 1855, a Norton soldier who had lost an arm at the Battle of the Alma, was appointed letter carrier from Woolpit to Felsham. Then in 1859 the bakers of Bury got together and decided to stop baking on a Sunday.

In 1857, the Rev. W. Sprigge of Brockley was charged by a Mrs. Sparke with assaulting her while in her pew in church. It appeared that she and her husband were owner occupiers of a farm in the parish, and alleged they had a customary right to a certain pew. Mr. Sprigge also claimed a right from long usage for the use of his servants. Mrs. Sparke, however, refused to let the servants into the pew, on which Mr. Sprigge, who was in his surplice, came and forced open the door and pushed the girl into the pew. In so doing he hurt Mrs. Sparke's hand and caused her to fall on to the pew.

The doors of Bury houses were numbered in 1868. One old lady, evidently a Suffolk individualist, objected to this, and as soon as the painter's back was turned rubbed out the number. The great Bury Fair was killed in 1872, because it had become a coarse and childish amusement, a temptation to servant girls, children, vagabonds and idlers. Friendly Societies began to spring up and rapidly flourished. The West Suffolk Friendly Society was founded in 1830. Odd Fellows began in 1840 and by the next year there were four Lodges in Bury.

Refuse collecting began in 1880, but because of bad sanitary conditions in the town, an outbreak of cholera was feared in 1885. The County Council was set up in 1889.

In 1855, Bury possessed five brewers, ten malsters and six coopers, and Sudbury had three maltsters and three coopers. Many public houses brewed their own beer. Public houses in those days, such as at Mildenhall, opened at 5 a.m. and closed at 11 p.m. Beer was indeed the national beverage and children at Great Barton, on St. Valentine's Day, were given half-a-pint, by a Mrs. Payne of Elm Farm.

The skill of farm labourers was commented upon in 1855. Ploughing and drilling could not be surpassed and very seldom equalled. But in those days a labourer was liable to be prosecuted if he took the day off from work. Stack burners, however, were busy. In 1868 a stack of barley was set on fire, but the culprit was caught in the act. In 1888 allotments at West Row were to be let to labourers and cottagers at sixpence a rod. And to show how keenly interested they were about wild life, a golden oriole was shot in the grounds of Mr. Edward Greene, M.P. at Ixworth in 1867.

The last public execution at Bury took place in 1851, when George Carnt (23), who had murdered a girl at Lawshall, was hanged in the presence of about 5,000 people.

In 1898 appeared this notice: 'We understand that Mr. James Last of the Meat Market, is the sole agent for Bury and Newmarket of the wonderful and interesting instrument, the Gramaphone. It recites, declaims, preaches, tells funny stories, sings quartettes, choruses, plays the piano.'

The greatest disaster of the Victorian age at Stowmarket, was the explosion at the gun-cotton works that killed 24 and injured two in 1871. Windows were shattered over a wide area and doors blown in.

A fitting end comes with the news that 1,575 plum puddings and 2,480 lbs. of beef were given away in Bury St. Edmunds to celebrate Queen Victoria's Jubilee in 1887.

Allan Jobson, born in 1889, of a Suffolk mother and a Lincolnshire father, both of true county blood. Was first brought to Suffolk in his mother's arms, a visit he cannot remember. Educated first (and too long, he says) at a Dame's school; then at an old church school, fee one penny a day, changed to sixpence per week for newcomers before he left. Served in First World War in a Field Ambulance of Kitchener's Army. Has never found anywhere better to live than Suffolk, about which he has written several books including A Suffolk Calendar, Under a Suffolk Sun, A Window in Suffolk, *and* Suffolk Yesterdays.

John Hadfield
The East Anglian House

ALTHOUGH the East Anglian landscape has its own distinctive charms, few people would say that in terms of natural scenery East Anglia is the most 'beautiful' part of England. But when it comes to the chief element in the man-made environment — buildings — there is only one other area, the Cotswolds, that seems to me to rival East Anglia. The churches and the secular buildings that arose from the prosperity of the wool trade between the 13th and the 16th centuries challenge comparison with those in any other part of England. (It is significant that the chief contender, the Cotswolds, also based its architectural riches on the wool trade.)

In this chapter I am concerned not with the churches but with the domestic buildings — the distinctive East Anglian house, whether it be farmhouse, manor house or 'stately home'. Apart from the multitude and magnificence of the parish churches, especially throughout Norfolk and Suffolk, the East Anglian house is the most characteristic and valuable element in our regional landscape.

When we try to visualize the typical East Anglian house I imagine most of us think immediately of a building like Willy Lott's house at Flatford, made so familiar to us in paintings and sketches by Constable. Timber-framed, with steep-pitched red-tiled roofs, the plastered walls colourwashed in cream, pink, ochre or earthy red, these yeomen's houses, dating from the 14th, 15th or 16th centuries, sit in our scenery with the same seemliness as the oaks, the elms and the hedges. They provide painters with perfect focal points of colour in an otherwise dun-arable landscape.

There are few villages in North Essex, in the whole of Suffolk, the eastern side of Cambridgeshire and the south-west of Norfolk, that do not comprise three or four farm-houses of this pattern, and a dozen or so smaller cottages substantially the same.

There are only one or two slight variations in the basic structure and layout of these buildings. The earliest had no central chimney-stack. The fire burned in the middle of a central hall, which reached from floor to roof, and the smoke rose to a central outlet. On either side of the hall was an aisle, separated from the hall by massive upright oak studs. At one end of the hall there would be a raised dais, where the lord of the manor or farmer and his family would sit for meals. Behind this there was a panelled screen, which separated the central hall from the parlour. Above the parlour there was an upper room called a solar. At the farther end of the hall there was usually another panelled screen, behind which was a pantry and a buttery.

The roof of the central hall in such a building would originally slope right down to ground floor level, and the two ends would have separate roof pitches running at right angles to the central roof, at a slightly higher level, to accommodate the upper floors.

This was the original layout of a vast number of the very early timber-framed manor and farmhouses, which still retain the original H-plan, though a central chimney-stack has replaced the original smoke outlet — a massive brick structure, with huge fireplaces at either side, dividing the original hall into two relatively small rooms. At the same time as this was built, a floor for upper rooms would be inserted, and either the central roof raised or dormer windows cut into it.

This very brief summary is intended merely to indicate that a large proportion of what seem, at first sight, to be very old and original buildings are in fact 16th century or 17th century adaptations of primitive buildings dating back to the 13th or 14th centuries. There is an admirable discussion of these early buildings in that wonderful book, *The English House through Seven Centuries* by Olive Cook, illustrated with photographs by Edwin Smith (East Anglians both). In many old farmhouses that remain relatively unrestored it is possible to trace the changes in structure brought about by 'modernisation' in the 17th century. There is an enlightening study of such a house — a derelict farmhouse in the middle of fields at Purton Green, Stansfield, Suffolk — in the *Proceedings of the Suffolk Institute of Archaeology* for 1965.

There are, of course, any number of minor variations in the decoration or internal detail of these old East Anglian stud-and-plaster houses. The arrangement of ceiling joists, the carving of rafters, and the shapes of door frames, can be subjects of endless study and theorising. Another variable element is the treatment of the plaster sheath on the outer walls, which was composed of lime, sand, dung and cow hair, sometimes mixed with chopped straw. The art of pargetting, which reached its height in the 17th century, and was carried out with a pointed stick, a 'comb', or a spray of sticks, created some enchanting patterns of scallops, zigzags or interleaving curves. These are particularly to be seen in North Essex or south-west Suffolk, and the treatment spread into Hertfordshire. Perhaps the most famous example is to be seen on a house at Clare. There is an elaborate coloured example, embody-

Playford Hall.

ing a vine and star design, on a house at East Dereham in Norfolk. Pargetting, thank heaven, is a craft that is still carried on by country builders today.

Another attractive variation in the structure of the basic timber-framed house, to be seen rather more often in town or village streets than on houses in open country, is the over-sailing of the ends of the upper floor joists, which project six inches or more beyond the line of the wall below. This can be seen to advantage in Lavenham or Kersey. Carved angle-posts with brackets, carved oriel sills and ornamental barge-boards are other decorative elements that lend endless fascination to the timber-framed house.

In two important respects many of these old and characteristic houses have suffered from restoration over the years, apart from what they gained by the building of chimney-stacks and the addition of staircases and upper storey floors in the 16th or 17th centuries. One alteration which is to be seen almost everywhere, and which can hardly be condemned, even though it may be regrettable, is the substitution of casement or sash windows in place of the original mullioned slits. Anyone who strips the plaster off the walls of an old building will almost always find traces of the original carved and shaped window mullions, which were covered over when new and larger 'modern' windows were inserted, usually in the 18th century. Sash windows came into vogue then, and window glass became readily available.

There is a temptation for architectural purists to remove the modern windows and open up the old mullions, which are usually arranged in elegant architectural patterns, with, say, a group of five deep narrow openings flanked at either side by groups of much shorter openings at head height.

I see no objection to this, provided the openings are filled with the appropriate leaded panes, either of diamond shape or rectangular. What is definitely *not* a true restoration — though a vast amount of unnecessary money is often spent on it — is the stripping of the external plaster off the external walls to reveal the faces of all the timbers. Occasionally these timbers were meant to be exposed, and certainly this was so if they were carved. But the vast majority of timber-framed houses in East Anglia differ from those in the midlands, Herefordshire, Cheshire and Wales in having had their timbers encased in plaster from the outset.

The interstices between the studs were very seldom filled with bricks — as they usually are in the (rather later) timber-framed houses of the midlands. There was nothing between the studs — except perhaps a certain amount of straw. The weather-proofing of the house was entirely dependent upon the lath-and-plaster covering nailed on to the outside of the studs — with usually another covering nailed on the interior. To remove the laths and plaster from the outer walls of such houses is as phoney an act of restoration as stripping the paint off Georgian deal panelling, which was intended to be painted from the start. It discloses merely the bare bones of the house, pitted with nail holes, and stripped of their 'skin'.

So far I have been writing about houses of relatively modest size, which are the true indigenous architecture of East Anglia. They are built of local timber, local lime, local sand — and local cow-dung. Originally they were almost all thatched with local reeds or straw — though tiles often replaced the thatch in the 18th century.

The chief reason for the use of these materials is that East Anglia is almost totally lacking in stone suitable for building. Such stone as is found in buildings here and there, for paving stones in houses or for corner-stones in churches, had to be brought in from Northamptonshire or Oxfordshire. There is, of course, flint to be found on the borders of Suffolk and Norfolk, and a certain amount of this was used for domestic building in Norfolk and Cambridgeshire. Along the coasts there are cottages faced with pebbles. But of stone domestic buildings such as one finds in profusion in Northamptonshire, Oxfordshire, Yorkshire, the Cotswolds or Dorset, there are virtually none in East Anglia.

Another reason for the initial dependence on timber and plaster and thatch is the fact that when the population of East Anglia was relatively high, in the middle ages, England had lost the art of brick-making, which the Romans had introduced, and which builders on the continent had maintained. Professor Sir Nikolaus Pevsner, in the volume on Suffolk in his invaluable Penguin series on *The Buildings of England,* says that the literature of

Seckford Hall.

building makes no reference to home-made bricks earlier than those used at Little Coggeshall Abbey in Essex in 1225.

East Anglia can claim one of the first brick-built houses in England, Little Wenham Hall in Suffolk. Built between 1270 and 1280, it is a somewhat gaunt building, looking more like a castle than a house, as its walls are castellated. But it marks the transition from the Norman fortress to the medieval manor house, and, as Sir Nikolaus Pevsner says, it ranks with Stokesay and Acton Burnall in Shropshire as one of the *incunabula* of English architecture.

Little Wenham is an architectural show-piece, but there is nothing especially East Anglian about it, except the home-made bricks, which are combined with two other characteristic East Anglian materials, flint and septaria — the smooth grey 'clay' dredged from the river estuaries. The really distinctive contribution to East Anglian domestic building in brick came a little later, when Renaissance styles were introduced into England by the Italian workmen whom Henry VIII brought to England. In East Anglia there is a group of ornate and exotic houses, built of brick with terracotta ornamentation, which have no real parallel elsewhere in England, and which have, in my view, never had their due as an extraordinarily imaginative and romantic 'sport' in English architecture.

Perhaps one reason why they are neglected is their inaccessibility (though this, for me, is one of their great charms). Few people driving from Bury St. Edmunds to Thetford turn aside to look at West Stow Hall. East Barsham Manor is in the middle of the no-man's-land of North Norfolk; Oxburgh Hall is hidden in the remote backwoods of south-west Norfolk; and Kirtling Tower is tucked away in the uplands south-east of Newmarket. How many people who pride themselves on their architectural interests have ever found their way to the desolate and semi-ruined Cressingham Manor in Norfolk, or Roos Hall near Beccles, or Great Snoring Rectory in Norfolk, Thorpe Hall — on the far side of a disused aerodrome near Stradbroke, or the old moated Hall at Parham near Framlingham, five of the smaller but no less romantic and exotic examples of this 'East-Anglian-Renaissance' art of building in brick?

Perhaps the most dramatic of these buildings is Layer Marney Towers, whose eight-storied gatehouse looms up above the featureless Essex landscape, a mile or two from Tiptree, at the end of a country lane. Obviously Lord Marney, who was Treasurer to Henry VIII, and may well have employed the king's architect, the Italian Giralomo de Travizi, intended to build a vast palace round a courtyard, and the gatehouse was the first instalment of his great undertaking. The rest was never completed. The gatehouse would appear to have been — and it certainly is now — purely ornamental. Unlike other gatehouses of its period it contains a vast number of large windows, tier above tier of four windows on either side of the gateway. The brickwork is arranged in elaborate diaper and zigzag patterns, and there is a vast amount of terracotta work combining Gothic and classical motifs. To come upon this extravagant building unawares is a startling but exhilarating experience.

Much simpler and more austere are the remains of another Essex 'palace', Leez Priory, near Braintree, built by Lord Rich in 1536 on the site of an Augustinian priory. The gatehouse here is only half the height of Layer Marney Towers, and has few windows. The decorative element is provided almost entirely by the pattern of the brickwork, which is strangely unsymmetrical — Layer Marney is a masterpiece of symmetry — the bricks being arranged in a diaper pattern on one side of the gateway and in a chequer pattern on the other.

Cambridgeshire is not as well endowed with Tudor buildings as Essex, Suffolk and Norfolk, and its most notable, Sawston Hall, is built of clunch, not of brick. But, hidden away on the borders of Cambridgeshire and West Suffolk, is Kirtling Tower, a gatehouse dating from 1530, which, as Sir Nikolaus Pevsner says, 'represents that moment in Tudor architecture when the Middle Ages and the Renaissance met'. Red and blue brick diapers, tall polygonal outer turrets, a two-storied oriel window, arched lights and a

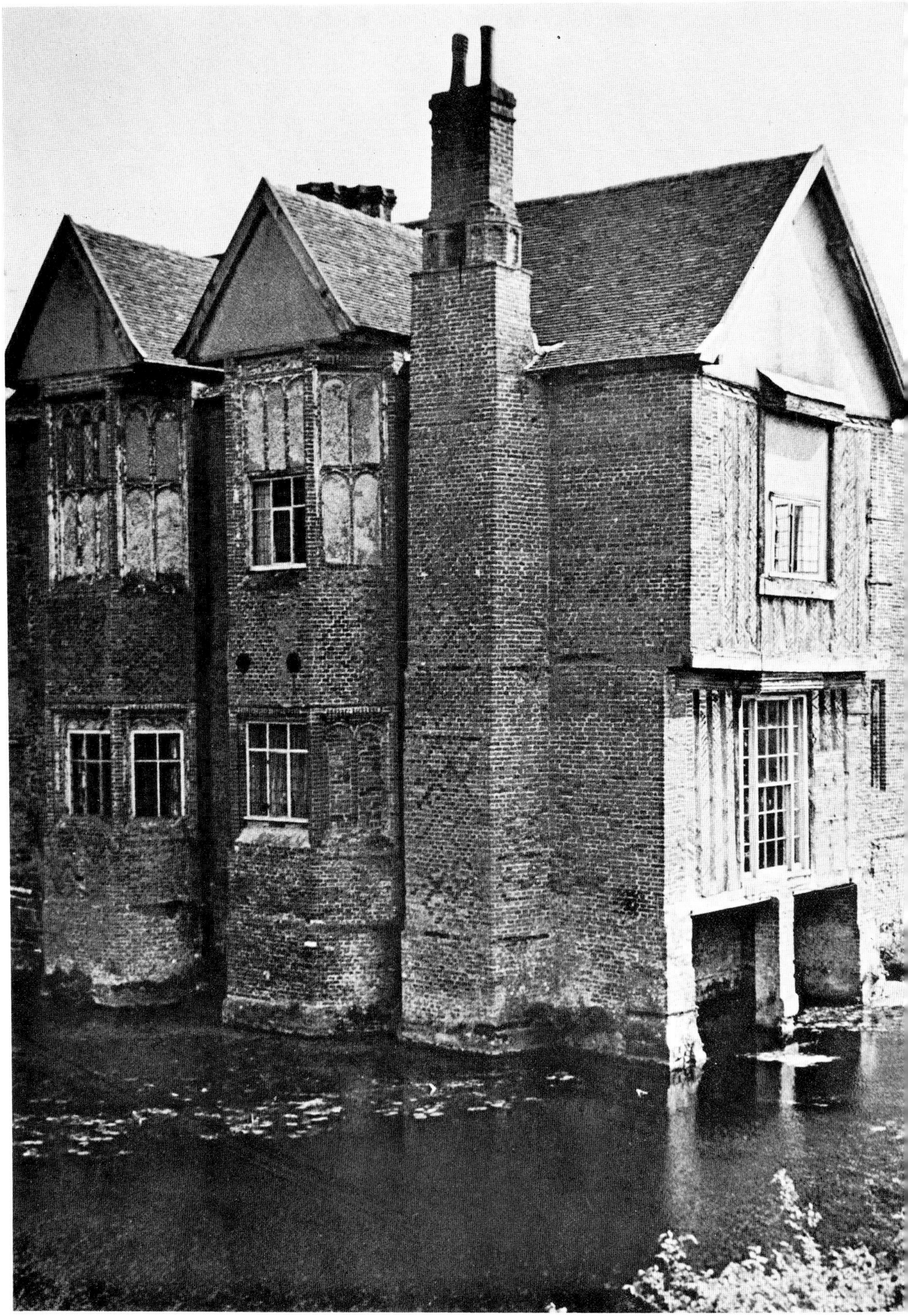

wealth of decorative Italian motifs indicate the showy extravagance of the original mansion, which was pulled down in 1801, leaving only the gatehouse standing. The present adjoining house belongs to the 19th century.

Suffolk has not any gatehouses quite comparable with these, though Erwarton Hall, now the home of the commanding officer of *H.M.S. Ganges* at Shotley, is an entrancing building on a much smaller scale, with a free-standing gatehouse, at the end of the driveway, built about 1549, containing a vaulted tunnel with a round arch at either end and round angle buttresses with round pinnacles. On the way back from Erwarton to Ipswich

John and Anna Hadfield.

one should not miss that engaging folly — also Italianate-Tudor — Freston Tower.

Even more odd and engaging — but terribly hard to find — is the gatehouse at West Stow, on the edge of Breckland, which is adorned with pepperpot domes and terracotta figures. West Stow dates from about 1525, though the famous wall painting of the Four Ages of Man, in one of its rooms, was done in the Elizabethan period. The handsome Deanery Tower at Hadleigh is of earlier date, 1495, and its very individual arrangement of trefoiled arches in pairs, above the 'blind' panels which decorate the polygonal towers, gives it a distinctly Gothic air.

There was once a gatehouse leading to the old moated Hall at Parham, in Suffolk, but the owners allowed it to be removed entirely to the United States in 1926. There is still a lesser gateway there, decorated with strange pagan images of wodehouses or wild men brandishing clubs. And the house itself, with two time-worn gabled bays projecting into the moat, is a

73

Left: Parham Hall.

wonderfully romantic, if desolate, sight.

There are, of course, many other ornate and early 'great houses' in Suffolk, such as Gifford's Hall, near Stoke-by-Nayland, which has a fine brick gatehouse, and Hengrave Hall, with its marvellously ornamental porch, but these have not quite the same air of Italianate extravagance and vertical eccentricity as have the buildings I have discussed.

Italianate, extravagant and eccentric, though not so dominantly vertical, is East Barsham Manor, in Norfolk. It has been much (and well) restored, but the gatehouse is original and is decorated with a bold coat-of-arms carved out of the brick *in situ*. The profusion of polygonal buttresses rising above the walls of the house, with decorative pointed finials, give a strange air of faerie-like delicacy to what is basically a very substantial building.

In several out-of-the-way corners of North Norfolk there are smaller relics of Italianate-Tudor brickwork. I have mentioned Great Cressingham Manor, which has a fantastically exotic pattern of brick and terracotta on the façade of its upper storey. The Rectory at Great Snoring, in Norfolk, is of the same architectural family — part of a manor house built by Sir Ralph Shelton in 1525. What survives is a plastered façade, flanked by octagonal turrets, with a more ornate façade at an angle to it. There are two friezes of moulded terracotta, above the ground floor and the upper floor, made up of Gothic panels and lettering.

Of all the Tudor 'follies' — and most of them can be described thus, as their most notable features were designed more for show than for use — the one that appeals most to me is Oxburgh Hall, the mansion which Edward Bedingfield built in 1482, and which houses one of the most exquisite treasures of English history, the bed-hangings embroidered by Mary Queen of Scots whilst she was imprisoned.

Perhaps my personal delight in this house has been heightened by my having used it — with some literary license — as the setting for a number of scenes in a novel which I wrote some years ago. Anyone who happens to come across *Love on a Branch Line* will find in it reasonably accurate descriptions of some of the chief features of Oxburgh Hall (though they must not be surprised if the scene sometimes shifts inexplicably to Blickling Hall in the same county!).

The tremendous gatehouse of Oxburgh, set in a sylvan scene of remote and gracious peacefulness, is, in my view, the *chef d'oeuvre* of East-Anglian-Renaissance. The polygonal turrets flanking the entrance rise to seven tiers, these being separated by arched and cusped brick friezes. There are double-stepped battlements on top. One could go on for pages describing the architectural details of this noble structure. All I will add now is that the staircase inside is constructed entirely of brick, to a highly ingenious design.

Perhaps the emotive impact of Oxburgh Hall is heightened by the fact that the building is entirely surrounded by a moat, which runs round the very edge of the building — just as it does at two other notable East Anglian buildings, Playford Hall and the Tollemaches' Helmingham Hall, in Suffolk.

The moat is really part of the characteristic structure of an East Anglian house — not only of the great houses, such as I have been describing, but of almost every medieval or Tudor manor or farm house, however modest. It is rare indeed to find an East Anglian homestead of any antiquity that has not got some water close at hand. It may be called a duckpond; it may not now

Oxborough Hall.

make a circle round the house. But investigation will nearly always show that once it did surround the house.

The original purpose of these moats has been the subject of interminable argument. They were not for military defence, since the houses they surrounded were far too many and usually too unimportant to be military objectives. Clearly they served the purpose of safeguarding the owners and —much more important—their cattle, pigs, and other livestock, from robbers. They formed an effective 'fence' for cattle at night. But I think they also had three other functions, which are seldom mentioned. By digging a deep and wide ditch round their houses the builders left a dry plateau on which to set their foundations. And by laying land-drains (I have found plenty of them, dating back to Tudor times, round my own house) they not only drained the surrounding land, but filled the moats with water for washing and drinking by human beings as well as the stock. Finally — and this is a theory of my own which relates to the main theme of this essay — I think the builders often extracted from these deep ditches the clay to make the bricks of which the houses — or at least the foundations and the chimney-stacks — were constructed.

I have put special emphasis on one individual type of East Anglian home, the brick-built Tudor house whose characteristics sprang from continental influences. I would be the last to denigrate such superb buildings of later date as Ickworth, Holkham, Wimpole Hall or Heveningham — the last named of which is a most exquisite and complete work of decorative art. But the fact is that the Queen Anne and Georgian periods, which so richly endowed so much of England with elegant 'boxes of bricks' and Palladian mansions in landscaped parks, made comparatively little architectural impact in East Anglia, since East Anglia was no longer prospering as it did in the heyday of the wool trade. A few of the 16th century farm houses were re-faced with Queen Anne or Georgian brick, but this was a renovation not a new architectural creation.

The Tudor-Renaissance brickwork of East Anglia, on the other hand, was a vigorous, individual, extravagant architectural style which has no parallel elsewhere in England. It is highly romantic and greatly underestimated. It brought into being a special kind of vernacular architecture which can be seen in less eccentric form in such buildings as Seckford Hall in Suffolk or Barningham Hall in Norfolk, and a number of 'crow-stepped' manor houses in Norfolk. In its original and uninhibited form it has given our East Anglian landscape, normally furnished with modest and homely yeoman's dwellings in stud-and-plaster, a rich sprinkling of Gothic splendours, Tudor fantasies and intimations of a Spenserian faery-land.

John Hadfield, publisher, editor and a former Director of the National Book League, has lived at Barham Manor, near Ipswich, for 19 years, in a Tudor brick house with crow-stepped gables that might be called a cadet version of the great houses he discusses in his contribution to this book. He has for a number of years edited The Saturday Book, *the famous annual largely devoted to the arts, and he has compiled a series of pictorial anthologies of which* A Book of Beauty *is the best known. Some years ago he wrote a light-hearted novel,* Love on a Branch Line, *of which the setting is the borders of Suffolk and Norfolk. The Branch Line of the title is assumed by railway buffs to be the now vanished Haughley and Laxfield Light Railway. In his chapter in this book Mr. Hadfield discloses that his descriptions of 'Arcady Hall' in his novel were based on Oxburgh Hall in Norfolk.* Love on a Branch Line *has just been reissued in paperback by Pan Books. Mr. Hadfield's home is graced by a pair of peafowl, and his wife Anna published a year or two ago an entertaining record of life at Barham Manor entitled* A Peacock on the Lawn, *which recently came out in a cheap edition.*

Mary Gilliatt
A Particular House

EAST Anglia has much the same effect on the juvenile mind as Jesuit education: give it to a child in its formative years and very likely it will remain imbued forever. Anyway, that is what happened to me. I was very happy to be brought up in Suffolk – and Fleet Street, travel, other people's country loyalties did nothing to change my mind about my first rural love. So I was particularly pleased after marriage to find that my husband, a Londoner born and bred, was at first willing, and then even anxious, to share my enthusiasm.

Since his enthusiasm, at least, was tinged with prudence, our first exercise in setting up house in Suffolk was to rent a dilapidated 17th century farm cottage in a more or less idyllic position. That is to say it was half a mile up a cart track, set in a cleft of dipping meadows with a shift system in appropriate season of cows and sheep. Superimposed on these assets were great oaks, spreading chestnuts, a lovely crumbling garden wall, two ponds, a stream, a prettily unproductive orchard and a glimpse of the village church through burgeoning branches.

Even idylls have their disadvantages however, and this was no exception. The cart track with its traffic of tractors got either so muddy or so snowed up during the winter that it became impassable; a tedious state of affairs to find after a long hard drive from London. The cows used to nuzzle along our pretty wall and munch our incipient climbers in the bud. The drainage was rudimentary with the ever-present danger of ordure rather than honeysuckle scenting the night air. The ponds, neglected for years, not only stank in the summer, but attracted more flies and mosquitoes than the south of Spain. And our benevolent landlord used to let the local dramatic society use the barn, whose members, apart from being unconscionably noisy, felt impelled, for some reason, to relieve themselves in our empty milkbottles.

Foolishly, because we only had a five year lease, we attempted to rescue the shambles for our aesthetic rather than financial advantage. We turned the lean-to chicken house cum carpentry shed into a nursery cum spare bedroom with the aid of a good deal of anti-damp liquid and white emulsion. We covered most of the floors with sisal matting, and bedrooms with off-cuts from a good carpet manufacturer (worth thinking about for small rooms). We painted the plaster between beams in some rooms in warm rich colours, as indeed they would have done at the period the cottage was built – (where do the English get their quite unhistorical penchant for black and white?) – and held together the more crumbling walls by covering up the ravages with wallpaper. We even persuaded our landlord to pay for knocking down a wall between tiny bathroom and windowless loo, which, I pointed out, or mildly threatened, was completely against all health regulations, and would, in any event, make the whole space more practicable.

With the aid of a marvellously helpful retired train driver who lived at the end of the track, we scythed, dug, erased brambles, raised seedlings, chopped down elders, cut away dead wood, dispatched a lorry load of ruined

'A pair of labourers' cottages...'

dog kennels, chicken coops, rabbit hutches, and sheets of battered galvanised metal to the local scrap merchant, planted trees and shrubs and herbs and bulbs, drained the most offensive pond, unblocked the stream, and totally astonished those in the village who were interested, whose consensus was that the cottage, or wreck, or ruin, or hovel was due for a bull-dozering some years before.

Alas, we grew too many for it, and although we tried to buy it with a view to adding on, and a resolution to re-drain, re-ditch, re-surface if we ever got the money or the chance, we never did get the chance. There was nothing for it but to look for something else.

We looked at a windmill with the loo on the first floor, bedrooms on three more floors and a precipitous spiral staircase in between. We examined decayed cottages and abandoned farmhouses almost invariably situated by someone's pig yard. Tripped in and out of tarted-up cottages with roses carefully curling through the wrought iron. Considered a splendid ramble of a farmhouse before we remarked its famous rural view of a double row of dead grey council houses. Considered, too, a lovely rectory with one end sinking gracefully below lawn level. And discovered a pair of labourers' cottages set at right angles, pre-packaged as it were with inferior mod. cons, by a go-getting rural developer who had managed to get there first.

We had almost bought the rectory before we came to our senses and decided it was an extravagance we could ill afford. Which left us with the labourers' cottages (one 16th century, the other Victorian), mostly because they were empty and available in a part of the county we wanted; a convenient size, being neither too large nor too small; and although not at all in the bucolic isolation of our last cottage, at least haphazardly and pleasantly rural with what could, with effort, be a garden, tapering off into woods and bound by a non-stagnant stream. Inside, the ground level had mainly brick floors, a major asset with children, fine, wide elm planks upstairs, and a large attic which, though at that time bearing great resemblance to an aviary, was obviously capable of being converted into more sleeping space at some time or other in the future.

The disadvantages were a kitchen not in any way adequate for my purposes, a scullery which was a damp and poorly constructed lean-to, a leaking roof, a rotting staircase at ladder-angle, dry rot, dark rooms, some horrible metal windows with superimposed criss-cross bars, hideous wrought-iron door furniture everywhere and, worst crime of all, the fireplaces had been bricked up and electric fires built in. Clearly the major task was to de-modernize; and, happily, the price gave scope for doing just that. We bought it.

After weeks of havering, disputing and changing our minds, we finally decided to knock down the lean-to scullery, and since it faced south, to build in its place a new kitchen with sliding doors leading out to a courtyard which we thought could be made in the L formed by the join of the two cottages. We planned to build a larder in the middle of the kitchen which would divide it into an extra eating area or breakfast room with the cooking, preparation, washing-up area out of sight beyond the wall. We thought we would try to find enough old bricks to match the existing floors and continue them right out into the courtyard; and that we would divide the old kitchen (which would be at right-angles to the new one) into a new utility room — washroom, cloakroom, and small spare bedroom with a French window opening on to the new courtyard.

Apart from replacing the worst of the windows, we would also knock down the walls on both sides of the fireplace between the sitting room and dining room, so that it would appear to be one enormous room, and indeed could be used as one enormous room for any parties we might have, although if you were in one section you would feel quite cut off from the other by the large fireplace we hoped we would uncover.

Upstairs, we decided, the large bedroom in the Victorian part of the house would obviously not suffer too much by having part of its space cut off to form a second bathroom, and we thought we could remove the pretty Victorian fireplace, which came just where the partition would have to go, and take it down to what we thought should be the nursery immediately below. One bedroom had a basin in it, so we thought we would turn this into a vanitory-dressing table unit and build a wardrobe next door, enclosing the whole thing behind cupboard doors. By cutting off half of the existing walk-in wardrobe, and making a door to it from the bedroom next door, both rooms could have adequate storage space. Particularly as the room next door had a gradient of one in three and would never have supported a free-standing cupboard.

To our astonishment, we discovered that a new staircase would actually cost less than a good quality staircarpet for the same area. As we proposed to have an open tread staircase, and did not want the new wood to have a

'We had to rethink the fireplace completely...'

utility air in contrast with the heavily beamed hall and landing ceiling, I decided to stain the whole thing red with a polyurethane stain which would be both tough and gay. To lighten and open the hall still more, we thought to restore an old window which had been bricked-up when the old lean-to scullery had been added, take it down to floor level, and fill it in with glass shelves on which we could stand a collection we possessed of old wine bottles and decanters. In this way, we imagined that people coming in the front door would be able to have a vista right through the hall, through the breakfast room and out through the glass doors over the courtyard to the garden and the hill beyond.

If this all sounds very detailed and tedious, I can only say it was. But then a house has to be the sum of its parts and the whole has to be planned like a campaign. Once the structural work was established and some local architects found to draw it all out, the decoration took its cue naturally. The new kitchen would be in whitewashed brick with a tongue and groove pine-boarded ceiling and exposed beams which we would stain red to match the staircase. On the whole, I prefer rich earth colours in the country, particularly in anything pre-18th century, so in the living room and dining room I decided to paint the walls a nutmeg brown, and the beams, with the exception of the lateral fireplace beam, would be white. Naturally, when heard about, this sacrilegious plan met with polite, and sometimes not so polite, murmurs of disapproval. (In fact, not only does the room look a hundred times lighter and bigger, but I still fail to feel horror and shame at painting anything white that had already been painted black).

The hall, staircase and landing area were to be painted a deep mustard, which would, I thought, look good with both the dark beams and the red stained stairs. And in our own bedroom, which faced north and could have been gloomy, I scheduled orange walls and ceiling, juxtaposed with blinds and bedspread of fresh green and white crewel work. In most of the other upstairs rooms I decided to use wallpaper, as at the previous cottage, and for the same reason, that it held the walls together, and I was lucky to find a new range of re-introduced Colonial papers which were introduced to the Colonies in the mid-18th century. *Plus ça change* ....

Because of the enthusiasm of our architects and the builder they found — who, I must admit, did give me a wondering look or two at the beginning when he heard of the colours I was ordering, and the things I was intending to do to the sacred beams — most of the work went well. True, I discovered an electrician chiseling up the up-till-then undamaged elm planks and putting switches in wayward places totally unrelated to the carefully drawn-up electrical schedule. But that might happen in any county. We were frustrated in our careful plans for the living room fireplace, because, when uncovered, we

'... *in the dining room I decided to paint the walls a nutmeg brown*'

'We planned to build a larder in the middle of the kitchen...'

found it had been so messed about in the past that we had to rethink it completely. However, the architects, after much experimentation and coughing, found that it smoked less on one side if we built up the hearth to waist level, leaving a niche underneath for storing logs, and kept the other side at the normal level with a basket grate. This disappointment, which in fact turned out rather handsomely, was more than compensated for by the discovery behind a wall in our bedroom of a great Tudor fireplace, judging by the narrowness of the bricks. So our late labourer's cottage must have belonged to a smartish yeoman farmer at one time.

The worst tragedy was caused by the drainage system. Profiting from our former often malodorous experience, we determined to remove the cesspit from its place, some 10 yards from our bedroom window, to a carefully picked site in the middle of the orchard (I forgot to mention that we had gained yet another fruitless but decorative gathering of trees). Knowing that we had set a moving-in date for mid-April, and that the architects had cunningly managed to swing a penalty clause for non-completion on to him, the poor builder was constrained to bring a bulldozer in to do the job in what must have been the muddiest week of the year. It got stuck. And in its efforts to recover its equilibrium it knocked down a couple of trees before getting permanently entrenched. The next day, another bulldozer came to tow it out, unfortunately reversing rather vigorously into two more trees in the process. Surveying the carnage, I hoped fervently that the sweetness of the air in the future would compensate for the sudden pruning of the landscape.

This pruning was carried even further, when we were told that a towering walnut in the garden had become rotten enough to be dangerous and should come down. As we reluctantly agreed, I stipulated that they would leave a good enough stump to be both decorative and useful, i.e. that it could act as both occasional seat and a base to grow honeysuckle, clematis or roses. The next time I arrived, I saw to my horror, a shorn, bald thing like a mast, some 12 foot high, stuck in the middle of a gaping pit. Hearing my expostulations they were truly contrite and, on my next visit, I found a nice fat stump, neatly re-planted and mossed, and the farm foreman from down the road, leaning over the gate and contemplating it with a pitying glint in his eye. 'That won't grow again, you know', he explained to me carefully. 'So I wouldn't try if I was you' ......

Since the bulldozers had already made such inroads, if that is the word, on one of our prospective lawns, we decided to turn tragedy to advantage and get them to finish the job by making a sunken lawn, with a curving bank rising up to some of the trees we had left, and the woods beyond. To our amazement and relief, not only did it work, but the whole thing was grassed over by the summer and looking as if it had been that shape for always. Rather a triumph, we thought, considering it had been half field, half stony farmyard before, certainly never a garden.

Now we are in our third year in the house. The climbing roses are beginning to shoot through the apple trees; the honeysuckles, vines, clematis and jasmines are thickly lining the walls of the courtyard; the shrub roses are arching and spreading, the hostas and euphorbia are widening nicely. Juni-

'I decided to use wallpaper . . . as it held the walls together . . .'

83

pers are disguising the man-holes and wisterias are camouflaging the drain pipes. Suffolk soil is very rich.

Inside, the walls, the tables, all flat surfaces, are getting covered with the sort of idiosyncratic things I cannot resist culling from the East Anglian antiquarians. Furniture is a mixture of old and new. The floors are so beautiful that they are only rugged. And I have put fabric blinds at the windows rather than curtains, partly because they are much cheaper, partly because they let in more light. It is all very simple, but every time we walk in the door we still feel delighted. As for the children, I cannot persuade them that anything other than Suffolk is country. We can be driving for miles through Hertfordshire and Cambridgeshire and they will still say: 'Oh, when are we coming to the country? Oh when are we getting there......?'

Mary Gilliatt has worked on the staffs of House and Garden, The Daily Express, The Times *and* The Sunday Telegraph. *She has written regularly for* Country Life, New York Times, American House Beautiful *and* American House and Garden. *At the moment she writes a monthly article for* Woman's Journal *and* Australian Home Journal. *Her publications include:* English Style *and* Doing Up a House. *Her book* Kitchens and Dining Rooms *was chosen American Book of the Month Club choice 1970. She, her husband Professor Roger Gilliatt and their children spend as much time as possible at their country house in Rattlesden, Suffolk.*

'We proposed to have an open tread staircase...'

Alan Bloom
Plantsman's Pie

IT'S not unknown for a hobby to grow into a business. There are not many professions that can provide a hobby as well, but some branches of horticulture can and several nurserymen I know have begun as amateur gardeners. With me it was the other way round, for having entered horticulture on leaving school, it was not until over 30 years later that I was able fully to indulge in a love of plants, as distinct from growing them for a living. The latter had still to come first, but the fascination for plants, and the making of a large garden in which to grow an ever increasing variety, became so absorbing that there came the need for a hobby of a very different kind. Like thousands of other men, I'd been attracted since early childhood by steam engines and, to obtain and cherish one of these old timers, was the obvious choice of a different hobby.

I never dreamed of having more than one, when it arrived just 10 years ago, and was thrilled to bits the first time I lit up this 1909 Burrell and coaxed her back to life. To own an engine and to play around with it occasionally would, I felt sure, fill my need entirely. But it didn't work out that way. Looking back I can see how well the stage was set for other engines to join the first one, to begin a collection which without any definite plan or ambition has now become the largest live steam museum in Britain. As a hobby it is rather overgrown, and though it has not become a business run for profit, it has to be run on business lines even if, for me, it is still a hobby.

It seems very odd that two such totally different subjects as hardy garden plants and steam engines should be so complementary to one another. The setting at Bressingham must have something to do with it. But the impetus towards it, the reasons for coming here in 1946, have their origin long before that date. Because I wanted to work amongst plants, I rebelled against school just before I was 16. I'd grown up with the notion that work was a virtue. Not only my parents, but pretty well everyone in that Fenland village of Over thought this way and manual work was for me infinitely preferable to swotting at a school desk. Not many temptations came my way to be deflected from work, as ambitions to become a nurseryman took shape, though the 'all work and no play' maxim applied and I enjoyed my ration of football and fishing. Speed skating could be safely indulged in because the weather that brought ice put a stop to work anyway. But I could never resist a pause to watch a steam engine at work, even if there was no time to learn in detail how it worked; and the study of differences between one engine and another.

In the process of learning about plants, I worked on five different nurseries in three years. It was also a process of becoming financially independent, and beginning with 10 bob a week at 16, I was receiving, if not earning, £2 at 19 — at a time when farm workers were getting 28s. to 30s. for a 52 hour week. How marvellous, I thought, to have an ambitious nature, but the next four years (1926 - 30) didn't yield the same rate of fulfilment. My parents had moved to Oakington and were struggling to make a living from a six acre market garden. Times were hard, and though I'd embarked on rearing plants for sale, as distinct from my father's flowers and fruit for market, it was not a good time to find customers who would buy my plants.

Market garden returns were often poor — flowers sometimes a penny a bunch, and plums often a half-penny a pound; but at least it was a cash return. I disliked market growing on the grounds that it was too chancy. You had to be content with what a salesman in some far city sent back, even if it didn't cover the cost of picking, packing and carriage. Apart from this, you had to cut flowers you'd reared or tended for a year just as they were about to look their best. But if father said it was no worse than growing perennials and rock plants and seeing them flower, but afterwards having a lot left unsold, he had a point.

Alan Bloom surveys the scene at the beginning of another open day at Bressingham.

It wasn't strong enough, I thought, to change my chosen ambitions and father was a very tolerant and unselfish man. He bought a near derelict glasshouse nursery at Mildenhall late in 1930. My brother George had come into the business, and he and father moved out, leaving me to rent the Oakington holding and get on with it. At least he knew I wasn't afraid of work even if I was headstrong and not very easy to get on with.

Gradually the purely nursery side of the business encroached on the market growing area, as more orders came in for plants. There was some retail business, resulting from flower show exhibits, but in 1934 I went wholesale only, with the strengthened belief that I couldn't go wrong if I produced top quality plants, set reasonable prices, and gave prompt despatch to orders. With 15 acres in 1931, I was looking for more land by 1936, and by 1938 had 36 acres under nursery stock. Still not satisfied, even if my earlier ambition of having one of the largest nurseries of its kind in the country was fulfilled, the idea came of competing with the Dutch exporters. Their type of soil, black peaty stuff, was pretty cheap to buy in the Cambridgeshire Fens, and I finally fell for a 200 acre farm at Burwell, at a cost of £1600.

I had, of course, leanings towards farming as well as nursery work. I was also attracted to land drainage and reclamation, and though within a year I was having to admit that I'd bitten off rather more than I could chew, the war came to offer ample scope to drain, reclaim and farm the 300 acres of Adventurers' Fen as well. This wild area of reeds, bushes, old turf pits and numberless bog oaks was a challenge I was glad, at the time, to meet. It was the subject of my first book *The Farm in the Fen* (1944), but by 1945, all went sour. Adventurers' Fen was again productive, but when I learned it was intended to let it revert, I lost heart, and sold out my own farm which was adjoining and sought a farm where both my interests could be practised. The choice fell on Bressingham Hall, with its 200 acres of both upland and fen, with some of the latter as wild as Burwell had been.

The move took place at Michaelmas 1946 and it proved, unfortunately for me, to be the worst possible winter in which to transfer the nursery stock. A wet autumn, then eight weeks bitter frost, a March flood and a May-September drought was disheartening. The exactions of a nurseryman's life, involving the rebuilding of the business decimated by the war, became so formidable that I decided to emigrate to Canada. This proved an utter failure. My only gain was the experience that comes from slogging against heavily weighted odds. It was not only business anxiety that had been the reason for this disastrous venture; but it gave proof enough that escapism does not pay. From going out in September 1948 to coming back in March 1950 it was one long struggle, and my bank manager had been right when he wrote saying if I didn't return quickly there would be nothing to come back to.

Part of the chastening process, having got to grips again with Bressingham, was the realisation that I'd shirked a duty — to the land I owned, to a business that was worth rebuilding, and to those of my helpers who had remained loyal. There was solace in handling plants, increasing saleable stocks, mastering weeds, restoring fertility, and even in digging a ditch, to say nothing of what I owed to my three children who had been in my sole charge throughout. Having slowly begun, restoration came much more quickly than I'd dared to hope, and in three years the nursery acreage was back to its pre-war level, and prospects were bright for the future.

Reclamation work on the fenny Waveney valley had been finished off, but drainage problems beyond my control scotched efforts to bring this black, rich-looking land into full production. In the main, it was sandy peat, even more like that in Holland than it was at Burwell. But in Holland water levels were under control to suit the type of crop and in the nursery areas it was lower in winter than in summer when extra was needed for irrigation. Here, it was the other way round, and with winter wet often a killer of plants and, because of the panning effect, any survivors failed to grow in summer.

Those fields by 1953 were sown down to grass and they grew heavy crops of hay and grazing for cattle. The more reliably productive upland carried the increasing stocks of hardy plants and, with the business showing modest profits, came the chance to begin a much postponed experiment in

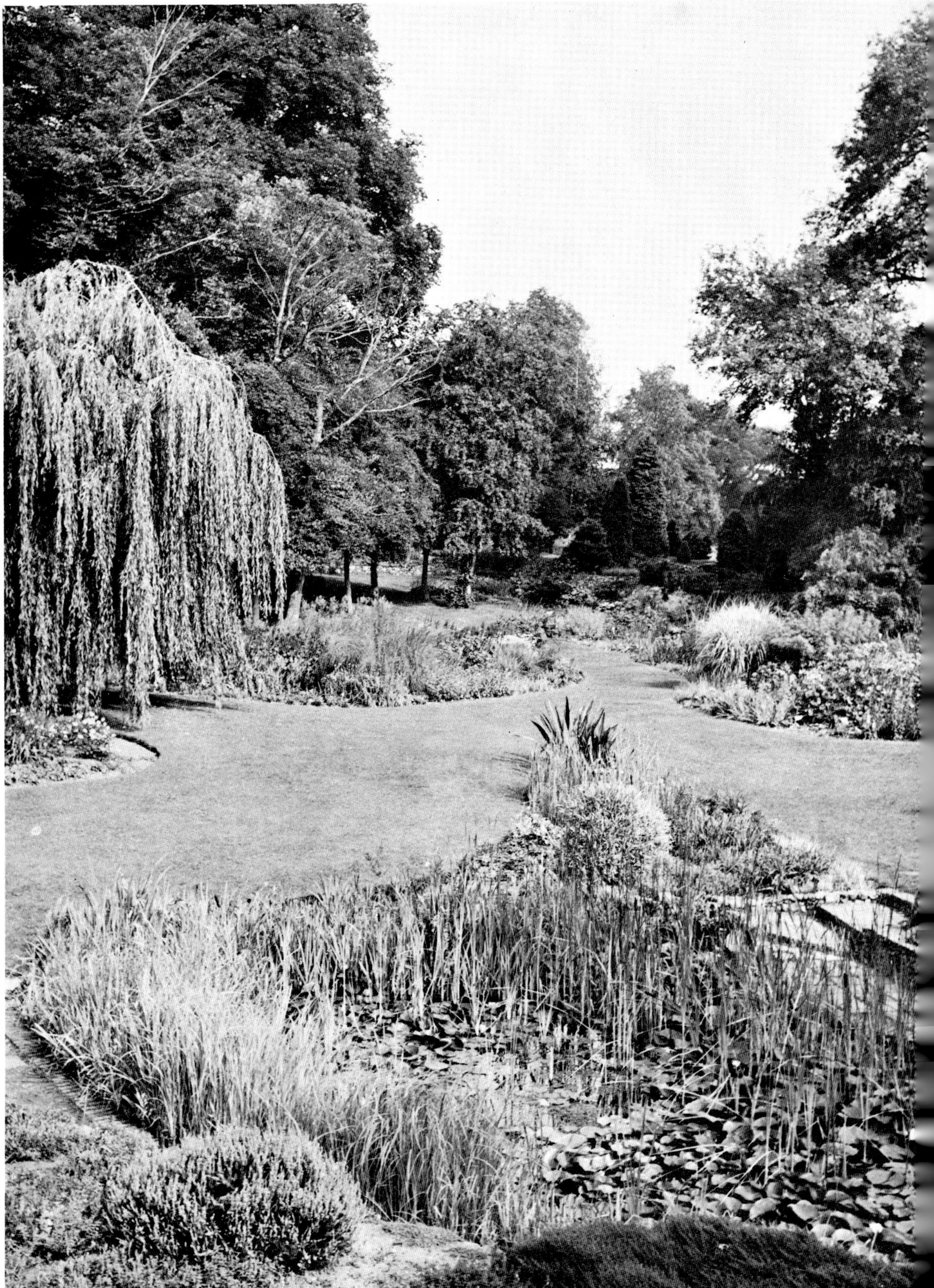

growing some — not for sale, but for display and interest. The notion had occurred that 'island beds' with all round access would be less troublesome and more effective than the conventional one-sided herbaceous border. With a large neglected lawn available, the first beds were made and proved such a success that I decided to develop and extend the idea into the meadow beyond.

The setting was pleasant and the soil was good. It offered, above all, scope for growing a much wider range of plants, of kinds some rare or obscure which till then had only been names to me, and some I did not know existed. Visits to botanic gardens began with the new garden extensions in 1957 and resulted in many a swopping. The newcomers became of quite absorbing interest and those that proved to be specially garden worthy were given special treatment, to be propagated somehow or other so as to add them to nursery stocks. In addition new plants were being bred and batches of seedlings were reared to try out, whittling down to the best by yearly selection. All this added zest to life as a plantsman. The garden grew year by year till it covered five acres and contained around 5,000 different species and varieties of plants, for, luckily, it was a site where almost every condition of sun, shade moisture and soil requirement could be met. Work was indeed a joy, but though scarcely aware of it, I was becoming over-absorbed and one-track minded. Plants had become a hobby that was too closely linked to the business to offer any relaxation.

Hankerings for a steam engine had been suppressed ever since my return from Canada in 1950. The Burrell traction engine I'd bought in 1947 had been used for pulling out bushes and driving a saw bench. It had served as a most enjoyable hobby too, and to find that it had been cut up for scrap just before my return made me very sore. But by 1961, with the garden project near completion and the nursery restored and reasonably prosperous, I saw no harm in indulging in steam as a hobby again. When 'Bertha' arrived early in 1961, I imagined it would be the only engine I would ever own. I also imagined that now and then I would put her in steam just for my own and my family's pleasure, to chug around the farm buildings. But I'd not taken account of other people's reactions. When summer came, with the garden being open on certain Sundays in aid of charities, I found people peering under 'Bertha's' covering tilt. They too were so obviously interested that from then on it became an excuse to put her in steam, and to give rides to children sitting up in the coal tender. It also generated the idea of acquiring more engines whilst they could still be had, and so build up a collection which would make an added interest for those who come to see the garden.

By the end of 1961 there were eight engines at Bressingham. Most of them were pretty derelict but, with some willing helpers on winter nights, one by one they were scraped and repainted, re-tubed and repaired. The offer of any engine, different to those I had already, held an irresistible appeal, as far as funds allowed. With the total up to 14 by 1963, my interest extended to locomotives. Contacts with British Railways led to inspection of redundant locos but the cost, including transport, was too formidable. Besides, it was steam alive both visitors and I wanted to see, and a full-sized railway engine running on rails seemed quite out of reach. So it was that I lowered my sights and found a miniature for sale. The track was 9½" wide, but right from the first, the fact that a passenger-carrying railway could

Left: The Dell Garden at Bressingham

be self supporting was an insistent thought. The other engines brought in nothing to offset outlay and maintenance, but this first little line beside the garden in 1965 was paying for itself, as well as being an added attraction.

With the nursery of necessity barred to visitors, it was but a step forward to plan taking passengers around behind steam. The closure of some Welsh slate quarries led to acquiring two 2 ft. gauge locos, and some workmen's trucks. The 1966 track was ½ mile round. In 1967 it was a mile, with 1½ miles by 1968. Another line through the Waveney Valley and some woods came in 1969. It was a mile around, but by this time other developments were fast taking shape. I'd learned that B.R. would consider allocating preserved locomotives to private museums, subject to adequate accommodation and care. A new shed of 12,500 sq. ft. was erected with only hope to go on, but it was fully vindicated with the arrival of three engines in 1968 — 'Thundersley', 'Oliver Cromwell' and No.2500, between them weighing nearly 300 tons.

They, and some industrial locos, were on permanent loan and with them came the realisation that without having had a live steam museum as an ambition it had none the less come into being; and there were responsibilities which were far removed from any ideas of this being just a hobby. Suddenly, it had become the most comprehensive live steam museum in Britain, and it would not only have to be self-supporting, but preserved for the future as well. My family used to grin wryly when I said a certain engine was needed to make the collection complete, but now I know that it will never be complete, I have also to admit that we have nearly as many as can properly be cared for. There are 35 engines of all types, including the little beauty that makes my wife's roundabouts revolve.

The most recent arrivals were a stroke of luck. To have the 'Royal Scot' at Bressingham is indeed an honour, and this goes for the comely 164 ton 'Duchess of Sutherland' as well. These were presented on permanent loan by Butlins Holiday Camps and, in a sense, they are a gift to the nation. They came because Butlins realised they could but deteriorate on seaside sites and, because they are of such historic importance, wish them to be restored to active retirement, to be seen by the public. In this case the public comprises not only enthusiasts — those strangely attracted by the power of steam — but also those whose memories are evoked. To the very young, steam engines are as fascinating as to our forbears who witnessed in wonder the coming of the Iron Horse.

I can and do think of myself as amongst the most fortunate of men in having the scope, both for the gardens and the engines which people flock to see. It would, in fact, be arrogant to think otherwise — as the man of action, wholly responsible for these displays. I do not see it as a personal achievement: I could not have done it on my own. This goes without saying, for I have no engineering ability worth mentioning; nor have I any knowledge of botany as far as the plants are concerned. It is simply a case of having the goodwill, interest and skill of others, to add to what impetus I have been able to provide, and of taking some of the opportunities that came my way.

I've reached a time of life when reflections are gaining precedence over ambitions. With hindsight I can see how many wrong turnings I took and how blind I was not to see them as such. Such turnings waste precious time, and the way back is often painful. Maybe my two sons who have now taken over the day-to-day running of the business will also take wrong turnings, and learn the hard way by their own mistakes. It would be as wrong for me to breathe down their necks or to try to direct their paths as to deprive them of knowledge I have gained and go into complete retirement. The thought of such retirement appals me, for I still enjoy working, and manual labour is more of a pleasure than it was 50 years ago. Perhaps this is because work was then under compulsion and now I can pick and choose. Zest for work comes not only from interest, but also because I believe the job, whatever it is, is worth doing.

Spring is the season for plants and gardens. The five acre garden I made would not hold its attraction for long if spring work were skipped or skimped. A large number of the plants grown are dug up every year, either to provide

Black Prince - the result of many hours of reconstruction.

additional stock for the nursery or simply because a better display comes from frequent replanting. Some kinds need annual attention because they have special requirements, and others are so rare or scarce that every opportunity of stock increase has to be taken. Some are so slow to increase that it takes years of patient handling before sufficient stock is available for sale. It is the caring for these which gives one of my greatest delights and though they are sometimes 'will o' the wisps', for me as a plantsman, they go a long way in providing hopeful and perennial expectancy, without which incentive might be lacking. It was thus even when my interests were centred solely on the nursery. Every year, there would be some failures as well as successes with propagating and planting. One seeks the reason and banks on the next year being better, not stopping to reflect that 100% success is never achieved when hazards are high and often unknown.

Close to the garden, I have my own little nursery of a few acres. Over the years it has served as land on which to work up stocks of specially good or choice plants, and as a trial ground for new varieties bred or imported. It is my pleasure to do most of the propagating in this area. When spring is past, with its replanting, replenishing work in the garden and rows of plants in my little nursery are complete; then comes the time for some relaxation with a hoe. There is nothing like hoeing to soothe jangled nerves. The weeds can become the frustrations and worries and as the sharp blade cuts them off, with the sun and wind to finish them off, then relief comes to the mind. In summer comes the joy of seeing the response of plants to rain. Ever since boyhood it has grieved me to see them suffer from drought. But rain is chancy and, if irrigation is not the same, the power to use it when the need arises is no less satisfying to me. In my time, I've dammed ditches, sunk wells, laid pipes, dug, delved and gone half crazy to bring water to plants that need it badly. But at Bressingham, luckily, we have artesian supplies and irrigation coverage for over 100 acres.

Autumn has sometimes found me trying desperately to be rid of water. It was like that in September 1968, when the whole of our fen land was flooded from the 4.36 inches that fell in 24 hours. Acres of plants on the fen fields were just ready for filling booked orders — the harvest time for the nursery. But when at last the floods receded, most of those plants were drowned, dead and stinking. It could be said that I've spent more time since coming to Bressingham in trying to be rid of excessive moisture than in trying to supply it when needed. Certainly, many more plants have died from too much water than too little; and the land, once flooded or gone soggy with wet, congeals and will not come to life again until it is broken up and weathered.

This is a factor we have to live with and, though the remedy would come with perfect drainage, I know it will never be perfect. The valley here is bottle-necked and it will be a battle unending to make the fen fields reasonably productive. Not even the spoil from a two acre pond I made a few years ago sufficed to raise the level of two adjoining fields to prevent sogginess. The addition of sand and clay certainly improved the quality of the land, and the pond itself has given us a lot of pleasure, not only from skating and fishing, but just because it looks now as if it has always been there.

In winter, the drab appearance of the place — farm, garden and nursery — belies the activity that must continue. The visiting public can have little idea just how much scheming and work goes in between autumn and spring to make it worth visiting in summer. But even those of us responsible for the work are apt to feel there is plenty of time, until by March we realise it is too late to do all that was intended. I've often tackled a piece of digging or embarked on some improvement involving axe, saw and a fire just because these are the kind of jobs I enjoy in winter. And then the rub often follows that a piece of newly-dug ground has to be planted, and any other improvement maintained. It is so much easier to let nature take over, but the kind of life I've chosen to lead is inevitably a constant tussle with nature.

This applies in pretty well every sphere of activity. The resurgence of weedy growth, the choking up of ditches, the overgrowth of plants and shrubs, and the rusting up of machinery through neglect and humidity are but a few ways in which nature hits back. And when it comes to increasing stocks of plants, we often kid ourselves that we are playing a trick on nature — or at least taking advantage of natural processes — but I've been at the game long enough to reflect that nature holds the trumps. This is the only philosophy that holds good, when failures come, though it doesn't stop us from trying a different suit next time.

Hope, to a plantsman, or for that matter any cultivator of land, is the mainspring of existence. No matter what one grows, the greater the variety, the higher the proportion of hazards are encountered, and the greater the number of failures one can expect. But because of the hope factor one does not expect failures. I find myself, year after year, blandly imagining that because the reason for certain failures becomes known and is obviated for the future, then next year all will be well. But this is where we fall down, because we just don't know what vagary, in the guise of weather and many other facets, nature will hand out. We may live and learn but, so long as we live, there is still a lot more to learn than we know or have already learned. I happen to have more space and more variety than most gardeners; but those with a surburban or cottage garden must feel as I do — that hope is a first requisite for any would-be cultivator. This may be the reason for gardeners being runners up to parsons in the longevity tables. One of them, still active at 92 gave me his advice — 'Keep a dewin' bor' — allus keep a dewin' '.

Alan Bloom was born a Fenman in 1906. He went to Cambridge High School but left when he was 16 because 'the appeal of growing things and the freedom of the landsman proved too strong to resist any longer'. His trade began at 10 bob a week for 52 hours' work at a Wisbech nursery. And today his beloved Bressingham Hall, near Diss is the largest herbaceous nursery in Europe. Apart from his love of the land Alan Bloom is also well known for his interest in steam engines. His publications reflect his interests and include Hardy Plants of Distinction, The Bressingham Story *and* Steam Engines at Bressingham.

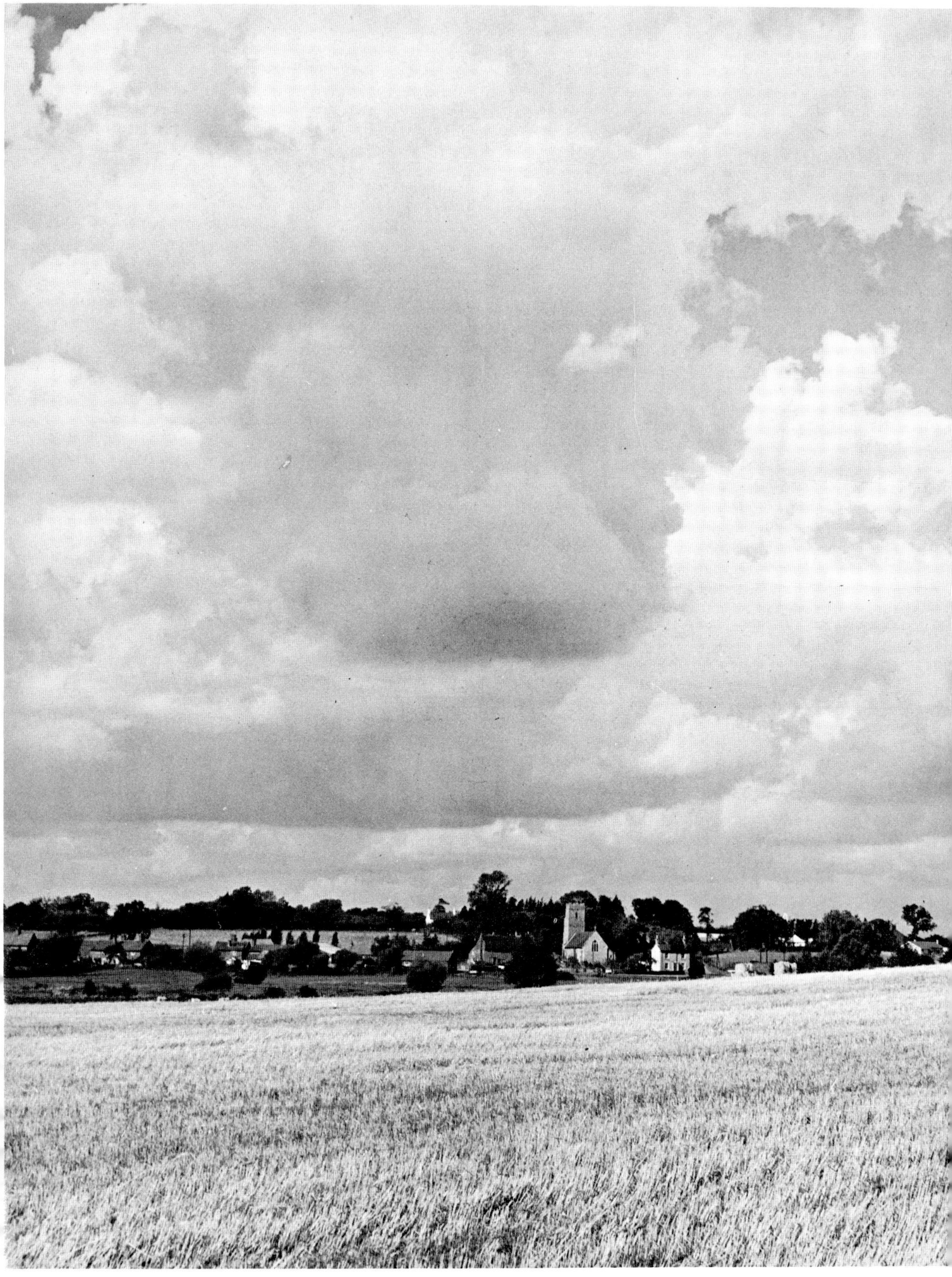

Rintoul Booth
The Rich Land

IT is a curious fact that, if ever I travel to another part of the British Isles, somewhere like Warwickshire, say, at first, it is a relief and delight to see trees growing, immemorial elms and spreading oaks, green fields with cattle grazing, friendly, welcoming inns; or Sussex or Kent, where everything in everybody's garden looks lovely.

Within less than 48 hours, the trees have become overwhelming; as one Suffolk farmer put it; they look like a waste of space that could be used for growing barley. Somehow the green fields and livestock take on the appearance of painted toys. The friendly inns, where Eric and Doris set out to be pleasant to their customers, provide endless 'ploughmen's lunches' of bread and cheese which seem largely to be eaten by travelling representatives in ladies' hats.

The cold grip of East Anglia tightens round the heart strings; it is time to return to the land of sugar beet growing, where, in most cases, it is a concession to weakness if the publican condescends to produce a packet of crisps or, as a delightful alternative, an emergency pack of hard cheese biscuits.

As in other parts of the country, East Anglia has its organised tourist traps but the majority of the native population is as much interested in the activities of foreigners as in the personal prospect of landing on the moon.

Like the old lady at a village near Stowmarket who told a friend that her son had emigrated to Canada:

'Did he go by boat or did he fly?'

'I don't know, but he took the bus to Ipswich.'

It was not so long ago either that a farmer was asked by a journalist what he thought of British farming prospects in the Common Market.

He replied: 'I don't know. I always sends to Stowmarket.'

All this is entirely as it should be, if there is still any value to be found in the Victorian attitude that a man should be content with his lot. It was the first Duke of Wellington who opposed the introduction of the railways on the grounds that it would enable large sections of the working population to move up and down the country, becoming discontented. I have been doing that most of my life, much of it in the course of agricultural journalism, which is not all plodding round farms and gently prodding pigs, while leaning on five-barred gates in the shade of those immemorial elms.

Often as not, it means going to London where the politics of agriculture have replaced the 18th century amusements of bearbaiting and cockfighting with majestic formalised battles between the civil servants of Whitehall and the farmers' champions of the National Farmers' Union at Knightsbridge. Where, on occasion, a new hybrid pig is presented on the end of a leash, held by a top model, or a new combine harvester is unveiled, under soft lights in the ballroom of a Park Lane hotel.

London is a curious place where it is virtually impossible just to run across somebody you wish to meet, as you always can in village or market town. He must be notified in writing at least a week ahead. As Claud Cockburn

Left: Stratford St. Andrew.

put it, 'What about Wednesday week?' is still the Englishman's idea of an urgent appointment. Try just standing still in London today. After 30 minutes you become aware of growing suspicion and resentment. You get the impression that somebody has probably notified the police of a suspicious loiterer. Suppose the occupant of the flat, the person you are actually waiting to see, is lying behind the door, murdered. You become neurotic — how could you prove you had nothing to do with it? Should you have left that note? How would you establish an alibi?

People are rushing by, like a solid wall of lemmings, all heading for destruction, yet each one glances suspiciously at the lone figure. You give up waiting. It is becoming dangerous. You hail a taxi and beat it to Liverpool Street and home across country, calling in at the local, in the heart of the sugar beet country.

'So one of the builders he say to me, just you come up on top of this church roof and see what it's like. So I goes up. Christ, I says ...'

'You said what? Not on top of a church roof?'

'You never saw anything like it. Sagging all along one side it is.'

'I'm not surprised with your weight on it.'

The same customers, standing in the same place, talking about the same things which have been around for years. If you went away on an interplanetary trip to Mars and back over five light years, the situation would not have altered.

On one occasion, I telephoned home to hear that a public relations officer of a national firm was waiting to see me. As my wife was just going out, I suggested that he waited till I returned when he could, if he wished, accompany me to a youth club where I was due to give a talk on the subject of foxhunting to an audience which was planning a hostile demonstration at the next meet of the foxhounds.

The P.R.O. looked slightly ill at ease in our heavily rural surroundings. Down to the local we went to find the normally sober-suited establishment had been enlivened, just a fortnight before Christmas, with a new and buxom barmaid, who served out drinks and insolence in equal measure, with the fine verve and style of an 18th century serving wench.

It was not too difficult for the lady to cajole us into buying draw-tickets to add to the useless collection that generally emerges in a crumpled heap from the breast pocket of a jacket during its annual spring clean.

We had not been there 10 minutes, when the lady appeared on our side of the bar and said, in awed tones, 'There's a man to see you.' The reason for her awe became apparent when the huntsman of the local pack of foxhounds appeared, still in hunt uniform, his scarlet coat — 'pink' it may be, it is still scarlet — spattered in mud, straight back from a day's hunting all ready to enliven the youth club with the notes of the hunting horn.

The P.R.O. looked surprised. I think he rubbed his eyes as though he had found himself standing on stage in an unrehearsed pantomime.

This was not all. In crashed a party of shooting farmers. One of them commandeered the hunting horn and, placing it to his eye, looked down the wrong end, like Nelson on the *Victory,* and focussed his attention on the lady's upper decks, at the same time giving vent to a nautical cry of some description, which was cut short as she jammed the 'telescope' back into his eyeball.

By now, looking glassy-eyed, which could scarcely have been due to two glasses of light ale, our P.R.O. accompanied the huntsman and me to the youth club. We managed to hide the huntsman out of sight till, on a given cue, he appeared at the appropriate moment blowing the 'gone away'. The anti-hunting faction was rapidly converted, in some cases, to become lifelong supporters of the sport.

We later returned en masse to the local to find that I had actually won a chicken in the raffle, which somehow set the seal on the whole occasion. Next day, the P.R.O. returned to London to report to his unemancipated colleagues that life in East Anglia had not greatly changed since the immortal days of Mr. Pickwick.

Of course, such occasions, even in East Anglia, tend to be the exception rather than the rule; there are even villages where such activities would be regarded as the work of the devil.

Worse than that, the alien fringe is moving in to bring the Joneses with it, the people that advertisers expect other people to keep up with in the race to buy commodities that nobody really needs.

To keep the Joneses supplied means building factories which must keep churning out goods designed to drop to pieces after a few hours/months, maybe up to two years in exceptional circumstances, so that more will be needed to keep the pollution rate in full swing.

At one time, there was a scheme afoot to dump 70,000 of London's overspill on the fringes of Ipswich in the interests of 'planning'. The scheme was only dropped when the planners discovered that the whole object had already been defeated. People were already leaving London, faster and in greater numbers than had been anticipated.

If all these people had arrived, the whole character of East Anglia would have been destroyed for all time because the urbanisation would not have stopped short at Ipswich but spread to the coast, till the area became as unattractive as the country in the London fringe areas.

To some people, developments of this type represent progress. They include the type of councillor who considers it fitting to provide car parks and toilet facilities at formerly remote beauty spots because they are brought into the reach of the destructive majority. Local residents who complain about the disruption of the solitude and beauty are labelled as selfish reactionaries bent on depriving John Citizen of his inalienable rights to leave his beastly traces everywhere.

As a Londoner once said: 'I always enjoy visiting East Anglia although it's such a feudal place.'

I replied: 'You mean you enjoy East Anglia because it is still feudal.'

Much of the unspoilt Suffolk coastline remains unspoilt only because it is still in the hands of a few private landowners who have been brought up in a tradition of continuity; the idea of passing on an inheritance, preserving their part of the national heritage rather than devoting the whole attention to profit on a time-and-motion basis.

One of the dangers of the instant, plastic society, which would encourage amalgamation of farms and countenance the disappearance of the rural way of life to make way for 'greater efficiency', lies in its very artificiality, its total divorce from roots and origins. Already there are London children who think that milk is always a bottled product — not a living substance which comes from a cow.

Man and his environment are interchangeable aspects of one another, speaking the same language, affected in mood and outlook by the weather, the fertility or otherwise of the soil and a millionfold subtle factors. This is the reason why each county has its own character and marked differences in the characteristics of its inhabitants.

Recently, an Italian entomologist, Signor Ottorino Ascani, discovered that air pollution in the industrial centre of Milan was severe enough to alter the colour of butterflies' wings and to cause profound changes in their anatomical development and reproductive systems. Butterflies may be amongst the smallest and most sensitive of creatures, but who is to say that the difference between butterfly and man is not largely one of scale?

Man, the technological master, only becomes aware of the effect of his environment usually in cases where the water supply may lead to irregularities such as undue developments of the thyroid gland, or similar problems, but the normal environment plays its part in moulding the character of the native; a fact which may be conveniently overlooked only for as long as the system works. A factory worker, doing the same job, day after day, in squalid surroundings, is asked to deny his own personality, to submerge his individuality, to go on working, whether there is any point to it or not. Many strikes are probably the result of sheer boredom with an environment which kills personality.

Private citizen or factory worker, people are expected by their masters to live in 'little boxes', to spend their evenings gazing at distant activities relayed on other little boxes, centrally-heated, cocooned away from the reality of direct experience.

At one time, most British citizens had the 'opportunity' to go abroad in the service of their country.

'Guarding the Nizam of Hyderabad, we was. He would have given us another shillin' a day if we'd been allowed to salute him but the bloomin' Government wouldn't play. They was bad old times but I enjoyed them.'

If it had been one of today's generation of cowmen talking, you may be certain that his conversation would be more likely to revolve round the intricacies of his business, perhaps the progress of the football team but, beyond that, his individual experience would not mark him out as very different from any of his counterparts.

It is this lack of opportunity for truly individual experience which threatens the whole character of the country. There is now an emphasis on the new in-business, which is 'training'. There is an assumption on the part of those set in authority over us to imagine that all 'problems' can be overcome by offering training, whether in matters of sex, industrial technique or in agricultural work.

If you know where to look, it is generally held, there is an expert who will do your thinking for you. Put enough experts together, in the form of a large-scale committee and you will end up with an Authority, say a Pig Industry Development Authority, or a Countryside Commission or an Agricultural Training Board.

No thought of listening to ideas coming up from the man on the ground. Once you have an organisation of this type, automatically, decisions tend to be made at head office and applied from above without prior consultation with the parties who are most likely to be affected.

On a smaller scale, the same type of process has been going on for years. Nobody in the hierarchy bothered to consult the stockmen, who were the only people going to use them, before putting up accommodation for them at one of the county shows. As a result the average man had to sleep in discomfort in a bed six inches too short!

The worst aspects of feudalism are with us still but, whereas, in the old days, the man at the bottom of the ladder could generally recognise his oppressor, the wicked squire or robber baron of melodramatic tradition, now responsibility has been diffused. Decisions are taken behind closed doors in Whitehall and presented by faceless men as a *fait accompli* in the hopes that the public will accept a new airport, reservoir or census form before the implications are recognised.

The stage appears to have been reached where the trick has been played once too often and the British public has slowly awakened to the realisation that its real freedoms are being rapidly eaten away under a smokescreen of trendy verbiage about the new liberties of the permissive society.

The better aspects of the feudal system, instead of strife and envy, the mutual respect of master for man and man for master, as both masters of their own affairs, has not yet entirely gone from the East Anglian scene.

Describing his employer recently, a farm worker said he was a hard man, who never gave anything away; but fair-minded. The farmer left his man to get on with the work, sometimes not seeing him for a month at a time, except on pay-day, when he never questioned the hours of overtime claimed. Yet, if the tractor driver asked for firewood which he had helped to cut, he was expected to pay for it at the going rate.

This exemplifies the old-time attitude that a man would be hired and entrusted to get on with the job without supervision. It was assumed that he knew his business and would not take unfair advantage of the boss. On the other hand the boss knew that, if he was to win the respect of his men, he needed to know how to turn his hand to any task and, if need be, to show his men a better way of doing the work. There was no idea of getting something for nothing.

Mutual respect was founded on the farmer's proud belief that he was the best man in the district and the farmworker's belief that *he* was the best man for miles around at his particular job. Perhaps, nowadays, both parties find it more difficult to believe their own myths, though the attitude has not entirely died.

A one-time farmer, who entered agricultural journalism comparatively late in life, told a Suffolk farmer that the more he discovered about his new work, the more he realised how little he knew about either journalism or farming.

The other man, taking this remark, in some way as an implied criticism, killed all further discussion on the subject with a prolonged: 'Whoy?'

Nowadays, the farmer is expected to contribute to the monolithic Agricultural Training Board. To claim his money, in the form of a grant, he must be prepared to allow his man time off for training. This intervention naturally weakens the direct link between farmer and man in an industry which, in spite of having the lowest wages of any comparable industry, has never engaged in the luxury of strike action since the war, though every year, thousands of workers leave the land to find more profitable employment elsewhere.

The men who remain are the most skilled all-rounders to be found in Britain, capable of driving a tractor, maintaining and handling a giant £5,000 combine harvester, looking after hundreds of animals single-handed. Though a farm worker spends most of his time working on his own, he does have the comparative freedom from the unending boredom of carrying out the same job of fitting nuts to bolts in the same surroundings day after day. He still has a sense of individual responsibility and pride in his work, which means that he would never down tools over a triviality; and he has the intelligence to work out his own answers to new difficulties.

More than one ex-farm worker, finding himself thrown out of his industrial employment, has returned to try to get back on the land, perhaps the very farm which he left years before, expecting an open-armed welcome, only to find that his former work has been mechanised out of existence. Some farmers prefer to tackle the whole task of looking after 300 acres on their own rather than rely on the off-chance of finding a man who will only stay till a better chance offers.

In the long run, the only sensible answer must be for the customer to pay the proper price for food in the shops, which would enable the farmer to earn his fair share of profits out of the market, sufficient to pay his men a real wage. This, in turn, would lead to a further shaking out of the labour market; and calls for further training, where essential, would come from the areas where they were really needed, for a better purpose than claiming a grant.

In effect, this would mean a return to a two-way system of communication which is badly needed if the country is to be restored to national health and prosperity.

How often have I, during the course of agricultural journalism, attended a press conference launched 'from the top' and met ministers, senior civil servants, agricultural co-operative society officials and others who speak a language which is barely comprehensible and is entirely divorced from the man on the ground, doing the job, who seldom has an opportunity to state his own views, on an ordinary give-and-take basis. It is all very well saying that there is always the National Farmers' Union or the National Union of Agricultural Workers, but the top dogs there too often become sucked into the artificial world created by Whitehall and lose the common touch.

In olden days, kings are reputed to have walked around incognito, to discover what their subjects really thought about their ruler when talking amongst themselves in inns, taverns and coffee houses. The wise king took action to put matters right. Our present-day rulers might try this technique for themselves, instead of relying on the results of market research surveys carried out at enormous expense by Mayfair agencies which attempt to replace individual judgment by pseudo-scientific methods of too-often proved unreliability.

If they did, they would discover that the phoney world of 'Observerland', with its trends and fashions, has made little impact on the hard core of England. If you want to hear commonsense, it will come from people like the tractor driver and the cowman, used to forming their own judgments because their very existence depends on it. Our rulers would earn more respect by showing a real interest in finding out the views of the majority of countrymen, who only complain in private, who have little time for superstructures of one-way authority. These are the men who always come to the rescue of the country when it is in real trouble.

Because they have a genuine contact with the land, their Britishness is an integral part of their character, not an assumed patriotism put on to 'sell' abroad.

The countryman stands for the real England, changing only with the seasons, adapting only according to need. The East Anglian has always been suspicious of the 'furriner', the innovator and, though this can be an exasperating characteristic, it provides a real stability to a region, which does not like to be pushed around.

When the Englishman is abroad, he does not think of home as the Balance-of-Payments situation, the white hot heat of technological competition, but recalls the annual point-to-point, the village green, the local pub, the cricket team, the sound of church bells. East Anglia still represents these realities.

In the interests of allowing room for modern machines to operate, miles of hedgerow have disappeared in East Anglia in recent years, trees have been removed, to give the region a spartan appearance but, as time goes on, these changes need not be for the worse. Farmers have started replanting, providing covert for game and wild life. Instead of maintaining hedgerows to prevent soil erosion they have planted shelter belts of trees. The land will take on a new appearance, a different character.

Farm workers do not all live in tied cottages under the constant fear of eviction, but many live in council houses with their own cars and television sets. Some even go abroad for their holidays; even some of the old boys who, at one time, would not have stirred beyond their own parish. No doubt the day will come when East Anglia is just like everywhere else.

For my own part, I prefer East Anglia in the bleak mid-winter when the tourists have gone and you can, if in a solitary mood, drive to the wild coast of north Norfolk through the forests of Thetford Chase. The imagination has time to work, particularly when you hear tales of stage coaches seen at night by quite sober Norwich businessmen; when on the way home a white hind appears in the car headlights, a princess in flight.

When looking back at the past, I think of the great stables at Denston Hall, a glimpse of a groom rubbing down a high-spirited hunter, a scene unchanged since the days of Stubbs. West Suffolk has its only strange magic: a wide, sweeping landscape, with islands of still trees, peopled at night with the spirits of long-dead poachers, gamekeepers and squires.

My father was rector of a country living in West Suffolk where the church organist cycled all the way from Newmarket to Ashley twice on Sundays. A little man, his hat-brim permanently bent upwards by the wind as he pedalled up the four-mile hill, on arrival at the church, he removed his cycle clips and placed them on the organ top. Accompanied by heavy breathing and grunting, he reached into his pockets and produced an array of medicine bottles and pills, which were swallowed in turn during father's sermon.

In school holidays I remember trying to keep up with another character called 'Tip' who looked slow and unconcerned when singling his row of sugar beet. He would leave me way behind and help finish my row. We would start level again but, in spite of all my efforts, he was well away in no time. He earned his nickname by a remarkable ability to lick the tip of his nose with the end of his tongue.

There was the point-to-point meeting at Cottenham when a wealthy Swedish undergraduate, not knowing the form, turned up fully dressed for Ascot, grey topper and tail-coat, formal striped trousers, slightly mudstained. Proper Swedish Charlie.

Out hunting, the land demands respect, as do the farmers' growing crops. The Master is undisputed field-marshal of the day whose word is law. The great gaping ditches have to be negotiated with care for the horse. The horse and rider learn to respect their own capabilities, to rely on one another, to know when to command and when to follow, real two-way communication. The land imposes its own discipline; there is a mutal give-and-take.

Take all the great 'characters', the eccentrics, the proud farmers, unashamed poachers, the struggling gentry, the independent-minded but loyal farm workers, the heathlands, the arable farms, the bullocks in yards, the smell of newly chopped sugar beet, the cry of the cock pheasant and East Anglia survives as an entity, jealous of its traditions but still in the forefront of modern farming.

The scenery may change and the character of the people change with it but, once the independent outlook disappears, the whole country will be the poorer.

Let Whitehall beware.

Rintoul Booth is 39. Author of the humorous The Farming Handbook to End All Farming Handbooks *and the four farming books in the Milk Marketing Board Project Club Series. Author, journalist, broadcaster, public relations officer, and animal sculptor — held first one-man show in London's Don Quixote Gallery in 1970.*

For 10 years agricultural editor of the East Anglian Daily Times. *Covered farming events throughout U.K., Europe as far afield as Moscow. In 1966, organised the first British Agricultural Export Trade Mission to Portugal and Spain, which led to record exports of livestock and barley and stimulated the setting up of the British Agricultural Export Council for which he consistently campaigned for over five years.*

Born in Western Australia, celebrated first birthday on ship coming home. Brought up in Yorkshire, parson's son. Father, after the war, held livings at Ashley, near Newmarket, and Linton, near Cambridge. On his death, returned to Western Australia for four years. Started journalistic career on West Australian Farmers' Weekly. *Won the first two West Australian show jumping events ever held under F.E.I. (Olympic) rules.*

After a brief spell in London, joined the East Anglian Daily Times *as assistant agricultural editor. Promoted three years later. Went freelance in 1969 to concentrate on writing and animal sculpture in bronzed welded steel. Keen horseman, has hunted with many East Anglian packs. Lives at Aldham, near Hadleigh.*

The Bishop of St. Edmundsbury & Ipswich
The Church

I HAVE been asked for a personal appraisal of the state of the Church in East Anglia. I can speak only for the Church in Suffolk, but I suspect our situation may be typical of the region. It is hard to generalise without distorting the facts, for one's view is influenced by one's mood of optimism or pessimism, and facts are valued differently in different moods. I find it hard to write of the Church in which I am so deeply involved; except in terms of paradox. St. Paul described himself and his fellow apostles as dying and yet alive, and perhaps this is a fair account of the Church.

At first sight the Church in Suffolk may appear dying. People look for two outward signs of the Church's presence in a village, one static, the other, we hope, active: the parish church and the parson.

In some villages everyone knows that their parish church is threatened. Many of our buildings are 400 or 500 years old, and the materials with which they were built seem to be disintegrating and need replacement at an enormous cost. In the last 20 years, for example, £80,000 has been spent on the parish churches of St. Peter and St. Gregory in Sudbury; now All Saints may need up to £100,000 for renovation. There is hardly a parish church in Suffolk which has not raised, or will not have to raise, a sum of money quite disproportionate to the number and means of the people who worship in it. We have to ask whether all these ancient churches are needed for the worship of God, the purpose for which they were built.

Very many people in Suffolk never use their churches for this purpose, except for marriages and funerals, and in some villages the usual Sunday congregation is elderly and small. Whether or not the English people retain faith in God, most do not support a worshipping community. At the turn of the century most people went to church, and the accepted social order was reflected in the seating arrangements and, indeed, in the difference in the congregation morning and evening. In parish churches there are still a few family pews left with fireplaces, and more common, uncomfortable benches at the back of the church for the lower orders. But by 1900 the days had long gone when a Yorkshire parson could set his people to sing the 119th psalm while he ranged the village with his hunting crop and raided the pubs, to drive any backsliders into church for the sermon; yet the social pressure to conformity remained powerful. England appeared to be a Christian country, and predominantly C. of E. The churches in the country districts were well used, at least on Sundays. Everyone was baptised as a matter of course.

This is not the case now, and the numbers of children confirmed have been declining steeply in recent years. There is now very little social pressure to go to church; in fact to attend church is to go against the tide of public opinion and practice. From a religious point of view this may not be a bad thing, but it is a sign of a great change in social custom, a swing from being a 'folk church' to a community aware of itself as in some ways standing apart from society. In my boyhood you could not ask a person without offence if he was a Christian. If you ask that question now, no offence will be taken.

Anyone who has discussed religion with the top classes of Secondary or Modern Schools knows how few boys and girls have a positive attitude towards religion, and how few come from homes that have any contact with the Church. This change of situation places our church buildings under threat because their maintenance must be done by those who use them; there are usually no endowments available for that work. If churchgoers are few and elderly, the burden can hardly be borne.

It is, however, people more than buildings which indicate the vitality of an institution, and, in England, parsons have been regarded as the real representatives of the Church. Here, too, the contemporary scene looks discouraging for a Christian. Parsons used to be found in every village, and once played an important role in the people's life. The parson was often the father figure in his community, the resource person for his people and the one to whom they took their problems. He and his wife usually did what they could to alleviate distress and encourage self-help. They also, with the squire, looked after the running costs of the parish. Collections in church used to be rare.

Now the parson's role has changed. The State cares for the education and health of the people and for an increasing range of counselling services. The parson does not have the kind of calls on his help which used to give him contact with people in need. There is a climate of non-faith, especially among younger people, which makes it unusual for people to seek theological advice and help. This has undoubtedly contributed to the decline felt by all the Churches, in the numbers of men offering for the Ministry. The number to be ordained in the Church of England is the smallest for 40 years. The result of these factors is that pastoral care has to be re-organised and parishes amalgamated, to give the parson a viable sphere of work, and to make the available parsons go round. In many villages the old rectory was sold years ago, and now the smaller, more modern house which replaced it will also be disposed of, as the parish loses its resident parson. This situation is forced on us, but no one can fail to see that loss is involved. The parson who worked in his parish for 30 years or more, if he was a good and conscientious man, was known and trusted by everyone. Now the parson is sometimes made to feel a visitor in some villages, and his contact with people may be less sustained and intimate than used to be the case.

So, as we look at the present situation we may decide the Church is dying, like much else that used to mark the English way of life. But I do not think this judgment is well-founded. I hope I am not guilty of wishful thinking in putting, briefly, something of the other side.

In Suffolk, as elsewhere, Church people as a whole are now taking responsibility for the affairs of their parish. In most cases they no longer leave everything to the parson (though in some places they still do), but are active in organising parish functions and taking responsibility for decisions made in the P.C.C. The Deanery Synods are extending this sense of responsibility from the narrow confines of a parish to a wider area. This sense that the responsibility for the life of the Church rests with the whole body of Church people, parsons and people together, is strongest in the towns, but it is also evident in many village groups. In villages as well as towns there are often groups of lay people meeting in their homes, especially during Lent, discussing their faith and its implications. This seems to me a most hopeful development.

The worship of the Church is changing slowly, and in many parishes the main service of Sunday is no longer Morning Prayer but a parish Communion, with a sermon and singing and often using the experimental service which has been authorised. Younger people especially seem to appreciate a service which gives more participation to the congregation and seems to demand more definite commitment.

Increasing participation of the laity in Church life has also led to a great increase in activities, worship and otherwise, shared with other Christian bodies. In many Suffolk towns close co-operation has replaced the aloofness with which we used to regard each other. The proposed change of Canon in the Church of England, by which baptised communicant members of other Churches will be welcome at Holy Communion, is very likely to accelerate and deepen this process of growing together and witnessing to our common faith.

One other sign of life is the dedication of many young people, Church based or not, to projects of service at home or overseas. Sponsored walks, voluntary service of all kinds, and imaginative fund-raising efforts for others are common. There is a quickened awareness of Christian responsibility to react positively to the needs of the world, and this is not confined to young people. In 1970 the Press carried a story of an old Suffolk lady of 85 who walked 17 miles over shingle beaches for Christian Aid, and she almost blind. There is a lot of that spirit about.

I believe that the commitment to Christ's way I have described demonstrates that the Church is not dying, but alive. The old ways of carrying on the Church's life may have to change and much re-organisation may have to be done. But the message of the Church is essentially the same simple proclamation of God's love in Christ and man's part in the purpose of God. If this is true, men will turn back to it.

After numerous ecclesiastical appointments, Dr. Leslie Brown was consecrated Lord Bishop of Uganda in Southwark Cathedral in 1953. He was translated to Namirembe and elected Archbishop of Province of Uganda, Rwanda and Burundi in 1961. After his resignation in 1965 he was translated to the Bishopric of St. Edmundsbury and Ipswich in 1966. He is the author of The Indian Christians of St. Thomas, The Christian Family, God as Christians See Him, *and* The Relevant Liturgy.

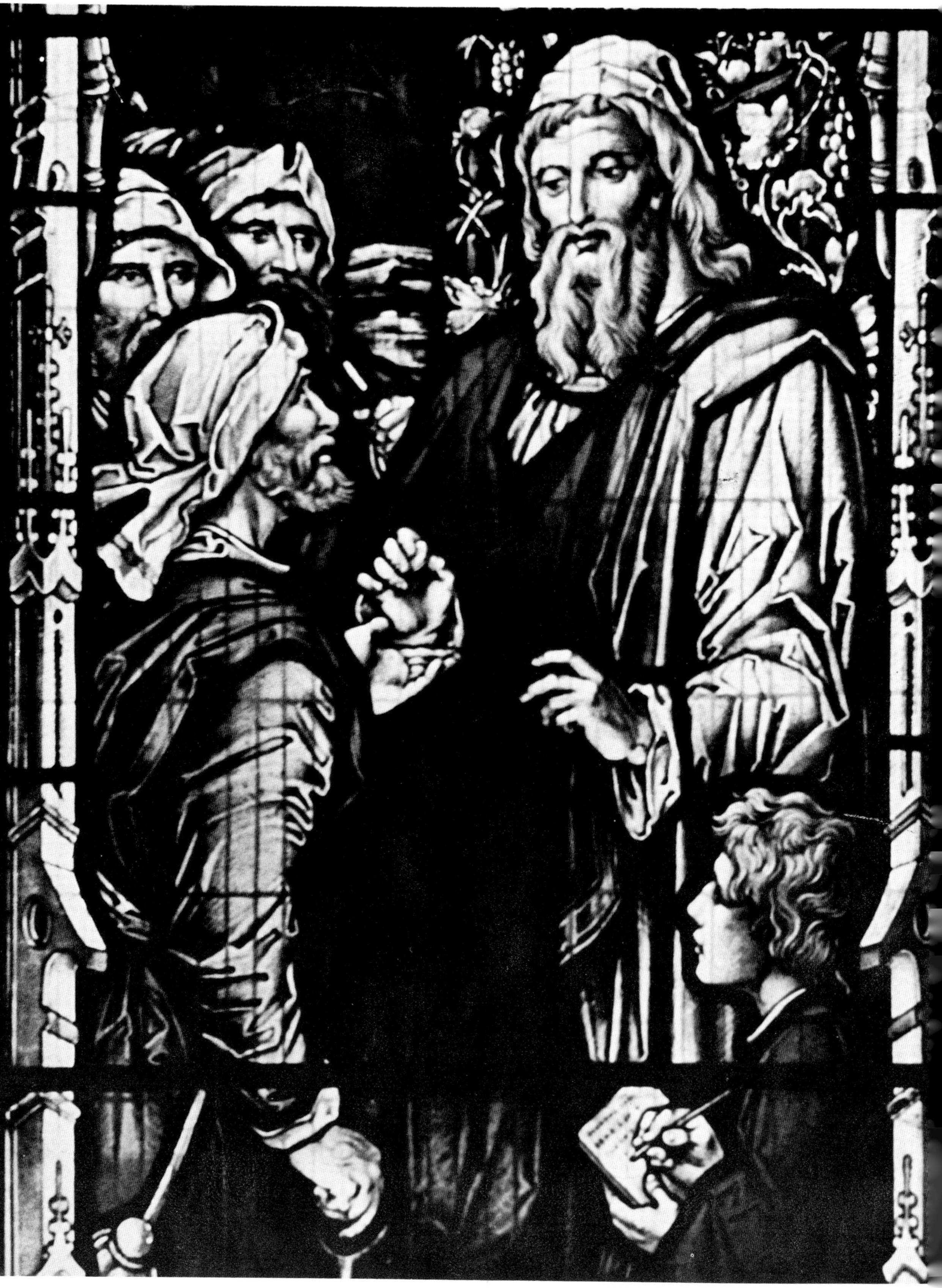

Simon Dewes
Some Churches

'ON the third morn He rose again', and that is just what we, in East Anglia, have been doing for more than 1,000 years — nearly 2,000, come to that — raising churches to God's glory.

You would have thought that, after the martyrdom of King Edward (the Danes used him as target practice with bows and arrows), we East Anglians would have given up the practice of our Christian religion as hopeless.

We did nothing of the sort.

In no time at all, as the centuries go, we were building our great churches, our abbeys and our priories: and, if anyone tells me — as they do — that these were built from the profits of the flourishing wool trade, he or she is quite wrong: because all these great churches were built by the love and labour of humble peoples' hands.

At Kersey, as an example, if you have an eye to see, you can see where, in about 1348-9, when the Black Death hit our part of the country, the labourers laid down their tools and went home to die. It was not until 10 years later that the sons or even the grandsons of these people were able to get on with the job.

And now, with a surge of faith, that may have been resurrected by the knowledge that they had been spared from this dreadful scourge, all of them set to work with a will. Thus the great churches at Lavenham, Long Melford and Hadleigh were built. And everyone had a hand in them, for this was a further age of faith.

The yeomen, whose flocks had been decimated by the lack of shepherds, gave gladly from their new-found profits (and, indeed, you may see in Lavenham Church two chapels which two farmers built for themselves and in which, no doubt, they prayed for the eternal resurrection of their souls) and the workmen, who must, at that time, have been living in utter squalor, gave their workmanship as a thank-offering that they — or their parents — had been allowed to survive the plague. And the women, too, Lords' ladies and the wives of their workmen got busy with their cloths and needles to make those vestments, threaded with 'cloth of gold' (there was, of course, no real gold in those days) which were in use until Henry VIII's rapacious ministers confiscated them to make bed-wraps for their mistresses.

At Long Melford, years before the great and gladsome and airy church was built, these East Anglian workers built what is now the Lady Chapel: and here, so humble were they (no Trades Unions in those days) that in the Chapel they also built an Ambulatory, where they might have the privilege to stay while their betters were in the main part of the Chapel.

But, now, we are not leaving Melford until we see two of their treasures in this everlasting treasure chest. The first of these is the memorable alabaster plaque of the Magi on the north wall.

Many years ago, when I first saw it, this image was on the floor — and it was richly coloured — but, later on, it was resurrected to the north wall; and here, today, you can see all its splendour and beauty.

Left:
This stained glass window of St. Mary's Church, Mildenhall, depicts the story of the Vineyard in St. Matthew, chapter 20.

Here is Joseph, getting a bit weary after all this unwarranted publicity; and here are the kings bringing their little bits of stuff.

And here, too, is the Mother of God, looking, as she might well do, very tired.

And here is Jesus; appearing remarkably adult for a little boy of — it can't have been more than — three months.

But — and this will cheer up our hearts more than anything else for us in Suffolk — from under the manger peep out two little heads of little cows who had come to adore but no one had time to milk them.

So no wonder they look a bit peevish.

I have to tell you about the most famous medieval glass in England. The church at Melford is dedicated to the Holy Trinity and, in one of the north aisle windows, there is the most marvellous bit of glass depicting three rabbits all interlocked together as, we are instructed to believe, the Holy Trinity is. This, and the alabaster plaque of the Magi are, in my opinion, the really outstanding things of Melford Church.

Let us go back to Kersey where there is a remarkable medieval screen which depicts — or is supposed to depict — three kings and three prophets but as numerous locals from Kersey have no idea who all these people on the screen are, except King Edmund, whom they couldn't possibly miss, with all his arrowed wounds, they have not been much help.

At Hadleigh I am not going to expatiate on the glories of Hadleigh Church, Deanery or Guildhall, but I would like to draw your attention to the vaulted ceiling of the Clergy vestry. (In this case, I am afraid you will have to get the key from the Dean. I believe there was once some trouble about the sacramental wine). I also want to point out to you probably the most famous bench end in England. You will find that in Our Lady's Chapel at the south side of the church, and it depicts the wolf who cried 'Here, here' and led these people to St. Edmund's body; but, before they found it, the wolf led them to the head — so that was what all the 'here, here-ing' was about.

Back to Sudbury, where I am not going to take you to Gainsborough's place or to St. Peter's Church which is rocked to its foundations by heavy traffic, but let's go to see the grisly little thing in St. Gregory's Church and this, if you can borrow the key again from the parson or the verger, you will find, behind a glass case — the shrivelled head of Simon of Sudbury who through no fault of his own had it chopped off by rebels following the Black Death and the consequent Establishment of the Paupers Act. Some chap who thought highly of him rescued Simon's head and brought it back to Sudbury, where it reposes in a glass case in the Vestry. It is bronzed in colour and rather resembles my brother-in-law's new suit.

As we are still rambling, let's go back to Hadleigh and see a little chapel which is far older than the church. This is known as the Row Chapel which simply serves the Alms Houses: it is a wood and wattle structure and has been there for more than 800 years. They have recently installed electric central heating in it which will, undoubtedly, muck up the ancient timbers which have stood for so many centuries.

And still we built to the Glory of God; and it didn't really matter a bit if we were Church of England, Wesleyians, Methodists or any other kind of body — because we were all, in our joyful way, going on the same footpath. But it needed the Salvation Army to show us how joyful that way was. They,

Right: The House of God. East Ruston.

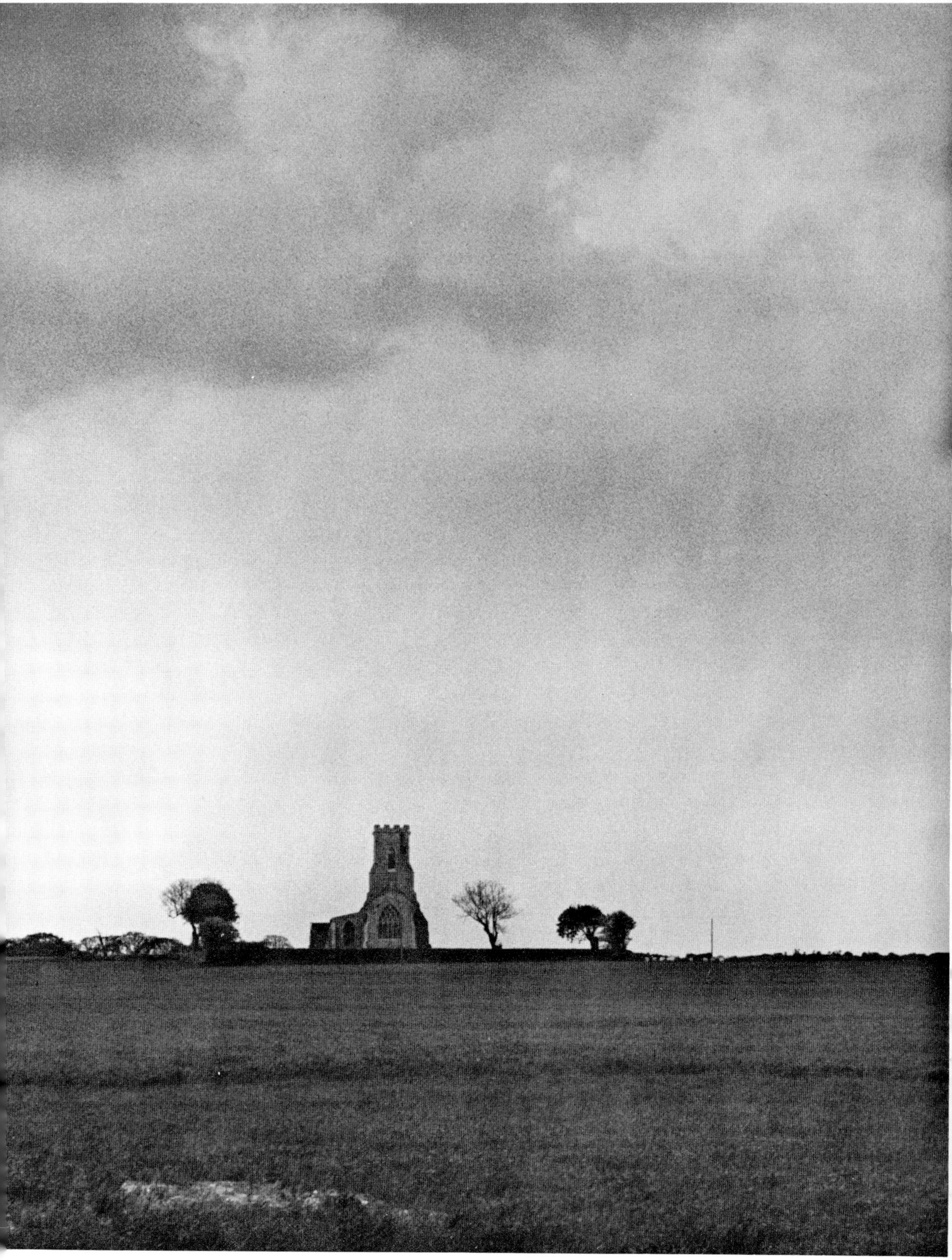

joyously, rent the skies with shouts of praise every Sunday afternoon outside my Father's house. He got a bit cross about this as he had already been to Church at eight and 11 and liked his Sunday afternoon nap.

At Thaxted there is the most beautiful church in the whole of Essex. At one time it was considered as the Cathedral of the Chelmsford diocese, created in 1914. But — and this was long before the days of Lord Beeching — it was decided that this splendid church was too far off any railway line, so they decided on a second-rate church in Chelmsford.

The great thing about Thaxted, apart from its church, was, for many

Long Melford.

years, its most remarkable parson, Mr. Conrad Noel, who resurrected this parish from hopelessness into one of the most wonderful bits of England. Here he built up a community of souls so that, although he put up the Red Flag in his church and a lot of scoundrels came and pulled it down, it was put up again by people who had seen the words underneath it which said: *'He hath made all people upon earth; and, of all blood, are we made.'*

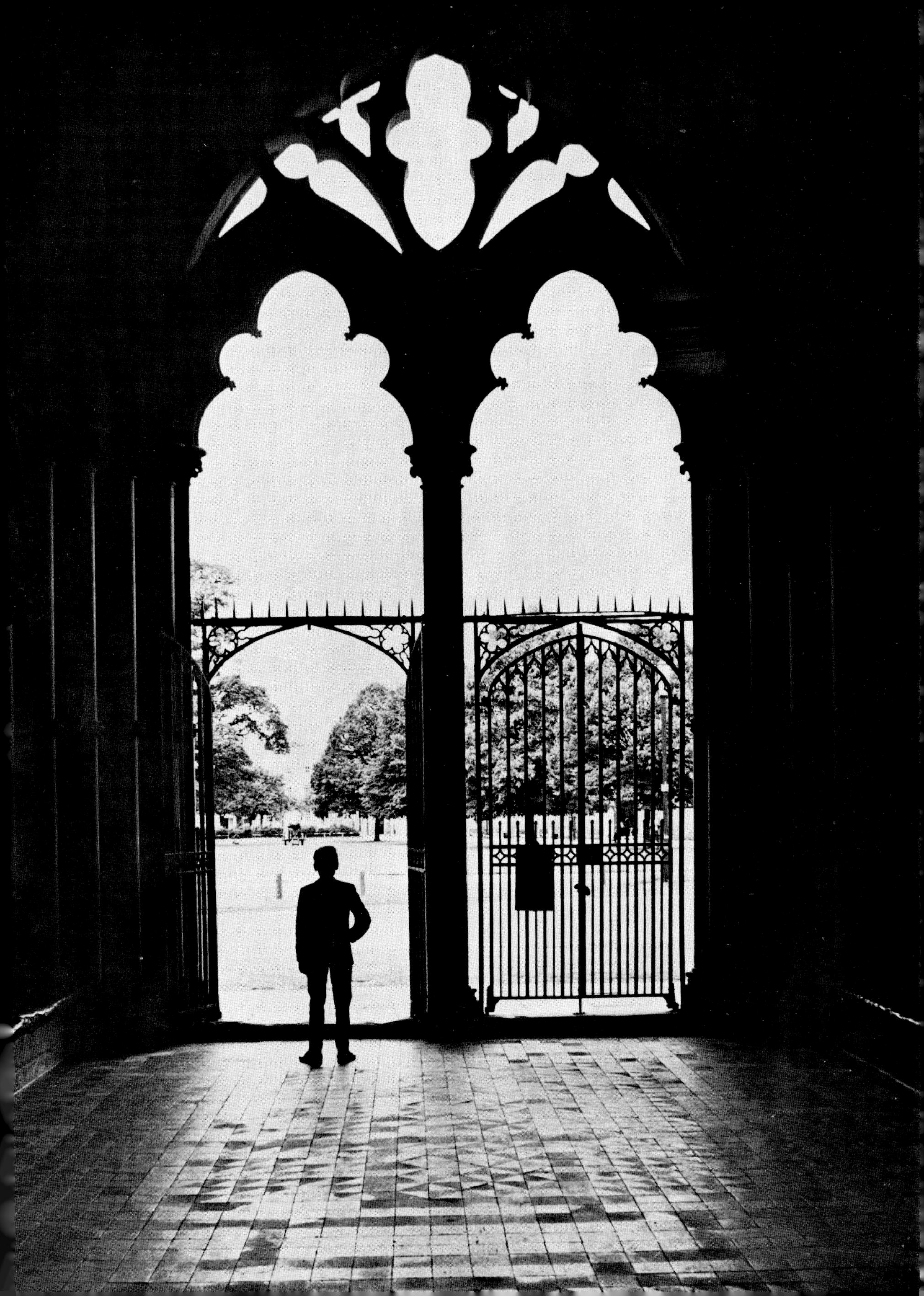

Ely Cathedral, a bit outside the proper East Anglia, is, perhaps apart from Durham, probably the most wonderful piece of ecclesiastical architecture in England. I cannot write of this without emotion, as many of my ancestors and relations are commemorated there. Through many centuries the great Lantern Tower of Ely Cathedral has guided the Fenmen home after their perilous trips through dykes and ditches to safety.

Blythburgh is the only notable landmark on the whole of the road from London to Yarmouth. This could be the coldest church in Suffolk, as it is the loneliest, but unlike Hadleigh which has always been a very cold church as all the light comes in on the north side, where there are no coloured windows, Blythburgh, looking inland to the marshes and outland to the North Sea, never gives the appearance of coldness. The remarkable 'Jack of the Clock' used to tell the time for many, many years, but he now only chimes once to herald the entry of the clergy.

We are leaving Blythburgh to get nearer the place where I now live; and this is Framlingham, where a certain almost miraculous thing happened to the present rector.

Until recently the early 18th century reredos under the east window was obscured by a rotten little altar and the result was that no one bothered to notice the centre piece, and no one realised its significance, which is a Glory; and had the present rector been offered a piece of canvas of the same size setting out some Biblical scene of Moses in the bullrushes or the Holy family, he would cheerfully have put it over the top. Fortunately no such offer was made.

Although there was no altar below the picture, a wooden table used in the choir vestry was discovered to be the old altar; so it was vested, and made into a small chapel behind the altar for week day services.

This was when the significance of the Glory dawned on the rector. He was celebrating the Holy Mysteries and when he raised his eyes from his work, they passed over the bottom curve of the clouds and he realised that he was looking, so to speak, through the veil into eternity.

'Simon Dewes' which, of course, is not his real name, was born in Hadleigh in 1907. His father was born in Hadleigh exactly sixty years earlier: but they are not really 'Suffolkers', as 'Simon Dewes'' family lived in Ely for nearly 1000 years. His family can't even pretend to be among the gallant Saxons, who, under Hereward the Wake, defended his stronghold in the Fens. His ancestors were of the Norman Invaders. He has written more than 60 books and more than 6000 stories and articles for which, he claims, probably rightly, he has never been adequately paid. He now lives near Framlingham with his beautiful wife who, although she is one half French, has now become more East Anglian than he is himself.

Edward Seago
A Place To Paint

IT is surprising how many painters have lived and worked in their native county. Perhaps this applies more to landscape painters; except that Frans Hals and Vermeer never moved from Haarlem and Delft. But I am thinking of Boudin who had the good fortune to be born in Honfleur and, except for a few excursions to Brittany and Holland and once to Venice, spent his life painting in his native district and died within two miles of the house where he was born. I wonder if this is why Corot called him the Master of Greys? All his life he lived with the infinitely subtle tones of Normandy grey — tones which anyone more used to strong contrasts would find so difficult to manage.

I am thinking, too, of Crome who made only one voyage from England — to Boulogne — and after a visit or two to The Lakes and North Wales, spent the rest of his life working within riding distance of his native Norwich, finding an endless variety of subjects by the banks of the Yare and the oak groves of Postwick. Maybe the familiar features which they had known since childhood provided all they needed for their work — a landscape in which they had grown up, with its own particular light and atmosphere to which they were completely atuned. I am sure this has been so in my case. My earliest memories are of reed-fringed Norfolk rivers and wide marshes.

I was probably about seven years old when I first sailed my model yacht on Salhouse Broad and I can remember the excitement of watching its uncertain voyage from one side of the broad to the other. At about the same age I first saw the mudflats of a salt-water estuary. I was staying with relations at Woodbridge and old Peg Gray, a local waterman, took me out in his fowling punt. I remember the delight of that first trip, and there were many afterwards because for the whole of that holiday I haunted the jetty where Peg Gray was to be found and he often took me with him when he was working on the river.

It was from him that I first learned the names of some of the waders which skimmed past us with fluting cries, and about the tide which ran swiftly between the piles of the jetty. I remember how puzzling it was that within a few hours the river could change from a vast sheet of water to a narrow channel winding between the mudflats. That place made an impact on me which has lasted throughout my life. My love of rivers and estuaries, of marshes and wide skies has never lessened. By the age of 10 I was trying to paint them with unbounded eagerness and heartbreaking disappointment; today I am still doing so, with the same eagerness and often the same disappointment.

Where there is water there are usually boats and at an early age I began making careful drawings of every boat I could find. I drew the black-sailed wherries of the Norfolk rivers and when I was 13 I painted an ambitious picture of a Thames barge lying at Beccles. Possibly in the past few years I have painted the same barge on the hard at Pin Mill. Walberswick is another boyhood memory, and there I drew the longshore boats and the old steam ferry. In those days Walberswick was a sort of artists' haunt and throughout the summer they were to be seen with their easels and large umbrellas grouped about the harbour; some of them had studios on the quay and there was usually a notice on the door inviting one to view the exhibition within — an invitation which, needless to say, I accepted and carefully viewed every exhibition there was. As these were the only exhibitions I ever saw, my knowledge of the painting world was rather limited. One notice I remember claimed that the artist was the only one to paint the gorse on Walberswick

'The Boatyard, Bawdsey, Suffolk.'

Common — a claim to fame which struck me even at that age as being a trifle strange.

I can remember, as a boy, making drawings of the sailing smacks at Lowestoft, but I must have been quite young because by the time I was 15 they were a thing of the past. But there were still the herring drifters, and each year I made endless studies of these when they crammed the quayside at Yarmouth.

From the beginning the sky played an important part in my approach to landscape painting. Perhaps because of the flat Norfolk marshland, the sky became the dominating feature and often filled two thirds of my pictures. An illness which kept me for many months on my back proved to be very helpful in my study of the sky; as it was the only thing I could see when I was lying in the garden, it was the obvious thing to paint. I painted dozens of oil studies, sometimes six in one day, and on the back of each I wrote such details as the time of day and wind direction. It was years later that I learned that Constable had done the same thing 100 years before.

I think we are more aware of the sky in East Anglia because, on the whole, the horizon line is low. But apart from this, the skies themselves are usually fine. I have been told that this is due to the formation of the coastline which causes the clouds to break up. From the cloud formations we get the shadows on the earth beneath and it is these shadows, sweeping across the fields, which bring the landscape to life with that elusive transparent East Anglian light.

It is this light which is the core of East Anglian landscape painting — it may even have been the cause of it. What the young Constable learned by observation in the Dedham Vale he applied later to Hampstead Heath, but if he had started life in Hampstead I wonder if the result would have been the same. It is a fascinating line of thought to which there is no answer.

Had John Crome been born in the West Country, it is very unlikely that he would have been influenced at an early age by Ruysdael and Hobbema or that he would have seen their pictures. His genius would have been the same, but his inspiration would have been different and he might never have painted his 'Moonlight on the Yare'. Although one of the largest and perhaps the finest of his pictures is 'The Slate Quarry' in the Lake District, most of his subjects were essentially local — 'Mousehold Heath', 'Pollard Willows' and 'Poringland Oak' — subjects which are still to be seen today. The pollard willows still border many of the roads across the marshes, planted so that their network of roots will support the bank on either side, and oak trees still line most of the hedgerows of Norfolk fields.

As a boy I grew desperately weary of those oak trees, I longed for stately elms which grew tall and upright with magnificent stretching limbs, but I could find only the oaks — distorted and ivy-grown. Within a mile or two of the coast they are often bent by the wind, when they become even more ragged. In the end, of course, I grew to love them and made careful drawings of their twisted boughs. When I think of a Cotswold vale I think of rounded elms casting long evening shadows in a fold of the hills, and when I think of Norfolk I see a wide horizon and low-eaved farms and the shadows are the swiftly changing shadows of the clouds. The pantile roof and the reed thatch are other features of the East Anglian landscape. The reeds are cut from the Norfolk broads and rivers and as a boy I can remember the lighters heavily laden, like floating stacks, with a lug sail rigged on top, crossing Heigham Sounds.

Although thatching is a dying craft, there are still reed stacks on the Norfolk ronds and, happily, there are still thatchers to use them. The pantiles are peculiar to East Anglia; originally they came as ballast in ships trading from the Low Countries to King's Lynn and Great Yarmouth and one is unlikely to find them more than 30 miles inland. The same ships brought the Dutch pictures which were purchased by the merchants of Yarmouth and the local squires. That is how young Crome became acquainted with the work of Hobbema, and it accounts for the influence of the Dutch painters on the members of the Norwich School, the Society which Crome founded with his friend Robert Ladbrooke.

The influence is most marked in the work of Ladbrooke, as it is with Vincent and the younger James Stark but, curiously enough, it shows very little in the work of perhaps the finest painter in watercolour England has produced, John Sell Cotman. To my mind he stands alone, not only for his mastery of the medium, but for his conception and power of design. His superb watercolours have perhaps overshadowed his work in oil, but in that medium also he was a master. One of his finest, 'The Lincolnshire Mills', still hangs in the Norfolk house where it first went from Cotman's studio. He was at his best, I think, in East Anglia and least successful in his Italian scenes, a country which he never visited, and the pictures were painted from drawings in the sketch book of a friend.

For some years Cotman lived at Yarmouth and the little white house still stands. Its windows face across a busy road to a line of warehouses and timber yards on the opposite side. But in Cotman's day there were no warehouses and he would have looked directly over the harbour to the sand dunes and the sea beyond. It must have been a wonderful sight with the harbour full of square-rigged ships and others lying at anchor in Yarmouth Roads; a wonderful subject for Boudin and, one would have thought, for Cotman

'Spritsail Barges on the mud.'

'Thurne Mill, Norfolk.'

also. But it would seem that he never painted it — at all events, I know of only one small pencil drawing of the harbour further upstream.

I have often wondered how the painters of the Norwich School managed to get about. They covered a wide area and found their subjects in some remarkably inaccessible places. Did they, I wonder, do much of their work on the spot, setting out with a horse and cart and sleeping in local pubs, or did they work from drawings in their studios and travel about on horseback with a sketch book in their pocket? How did Crome see his 'Moonlight on the Yare'? Did he perhaps journey with the wherrymen from Yarmouth up the Yare to Norwich and moor for the night by Reedham Ferry where the cone of the mill still stands? Indeed, it was not so many years ago that its sails were still turning.

Two miles from my house, the ruins of St. Benet's Abbey stand by the River Bure; it is a mile from the road and can only be reached by a rough track across the marsh or, of course, by water. At some time a mill was built into the foundations of the ruins, considerably taller than the other drainage mills because its cloth-covered sails had to clear the gateway of the Abbey. To enable the marshman to rig the sails, a wooden platform, supported by scaffold poles, surrounded the cone about 30 feet from the ground. One can well understand its attraction as a subject and it was painted many times by most of the Norwich School but how, I wonder, did they get there?

Their favourite painting grounds seem to have been the wooded country of Postwick and Marlingford and the river banks of the Norfolk Broads. Again and again they painted the marshmens' cottages, the windmills and of course the wherries; sailing yachts had hardly appeared on the Norfolk rivers. There are one or two pictures of regattas, but I imagine these occasions were more in the nature of a water frolic. The white sails were to come later and provide those sunlit accents across the marsh.

The marshes themselves are another link with Holland: until the year 1600 the whole of that area was a vast swamp of reed beds and mudflats through which narrow channels wound their way to the estuary which ran out to sea at Yarmouth. Over the years a sandbank had formed across the greater part of the estuary mouth and on this bank the town of Yarmouth was built. In 1600 the Dutch engineers were asked to advise on the drainage of the swamp. The estuary of Breydon Water remained and the channels became rivers with revetments to prevent them spilling over to the reclaimed marsh which was often below water level. Drainage mills were built to pump the water from the dykes and the huge, disused, peat diggings filled with water. Cattle grazed through the summer months on the rich marshland grass and the shallow-draught wherries carried tons of commerce along 350 miles of navigable waterway. Thus the Norfolk Broads as we know them today came into being and a part of England, unlike any other part, inspired some of the best in English painting.

My own house, which was built in 1603, is of Flemish bond and Dutch gabled; it stands only 12 feet above sea level and the garden runs down to a reedy creek. It overlooks the marshes by the river Thurne and perhaps it was built by one of the Dutch engineers who worked on the original drainage scheme.

To me it would seem natural for a landscape painter to turn to the subjects he knows, and thereby express himself with understanding. Knowledge must surely be the basis of that expression. The mere putting down of what one sees is not landscape painting. It is the knowledge beneath that matters and with it the ability to convey an inspiration. Maybe it is not surprising that painters linger in the locality of their childhood. This is their environment, the instrument to which they are atuned — what better one to play upon? It would, of course, be difficult for someone brought up in a large city. Would they, I wonder, continue to live in a city, finding their subjects in the streets, or would they go elsewhere to find something which suited them better? There is no rule, of course, and it depends upon the individual. There have been many painters who have found in the city something suited to their own form of expression; men like Toulouse Lautrec and Utrillo and Whistler, who discovered a London river which existed never before nor since, but only for him. Others, city born, went far afield like Gaugin who found his answer in the South Seas.

Although I was born in the suburbs of Norwich I have never thought of myself as city bred; when I was 14 we moved to Brooke, a village about six miles from Norwich, where my working life really began. Until then I had made painting excursions on my bicycle and indoor work involved the use of the dining table. Suddenly everything was at hand. All the things I so wanted to draw were within a stone's throw of the house; a farmyard with its wealth of subjects — the binder and the ploughs, the wagon shed, the stack yard, the cow-house and the stable.

A bit at a time I drew them all. Looking back it seems that I always worked a bit at a time; the hind legs of cattle, the wheel of a wagon or the horse-collars hanging in the harness room. There was an attic above the boiler house which I used as a studio, but I hardly ever worked in it. My work was done outside, sometimes drawing, sometimes painting in oil. I remember I used small panels for oil painting. I think they were 11 by nine inches — they were little more than colour notes. From the beginning my ambition was to paint atmosphere and light in landscape. That ambition still remains. The sort of light I wanted to paint never lasted long, and endless colour notes seemed the only way of learning. In these notes I never bothered about form; form did not run away and I took my time about it; I drew it carefully in detail.

Had I lived elsewhere I imagine my work would have been different and would, I suppose, have developed in quite another way. I might in time have come to East Anglia, but I would have seen it with a different eye. Over the

'The road near Upper Horning.'

years I have worked in many different parts of the world; some countries, of course, appeal to me more than others and there are certain places for which I have a particular feeling. I see them with the eye of a painter, but I do not belong, and have very little understanding beyond what I see. This in no way detracts from my appreciation of them or from my enjoyment and I can work quite happily for months at a time, but eventually I want to return to East Anglia, where I am so firmly rooted. The same applied, I suppose, to the painters of the Norwich School. Cotman went to London but returned to Norwich. Vincent and Stark left East Anglia, but the rest, I believe, remained.

Crome, I think, was the most firmly rooted of them all and he, of course, was city bred. He truly belonged to Norwich — he was born there and he died there; he never lived anywhere else.

No one can explain how the Norwich School came into being or the nature of the spark which kindled such a flame. Why, at one time, should there have been such an eruption in the City of Norwich? It cannot have been because a few Dutch pictures had found their way to houses in the vicinity; neither was it a revival of a previous school of painting. Whatever the spark, it found its inspiration in the landscape of East Anglia.

Painting has changed a good deal since then. The Romantics have gone. Traditional work gave way to Abstract, while light and atmosphere have been exchanged for design and colour. In fact, the landscape painter who strives to put air in his pictures does not exist. Crome was the first to do so and he died in 1821. In 150 years that approach to landscape painting was born, flourished and died. One 'ism' follows another in rapid succession and one day, I am certain, there will be a return to traditional work. It will be rediscovered and landscape painting will begin again. Men will once more go into the fields as Constable did, and nature will no longer be an ugly word. When that time comes I think the landscape of East Anglia will be a part of it.

'Sunday Afternoon - Waxham Beach.'

Edward Seago was born in Norwich in 1910. He held his first one-man exhibition in London at the age of 19. Between 1930 and 1933 he spent most of his time with travelling circuses in Britain and on the continent. 1933 saw the publication of his first book Circus Company *and his second exhibition in London. At this time he was drawing for magazines including* Punch *and dividing his time between Norfolk and his studio in Chelsea. Served with the Royal Engineers in the Second World War and was invited by Field Marshal Alexander to work in Italy during the Italian Campaign. In 1945 he held his first exhibition at Colnaghi's in London — Italian war pictures. In the same year he bought the Dutch House, Ludham, where he now lives. Edward Seago has exhibited in Glasgow, Toronto, New York, Oslo, Belgium, Los Angeles, Brussels, Johannesburg, Chicago — but still prefers the quiet of the Norfolk Broads.*

W.G. Arnott
The Past

THE story of East Anglia, the country of the Angles who were called the North and South Folk, and including for our purpose the northern part of the kingdom of the East Saxons (Essex), is not a story of a settled established countryside but of a land peopled with fugitives and invaders who first set the course of our history.

We know little about the primitive tribes who came and went during the intervals of that extraordinary period of time known as the Ice Age when the weight of the ice caps forced the land downwards and so flooded the North Sea basin to form the shape of Eastern England somewhat as we know it today. Nor do we know much about the Bronze and Iron Age men who came afterwards, more advanced in their culture and making pottery urns and socketed axe-heads. The East Coast, however, is changing still; Easton Ness north of Southwold, once called Extensio, the most easterly point of England, has gone and medieval Dunwich is no more. Great Yarmouth has grown up on a shingle bank which was not there in Roman times.

Perhaps it is with the Romans who came to England in about AD 43 that we may more easily begin. These invaders turned this part of the country into a province of a vast and powerful empire, subduing the local tribes like the Iceni and imposing a civilized culture with walled towns such as Colchester and Caister, near Norwich, long straight roads, country villas with sun parlours and underfloor heating, and schools where the native British children were taught Latin.

What a fascinating period this must have been and what a disaster when, almost precipitantly, the Roman legions withdrew during the 5th century owing to pressure at the centre of their empire. When they retreated they left their roads and buildings to the mercy of unskilled natives and barbaric invaders who cared little for the culture and treasures of Rome.

The massive forts the Romans built for defence against the Saxon pirates along the coast at Bradwell in Essex, Walton near Felixstowe, Burgh near Lowestoft, and Brancaster on the Norfolk coast fell into ruin or were eaten up by the sea, as at Bradwell where St. Cedd, about 654, built the first cathedral of Essex amongst the remains of the Roman Fort. Bede, in his *Ecclesiastical History,* speaks of Grantchester near Cambridge as 'a certain little city left desolate and uninhabited' where, later on, the Ely monks found a white marble tomb which they used for enshrining the body of St. Etheldreda, their late abbess.

In the bloody battles which followed the Roman withdrawal, when Angles, Saxons and then the Danes ravished the land, the primitive inhabitants came to be sustained by a new hope called Christianity, which had spread slowly across the empire during the days of its decline. Inspired by Felix, Cedd and Fursey, who were all later canonized, men learnt the virtues of mercy and forgiveness and how to live in a law-abiding world wider than their own tribe or kindred. Christian teaching gradually took a firm hold and gave the ideal of stability to native kingdoms which had not had it before.

Churches and monasteries arose throughout East Anglia only to be plundered and burnt later by the heathen Norsemen.

The Anglo-Saxon invaders, blue-eyed and phlegmatic, turned out to be good farmers and intermarried amongst the defeated Britons. They settled throughout Norfolk and Suffolk and on the Isle of Ely, as we know, from tribal place-names like Impington (Cambs), Bealings and Framlingham (Suffolk) and Walsingham and Sandringham (Norfolk). Local kings such as the Wuffingas, who gave their name to Ufford in Suffolk, achieved some sort of organised government, having their palace at near-by Rendlesham and their burial ground at Sutton where the cenotaph, believed to be that of Redwald, the last of the pagans and a nominal Christian, displayed — when excavated in 1939 — the rich, almost sophisticated treasures of jewellery and regal objects which these barbaric rulers amassed.

During the ninth century the Danes ravished much of the countryside and in 869 captured and brutally murdered St. Edmund, the last of the East Anglian kings, possibly at Hellesdon outside Norwich, although there are some who think that the place of martyrdom may have been at Sutton, near Woodbridge. Many village names, particularly in the Yarmouth — Lowestoft area, ending in -'by', indicate places where the Danes settled.

Thanks to Alfred, king of the West Saxons, the Danish king accepted baptism, and Englishman and Dane at last settled down together. From this time dates the foundation of many of our East Anglian towns, some of them built on or near the ruins of the desolated Roman settlements. During this pre-Conquest period two remarkable buildings were erected, the 'Old Minster' on an isolated Roman enclosure at South Elmham near Bungay, probably as a kind of college of priests for the surrounding countryside, and the cathedral at North Elmham in central Norfolk to serve the northern diocese before Norwich became the see city. It is the only Saxon cathedral which survives above ground in the country.

Some sort of administrative order seems to have been maintained in East Anglia in spite of the Danish incursions. By means of the Hundred moots or meeting-places, more general in Suffolk than in Norfolk, rough justice was meted out at open-air courts often held in the shadow of the gallows. Jurisdiction through the great ecclesiastical franchises or liberties granted to the religious houses of Peterborough, Ely and Bury St. Edmunds has left a stamp upon our local government even today, causing the Bury St. Edmunds district to be parted from the other half of Suffolk to form its own administrative unit. The Liberty of St. Etheldreda of Ely retained the right to appoint its own coroner at Woodbridge until 1933, when the last coroner died.

William of Normandy, coming to an England grown tired and sluggish, had the sense to leave the administration of the country much as it was; but saw to it that it was controlled by what it had previously lacked, an effective central authority visually represented by the high circular moated castles raised to overawe the neighbourhood at Castle Rising, Norwich, Bungay, Eye, Orford and other places.

In the Domesday Survey of Norfolk and Suffolk, which recognised the separation of the two counties, are recorded with meticulous care the value of the various manors or estates, the number of farm workers, head of stock, ploughs, even salt-pans and beehives. East Anglia, heavily populated, was a land of yeomen small-holders and characteristically showed a far greater number of small manors than Saxon Essex with its great estates like Audley End. Thus you find, particularly in the Suffolk villages, as many as five or six halls or manor houses in one village, often with a moat around them for defence and water supply.

Among the towns, Norwich stands pre-eminent in importance, by 1150 becoming the sixth largest town in England. Ipswich, Bury St. Edmunds and Dunwich also developed early, and trade with the continent caused the small Saxon settlement of Lynn to grow into one of the largest ports in England.

Under more settled conditions after the Conquest, a great spate of church building began and many of our village churches bear witness in a lancet window or round-headed door to their 12th century origin. On the site of some of the small early churches great monasteries arose, magnificent with their lofty vaulted roofs and towers, as centres of learning, worship and charitable works. Such were Ely, Norwich and Bury St. Edmunds with its massive Norman gate leading to the abbey church, the nave of which, 300 feet long, surpassed that of our largest cathedral today. Stone for these vast buildings came from abroad, shipped up the many rivers which must have run deeper in those days. In Suffolk brick was also used as is shown in Little Wenham Hall near Ipswich, built in 1270, although it did not come into general use as a building material until the mid 1500's. There is much brickwork of this period in the Cambridge colleges.

The sea routes were the main lines of communication, which gave East Anglia its unrivalled place in the wool trade. On the sheepwalks of Norfolk and Suffolk grew the sheep which contributed so much wealth to small towns such as Halstead, Dedham, Lavenham, Sudbury, Aylsham and Dereham. The abbeys, as large landowners, went in for sheep-farming in a big way and the memory of those days is still retained in the name of Ely Hill at Boyton, amongst the Suffolk sheepwalks. From Worstead near Norwich came a fine woollen cloth, almost like silk, of which William Paston wrote 'though it be dearer than the others, I shall make my doublet all worstead for the glory of Norfolk'. Worstead parish church standing magnificently in the middle of the village is one of the glories of Norfolk.

The great expansion of trade with the Low Countries in the 14th century brought prosperity to the ports along the eastern seaboard. Small ships of light draught, seldom exceeding 100 tons, the size of the old spritsail barge, crowded the shingle-barred estuaries, bringing fish from Iceland and wine from Bordeaux. Shipwrights plied their trade in the dockyards of Harwich and Ipswich and the smaller yards at Woodbridge, Orford, Blakeney and Wells, earning their pay of a shilling a week and no holidays except on feast days which, until the Reformation, were frequent.

The medieval equivalent of holidays was the pilgrimage, and records show that pilgrims set off from Harwich, Wells and Lynn for the shrines of St. James at Compostella, and Our Lady of Walsingham. A large part of Edward III's battle fleet at Sluys was composed of Yarmouth ships, and later on many of the local ports contributed men and ships to the defeat of the Armada, the Woodbridge ships being only about 130 tons in size.

The accession of Henry 7th in 1485 ended a long period of strife and brought in a time of transition from the feudalism of the Middle Ages to the self-confidence, adventure and commercial progress which Elizabeth's reign was to inspire. But the age of church building which produced such masterpieces as Thaxted and Lavenham, fine timbered roofs, screens and font covers like those at St. Peter Mancroft, Norwich, and Ufford, was coming to an end, checked by the Reformation. Out of the ruin of the monasteries the people of Wymondham and Binham, for example, were able only to save the monastic church for their own use.

Elizabeth was hailed with acclamation throughout the countryside. In the fertile lands of East Anglia large landowners, enriched by the break-up of the monastic estates, built great houses at Blickling, Hengrave, Long Melford and other places and many lesser farmhouses show, by their twisted chimneys and gabled ends, their origin in those flourishing days. Merchants like the Seckfords of Seckford Hall near Woodbridge, and the Sparrowes of Ipswich enlarged their houses, the latter adding a fine pargetted front with symbols of the four continents — but no Australia because it was not then known.

Through ports such as Ipswich came books of the New Learning, often hidden in casks for distribution in the countryside where ideas from abroad seem swiftly to have taken root. The first books were printed in the town in 1547, probably the earliest in the Eastern Counties. Thomas Cavendish and others fired by the spirit of adventure circumnavigated the globe and his exploits are described by Richard Hakluyt, a Suffolk man from Wetheringsett. It was an era of great adventure, giving a new feeling of security and confidence.

About this time plans were put in hand for draining the Fenland area between Ely and the Wash by engaging Dutch engineers such as Cornelius Vermuyden. The East Coast rivers were walled in with grass banks to confine the waters to a deeper channel and so give access to the ports for larger ships. Dutch architecture can still be seen everywhere in the villages, notably in the Town Hall at Woodbridge and the White Hart Inn at Scole; but the graceful Customs House at Kings Lynn belongs to a later date and was erected in 1683.

During Elizabeth's reign and the following years Suffolk oak provided timber to build ships up to 600 tons burthen and in 1674, through the recommendation of Samuel Pepys, Harwich became a Royal Dockyard with Anthony Deane as Master Shipwright. The old treadmill crane from the Dockyard is still preserved on Harwich Green. In the Dutch wars of this century much work was brought to the local yards, where ships put in for a refit. Letters from Woodbridge written in 1666 tell of the bloody sea fight off Southwold (Sole Bay) which lasted for four days when the flagship *Royal Prince* was burnt. A year later 1000 Dutchmen succeeded in landing on Landguard beach near Felixstowe, but were repelled by the defenders firing into the shingle and showering the invaders with stones. This was the last time that the East coast of England was invaded.

Increasing prosperity led to the enclosure of the medieval land strips and the common fields so that the countryside began to take on a new look. Much of the poor marginal land was abandoned or put down to grass, causing whole villages to be deserted, as can be seen especially in Norfolk where these deserted villages are represented by the ruins of a church and the outlines of fields and houses.

Many of the farmhouses built at this time were later enlarged to form the substantial Georgian and Victorian houses which we see today on the outskirts of nearly every village. Landowners like Viscount Townshend of

Raynham and Thomas William Coke of Holkham — where the magnificent house was completed to William Kent's design in 1734 — experimented with crop rotation and new methods of cultivation, although as early as 1557 Thomas Tusser of Cattawade on the Stour had published a book on good husbandry. Everything slowly became more orderly and the countryside now began to look something like it does today — or did yesterday. Eminent architects such as Robert Adam and James Wyatt were brought in to design or embellish the mansions at Heveningham, Suffolk and Gunton, Norfolk but, alas, with the changing times many of these fine houses are today empty or derelict.

Landowners had their parks landscaped by Humphry Repton, a Bury St. Edmunds man, or Capability Brown, who laid out Holkham with lakes, arbours and gazebos. Richard Digby of Mistley Park, near Manningtree, employed Robert Adam to transform his estate into a spa and a port with a saltwater bath, a curious two-towered church (of which the nave has been pulled down) and a ridiculous swan in a round basin in the little square.

In the Napoleonic wars early last century, when the price of corn rose to astronomical heights, many of the old sheepwalks of East Suffolk were ploughed up and, if you walk across such of those heathy wastes as have not again been ploughed up, you can still see under the bracken the ridges and furrows of earlier days. The Martello Towers, which stretch along the coast as far as Aldeburgh, were put up at this time as a defence against Napoleon's proposed invasion in flat-bottomed rafts across the coastal shallows. In rural Suffolk you can still hear the country people calling the weather 'rafty' to describe the raw, misty days when it was thought invasion might take place.

The Industrial Revolution of the 19th century touched the countryside far less than many other parts of England. Old maltings and warehouses like Cowell's Paper Warehouse at Ipswich and Jarrold's factory in Cowgate, Norwich still survive; but the small ports were greatly affected when the railway came. Instead of bringing more trade as was first thought, the railway took it away to London. The larger towns drew in people from the villages, as they still do, and new industries and methods have prevented a decline. With the rise of the holiday industry, East Anglia is well set to take advantage of the increase in leisure time. The famous Norfolk Broads, once thought to have been part of a large open estuary, are now known to have been formed by flooded peat excavations in the 14th century. Norwich Cathedral records show that there was once a very extensive industry of cutting turves to provide peat for firing.

East Anglia has now become known as something of an artistic centre with increasing appreciation of its Norfolk painters who formed the 'Norwich School'. Both Constable and Gainsborough were born in the Stour Valley of Suffolk, and lesser artists such as John Moore, Thomas Churchyard of Woodbridge and the Smythe brothers of Ipswich have achieved world-wide recognition. In the literary world we must not forget George Borrow and Edward FitzGerald, the inimitable translator of the Rubayiat. Of Geoffrey Chaucer, the greatest of English poets, we do not know if he ever visited his father's home town of Ipswich.

Every year East Anglia becomes known to more and more visitors because there they can still find large tracts of unspoilt countryside. But it must not be forgotten that their desire to savour the 'backwardness' of the countryside is equalled by the determination of the 'natives' to catch up, and perhaps before very long we, too, will find ourselves in surburbia.

One of the richest legacies from the past — the Saxon ship discovered at Sutton Hoo in 1939. Here part of the British Museum team is uncovering the ship's framework.

George Arnott has lived at Woodbridge all his life in the same house which his grandfather bought in 1877. He was educated at Woodbridge School and was later articled to his father as an auctioneer. He has spent most of his leisure hours on the River Deben and the East Coast and in sailing his boat to Holland and Belgium. He has written books about the rivers Deben, Alde and Orwell and the place-names of the district.

Peter Pears
The Music

THE beginnings of music in East Anglia are lost like most other beginnings, in the mists of Time, and if much, indeed most of early East Anglian music-making can never now be charted or documented, we can comfort ourselves that it was never meant to be.

Perhaps we can even envy the unselfconscious performances of folk-songs and morrises, motets and madrigals in abbeys or homes, stately or humble, where there was no possibility of the inquisitive tape-recorder putting in an appearance, or a local critic staking his claim as a historian of today. On the other hand, without the passionate enthusiasm of the folk song collectors in the early years of this century Essex might have lost such a lovely tune as *'Bushes and Briars'* for ever. There is still research in progress (as well as difference of opinion) about such matters as the identity of lay-clerks at Ely Cathedral in the 15th century and the attribution of the music they sang, and about musical settings of the Liturgy written in honour of Saint Edmund, *Rex Angliae,* much earlier.

In Elizabethan times when all England was 'a nest of singing birds', the most beautiful sounds of all must have been heard at Hengrave Hall, near Bury, where one of our greatest musicians, John Wilbye, was employed. If one realises that, mentioned in the 1602 Inventory, there were at Hengrave six viols, six violins, seven recorders, four or five cornets, four lutes, three oboes, two flutes, several virginals, as well as other stranger wind and string instruments, together with quantities of books of songs and dances of all sorts, English and foreign, it is not difficult to accept Thomas Morley's story of the guest who was put to total shame by his bad sight-reading of his part in a madrigal. 'Unto John Wilbye *my servant* I do bequeath the bedsteed and all the beddings and furniture in the chamber called Mr. Long's chamber,' wrote Lady Kytson in her will. But when Wilbye made his will he wrote 'I John Wilbye of Colchester in the County of Essex *gentleman'* and he left his best viol 'unto the most excellent and illustrious Prince Charles, Prince of Wales'. Musicians were properly looked after by the Elizabethans, nor was Hengrave so very exceptional. There were probably more resident musicians in the East Anglian great houses than in any other part of England. Apart from Byrd at his home in Essex, and the Cavendish group, there was Kirbye at Rushbrooke, and of course the great John Dowland at Audley End, near Saffron Walden.

Musical life during the Civil War must have been rather thin, and when Charles II came back with his new musical ideas, the court was the place where most music appeared, and it was in London that opera ruled and grew. Unlike the German countries where every duke had his opera-establishment, here there was really only London, and resident musicians disappeared from the provinces.

Would it be worthwhile knowing more about Joseph William Holder, who was organist at Bungay and whose Op. 6, *Catches, Canons and Glees for 3, 4, 5 and 6 voices* was published in the 18th century by Longman, Broderip?

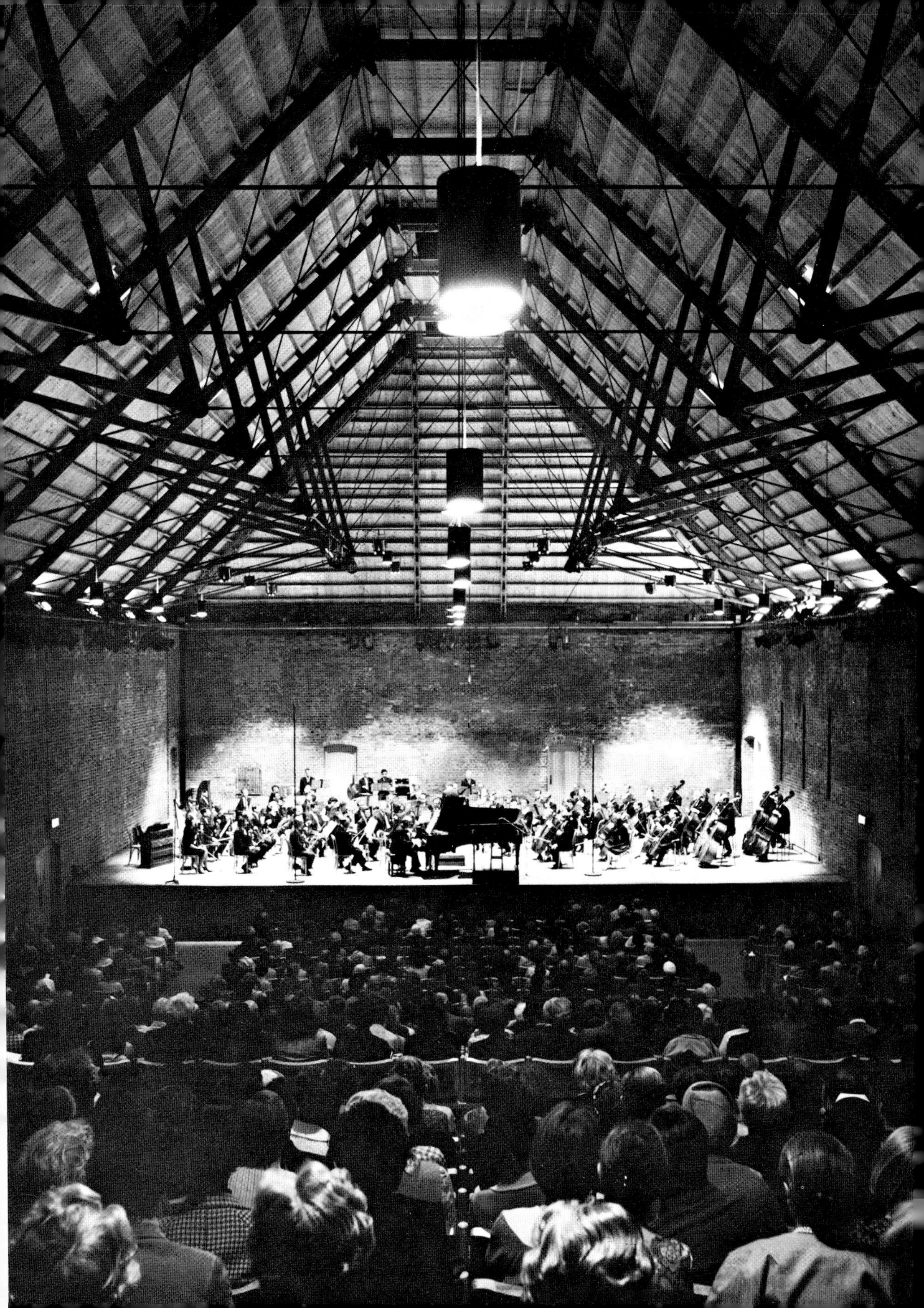

The subscribers' list included famous East Anglian names — Adairs, Bacons, Bunburies, Bedingfields, Brokes, Cokes, Rouses, Upchers — as well as contemporary musical men like Dr. Arnold, Atwood (Mozart's pupil), Dr. Burney, Muzio Clementi and many more. Among the glees were settings of Collins, as well as a topical catch:

> Too poor for a tribe and too proud to importune,
> he had not the method of making a fortune,
> Could love and could hate, so was thought somewhat odd:
> no very great wit, he believed in a God:
> A post or a pension he did not desire,
> but left Church and State to Charles Townshend and Squire.

Some were convivial and very slightly suggestive; some devout.

Was the composer perhaps the grandson of William Holder whose *Inquiry into the natural production of Letters: with an appendix concerning persons Deaf and Dumb* was commended by Dr. Burney (of King's Lynn) in his *History of Music?* The elder Holder had composed too; some anthems and an Evening Service in C have survived, as well as the nickname he earned for himself as sub-dean of the Chapel Royal on account of his discipline with the choristers — 'Mr. Snub-Dean'. No doubt at the parties in the big 18th century houses the walls would have resounded to the harmony of the squires and farmers (and their ladies), voices probably never so resonant or lusty as those of the North or 'West-cuntrie' who, in the 12th century, were already recorded as singing in as many parts as there were singers, while the rest of England were still unison-ing.

In the 19th century East Anglia had its staple diet of oratorio *(Elijah*, in particular) no less than any other part of England, but the musical life was as erratic then as it has been since. Though royal patronage was widespread (the English Glee and Madrigal Union had Queen Victoria for its patron), it was possible to write in 1852 that 'the musical history of Ipswich has been of a very chequered character. Societies have risen and fallen so rapidly that lovers of music have almost despaired of finding any sound basis for the permanent cultivation of music in either a secular or Oratorio form.' The Norwich Triennial Festival has consistently functioned since 1824 and indeed there has always been a lot of music-making at Norwich, as at King's Lynn, and of course at Cambridge.

No doubt the programme which Mr. Lindley Nunn, (recently arrived in Ipswich from Bury, via the Royal Academy of Music), directed as his first concert there in 1851 was typical of provincial English musical life all over the country, consisting of a Mozart quartet, Mayseder's trio, a concertina duet, and songs by Sims Reeves, the greatest of English tenors, whose principal song was *The Death of Nelson* ('the combative feelings of the people gave to this composition a more than usually intense interest'.) A rarer programme was a grand amateur concert in 1870 in aid of the Suffolk Convalescent Home at Felixstowe when the Overture to *Figaro* was played on 10 pianos. 'The difficulty I experienced in obtaining anything like precision I have never forgotten,' wrote the conductor, mildly. In 1897, on the other hand, *Elijah* was 'conducted very efficiently by Mr. Bunnell Burton aided by a powerful band'. As elsewhere, singing lessons were for a long time *de rigueur* among the gentry, and Richard Garrett at Leiston had his two daughters taught along with Mrs. Garrett Anderson and Mrs. Fawcett by a teacher from

Left: Richter playing at the Maltings

Ipswich, who on Mondays set off on his horse at 4.14 a.m.

Though choral societies have been in existence in East Anglia for generations, they have never acquired the security or fame of the great northern choirs. Perhaps there is too much of the east wind in our lungs. For the most part our glorious churches have not possessed choirs worthy of their architecture, so one was doubly grateful to Gustav Holst and his Whitsun music-making at Thaxted in the 20's, helped as he was by a passionate parson.

England has had to rely on individuals or groups of enthusiasts for launching new musical ventures or sustaining old ones. And the founding of the Aldeburgh Festival (and indeed of its friend and colleague, the King's Lynn Festival) was no exception to this. Characteristic too of its inspirer, Benjamin Britten, a passionate East Anglian, was the practical realisation of the Festival idea. There was a newly formed Opera Group looking for a home, a county wanting more music, a borough of charm ready for visitors, beautiful churches and an 1897 Jubilee Hall for performances, and willing colleagues and friends, enthusiastic to help the resident composer.

It started modestly but firmly, overcoming some conservative native resistance to the arts and, after a few years, the demand for seats was such that the complaint that 'you can never get seats for Aldeburgh' rang true. As playing or singing at Aldeburgh has attracted more starry artists, so audiences have become keener. Benjamin Britten has composed almost exclusively for Aldeburgh performances, and it was natural and inevitable that when expansion seemed possible, it should be greeted enthusiastically, and when a block at Snape Maltings was planned to be converted to a Concert Hall, subscriptions came pouring in, with substantial contributions from the Arts Council, the Gulbenkian Foundation, and the Decca Record Company.

The Concert Hall was opened by H.M. the Queen in June 1967, but two years later a disastrous fire gutted it. Work was immediately begun on the rebuilding and it was ready for use again a year later with the Concert Hall just as it had been before the fire; the simplest, most beautiful Hall in the country, with a wonderful acoustic and a unique position.

The response to music at Snape Maltings has been so strong that a week's season of *Opera at the Maltings,* first put on in 1970, and again in 1971, went with such success that it is hoped to become an annual event. One of the most interesting points in all this new music-making is that a large majority both of subscribers to the Aldeburgh Festival and of ticket-holders for the September Opera at the Maltings would appear to be East Anglians, which suggests that nearly 25 years of devoted work by musicians and non-musicians has produced strong roots for music in this area. And because time will not stand still, a new development has been the formation of the Snape Maltings Foundation Limited, of charitable status, whose prime aim is to extend the activities at Snape (as well as continuing the present ones) to include an Arts Centre, with a Music Library, an Art Gallery, and a Crafts Exhibition Hall, with amenities for study-courses in Music and the Arts.

Here, one hopes, the chequered history of music in East Anglia may continue with more confidence in its future, assured of a genuine interest from those who have helped the whole venture to become a reality, and that East Anglia may again have 'a nest of singing birds' as it had 350 years ago.

The Queen with Benjamin Britten at the opening of the Maltings in 1967.

Peter Pears and Benjamin Britten surveying the ruins in 1969.

Re-erecting the roof.

Co-founder of the Aldeburgh Festival, Peter Pears is an Honorary Doctor in the Universities of York and Sussex, a past President of the Incorporated Society of Musicians and was recently awarded the Charles Santley Memorial Prize by the Worshipful Company of Musicians. Benjamin Britten has written no fewer than 11 principal operatic roles for him, seven song cycles and a number of other works. His interpretation of German lieder with Britten has been acclaimed throughout the world.

Adrian Bell
The Two Suffolks

SINCE a life-story hinges on coincidence, I can see that the most important event I look back on in mine was moving from West Suffolk to East Suffolk. I have not travelled much, but have travelled fairly far — to the New World as well as the Continent. To swan around the globe means nothing (which may be why travellers can be such great bores); to burrow into one place is what gives it meaning to you, and ultimately you to yourself.

I was not too happy to move from my West Suffolk clay, which I did about the time the Air Force moved into Stradishall next door. The Air Ministry in those days must have been curiously amateurish, to have sown down to grass Frank Clarke's 400-acre farm, having demolished house and buildings, and think that bombers could land on and take off from the resultant sward. They lay bogged there, hippopotamus-like, as every farmer and farm worker who had trudged that clay behind his swing plough knew they would.

I was sad also to leave Bury St. Edmunds, which had been my market town, and my first love among towns. It was then a town which agriculture took over, literally, every Wednesday — strewing wheat and barley over the pavements near the Corn Exchange, and infiltrating its traffic with droves of cattle, pigs and sheep on their way from and to the railway station.

'Just you listen,' said Farmer Colville, stopping me on the pavement beside the Corn Exchange. 'That sounds like a hive of bees, don't it?' A vast hum vibrated to us from inside, of hundreds of deals going on over samples of grain. It was the counterpart of the huge activity of the stock market, which could have done for an illustration of one of the more tumultuous moments of the not-yet-written *Animal Farm*. It was here, at the Suffolk Show, 1921, that this city-bred boy of 19 felt pulled into the rough embrace of still-traditional farming — all the red-faced brag and flourish of it. A gig with bright yellow wheels was driven down Abbeygate Street, paused at Oliver's, the grocer's with the Gothic windows, took on a country cheese, and continued its way.

The town itself provided all that farming required, from harrows to hedging darnocks, heavy shirts and cords.

Really, to leave West Suffolk was to say goodbye to the horse; not only the working horse, but those informal point-to-point races over courses created overnight out of a farm's hedges and ditches, for horses that local farmers rode and hunted.

It was still a home-made culture, of blacksmith, wheelwright (those balance tumbrils of Whiffen of Clare — you could tip them, loaded, with one finger). Its standards of workmanship were strict.

When I moved to East Suffolk everything was different. The day of the horse was nearly done; exigencies of the 1939 War abolished the old pride in the look of the job. It was all a great muddle for a time — a frenzied plough-up policy with small paraffin-burning tractors. The tractor to the horse was as a powerful idiot to a sentient being: the horse could be so clever as to walk

Euston Hall, West Suffolk.

unled pulling a hoe between just visible seedlings and not trample them. The tractor was hitched to the old horse implements, juddering the beautiful old wagons and tumbrils to pieces, not to mention those splendid wooden Smyth corn drills so suited to the Suffolk soil.

By now, tractors are mounted with specially designed tools and trailers. But not then. The most damned-awful thing ever invented (apart from the three-wheel water-cart) was the trailer tractor-plough, with an uncertain trip-gear to lift it out of the work at the headland, activated by a piece of string. If it failed to work first pull, you were almost into the ditch, unable to go forward or back (the plough just jack-knifed and stuck). It was a maddeningly clumsy combination, after the sweet and sensitive, if slow, progression of a horse team pulling the wooden swing plough, whose every vibration was communicated instantly to your hands and muscles, so that you knew every variation of the soil and subsoil you were ploughing as you went along.

Wartime farming in East Suffolk was a crazy business after the slow quiet routines of the horse farms of West Suffolk. In wartime farming we had land girls, Italian and German prisoners, conscientious objectors, as farm workers at various times. The law decreed that land girls must not work on the same stack as prisoners of war, lest fraternisation occur. Planning a day's work became like a game of chess. A gang of German prisoners came to hoe the beet. They were splendid workers, but as they walked off the field to their dinner their 60 great boots trod the weeds back into the soil and rerooted them. I had to get them to drill themselves: form fours, form two-deep and march off down two rows, which they did with a precision that looked like Hitler Youth. But as for that Nazi who said, 'When I hear the word culture I reach for my gun', these boys said to my old cowman, 'Your boss writes books'. Walter was then unaware that I wrote books — our only joint literary effort was the daily milk record sheet. And we both had some difficulty spelling 'heifer'. Then the land girl came in and wrote 'hepher'. One of these prisoners asked me had I any spare copies of the English poets? I found duplicates of Keats, Shelley and Byron from my father's library and gave them to him. He was deeply grateful.

Crazy it was, to be working beside these friendly boys, while overhead bombers from the nearby airfield were assembling to make another raid on their home cities.

A couple of G.I.s stopped at our farmyard one day while we were threshing: they were amused to see an old steam engine still at work. There were as yet hardly any combine harvesters available here. A few days later the engine driver said, 'Me tubes've gone', and, twirling his little steerage wheel, turned and made off back to base in a lumbering race against time with his engine's crumbling intestines. That was the last time I had a steam engine working for me — that which had been a prime wonder of my first day on a farm in 1920; a mighty cable ploughing pair, anchored at either side of a 30-acre field.

East Suffolk was that sort of muddle, farming-wise, when I came to it; neither the old nor the new. A 25 horsepower tractor pulling a wooden one-horse tumbril was its apt symbol. A 150 h.p. machine came to pull out tree roots from a field to restore it to cultivation, while, two fields away, I was rolling with my last horse a newly sown field of beet with a roller made of a

Dunwich, East Suffolk.

trunk of crab apple, hooped with iron.

At the same time we had, surrounding our by no means romantic redbrick Victorian East Suffolk home, two sour paddocks, in which came up those pretty things that love sour land — primroses, cowslips, orchises and moon daisies, in contrast to the fields sweetened by applications of lime which utility crops required. The good moments were leaning out of the bedroom window in April, the air full of nightingales singing from a 100 acres abandoned to thorn bushes between the wars. The acres were reclaimed and the nightingales left. In June, in the moonlight, the marguerite daisies seemed clotted together like one pale face of mist. We had them always, and the cowslips, (we did not 'sweeten' our two paddocks), and three children in that home.

West Suffolk farmers hated cows. A few cows there were for the wife's butter money, that was all. I recall the competition each week in Haverhill market as to whose butter made top price in the auction. Many years later I saw a newspaper picture of housewives in an industrial city during a bakers' strike, queuing in the rain for bread rather than make a loaf in their own kitchens, and I began to think that civilisation was petering out — not what goes by that term today, but that which I learned to mean by civilisation, when I had learned how to look at things, how to taste things, how to know quality by eye and touch, from those fellows who cut the hay and their so capable wives, in the long ago when Bury St. Edmunds was the home of cattle, sheep and corn. The farmers of West Suffolk loved beef animals, and prime porkers and baconers. Their Sunday afternoon occupation was to take a neighbour round their straw yards, rattle a stick on a gate, cry 'Ho-ho-ho!'

and see a score of clean pink pigs leap out of deep straw — or prod a roan steer to its feet and judge his top-line and depth of body with a subtle eye.

We had a rib of beef recently which reminded me of the beef of those days. It was extra good for these days. I said, 'When shall we taste another piece of beef as good as this?' We ate it cold day after day — sacrilege to hash it up. I said, 'I used to think our diet in the old farmhouse must have been dull. But I had forgotten how good the home-bred beef used to be, marbled with fat, in West Suffolk — none of this Friesian cow — and those great apple pies (the only sweet a farmer would touch).'

But here in East Suffolk cows were the mainstay — so I had to come to terms with cows. In those war days we still grew enough straw to bed them comfortably in the yard in winter — polled cows. Now the scientists have been so clever as to breed most of the straw out of cereal crops, and what there is is chewed to chaff by combines. So we get no more bedding of cows, but hosing-down of concrete. And we get this abomination called 'slurry' — the hosed liquid muck which (given unlimited piped water) is drowning our already sodden upland clays. In West Suffolk we had solid manure heaps, built by handfork, not a foul slop tipped from a tractor's jaws — heaps built with tall straight sides, and when the stuff was carted, it dug out like dark cheese, and smelt of ripeness and fertility, nor putrescence.

Today, when I see the slivers and gashes in a hedge which the mechanical hedger leaves, I can't help reverting in thought to those hedges the old hedgers cut so featly with their sharp bills, the neat almond-shaped cuts. Of a single sliver they would have been deeply ashamed.

But of course, the old farming ceased to pay; the yarded beef cattle ceased to pay. Bury St. Edmunds has to import other industries. Cows go on paying — just — in East Suffolk. I learned a lot about cows here, and bag trouble, and maintenance ration and production ration, not to mention having to light a fire under a boiler every dawn and turn myself into a washer-upper at a steel trough beside a steam sterilising chest, and wear a monkish sort of outfit of white skull cap and white overall. After those buskined West Suffolk days behind the horse plough, I felt a sort of fool.

But all in all I'm glad I came to East Suffolk. The tides of London, once so remote, lap even to the banks of the Stour today. The Stour Valley — Clare, Cavendish, Long Melford, even to Nayland, is known now as the Cocktail Fringe among surviving friends we have there. Sixty miles north-east, on the other river boundary, the Waveney, we have still a native life: we look to Norwich, which is a truly regional capital, and not to Ipswich, which from here looks like a staging-post of commuterdom.

So hail East Suffolk, and those parishes known as 'The Saints' whose mud is as cheesy as any that engulfed the first bombers of Stradishall Airfield, or was pared from the breasts of the West Suffolk swing ploughs. Hereabout you can still get locally brewed mild beer out of a barrel in a country pub among the 'crink-crank' lanes.

And there is still a horse in sight; a grey horse that was the faithful servant of a neighbour, now pensioned off to pasturage. And in Bungay the other day I found in a secondhand shop a bean-box. What is a bean-box? It is a hopper-shaped box running on a wheel, which was fixed to the back of the wooden plough and filled with seed beans, which a brush on a spindle (turned by the wheel) dribbled into the furrow behind the plough.

I turned up my farm diary for 1923. Beside October 11th, I read, 'Ploughing-in beans', and that entry was repeated for the next 10 days. A rule-of-thumb, on-and-on life was farming in 1923 in West Suffolk; its only sounds the creaking of harness, scrape of ploughshare and voices of birds. A monotony rewarding in everything but money after the repeal of the Corn Production Act. In East Suffolk the job was made to pay again, noisily. Hobnails and a healthy glow were exchanged for gumboots and freezing on a tractor seat — regular meals (because the horse too needed them) were exchanged for sandwiches in the toolbox eaten to time so that you had both hands free for the turn at the headland — and most important of all the built 'dungle' (dunghill) for slop and 'slurry'.

What I am most glad of, is that I came to Suffolk in time to see it still being farmed entirely by horses — its fields full of stepping Suffolk Punches, that will never come again. In the dins of later days, the strenuous quietness of that huge operation of growing bread corn is what impresses me.

And the parish windmill was still turning, to which I took a tumbril-load of my barley to be ground every week. And drank with the miller a glass of his home-brewed beer — *not* 'Keg Bitter'.

Adrian Bell has, over the years, become a distinguished Man of Letters in East Anglia. He has farmed in West and East Suffolk. Among his many publications he has written Music in the Morning, A Suffolk Harvest *and* A Street in Suffolk *and that great classic* Corduroy.

Alan Savory
The Wild Life

    THERE was a form master at Ipswich school during the Kaiser's War who did his utmost to beat history into me by the means of what he called 'Tags' and a cane. He was a jolly good schoolmaster in a very difficult period of our Island history; I forgive him wholeheartedly for his sudden outbursts of temper, although I can still see him grabbing me by the collar and shoving me over a form, swishing his cane and shouting 'Will you pay attention?'. His favourite history tag, or at least the only one I can remember, was '1665 scarce left one alive, 1666 London burnt to sticks'. The Great Plague and, the next year, the Fire of London. It made a great impression on me in more ways than one. During those terrible years when the almost savage population died in thousands and looting and robbery with violence were normal every day occurrences and there were gallows-trees at every street corner swinging their grisly fruit, the wild life of East Anglia was possibly at its highest variety and numbers since prehistoric times.

    The fens were undrained and stretched for mile after mile of water and reeds and wash lands, and the heaths and great tracts of sandy warrens reached from the fenland to the forest edge. The local peasantry who worked the land, sometimes for the Lords of the Manor, sometimes for their own small holdings, ate anything they could get hold of in the way of wild life. They seldom lived to a ripe old age and the plague which was brought into the country by the town dwellers depopulated the countryside, so that whole villages disappeared leaving huge empty churches surrounded by derelict hovels. In those days the household garbage was thrown into the streets and kites which fed on it were common birds as were ravens in Norwich and Ipswich.

    The bodies of the plague victims were thrown into open pits in what is now called Tombland in Norwich, and the stench was so terrible that the bishop complained that he could no longer compose his sermons at the open Bishop's Palace window. Men said that 'God was asleep', but the wild life of the countryside swarmed and multiplied. There were droves of great bustards on the sandy heathlands, and the fens and meres thundered with the wings of mallards and wigeon. Spoonbills bred in the heronry at Reedham on the River Yare, and also at Claxton; and avocets and ruffs and black tailed godwits were common nesting birds on the Breydon marshlands, as were the black terns. The only way of taking wildfowl was in decoys, of which there were scores all round about the country.

    For sport the gentry of those days went hawking. Every manor had a falconer who looked after the hawks and there were a great many trappings for each hawk and falcon. It was one of the great sports of the times and there was a great deal of pageantry attached to it. There was a lot of class distinction too. Only the most noble of the people were allowed to hawk and sport with the most noble of falcons such as the peregrine and goshawk. There was a list of the snob value of the hawks. The only piece I can remember was 'A merlin for a lady and a kestrel for a knave'. Class distinctions were rigorously kept and if one of the noble lord's servants got a bit above himself, he got himself hanged from the village gallows. For a lesser misdemeanour he was put in the stocks for 24 hours or so, to be pelted with filth by the village boys. There was no sanitation at all and refuse of all kinds was just thrown out on the heaps called the village middens, to be eaten by the kites and ravens and crows. Life in those days in England was very much like life today in a primitive African village, with the heat turned off.

The old time fowlers of the Lincolnshire fens took untold thousands of wildfowl, mostly mallard and wigeon and teal, in their decoys. The old records of some of the decoys have been preserved and on one decoy at East Somerton in Norfolk a new decoy worked by a skilled Lincolnshire decoy man took 1100 teal in seven consecutive days, and this was only about 100 years ago. Some of the takes in the old fenland decoys before the drainage of the fens was finally completed in about 1851 were enormous, and in the ten decoys around Wainfleet the fowlers sent over 31,000 ducks to the London markets in one season.

The life of a fenman in the old days must have been reasonable in the summer time, but in the autumn and winter it must have been extremely hard. He lived in a hut on an island amid the swamps, with nothing but what he could get out of the fen to eat. His hut was made of grass sods and marsh hassocks, and was full of smoke from a turf fire. He drank tea made of swamp water and poppy heads to ward off 'shakes', which was malaria, and he died at an early age, crippled with all the rheumatic complaints which even modern science cannot cure. If he lived till he was 40 he was a very old man; but anything like typhoid would just wipe out whole families. In the times when he could get about, the family would eat fish like eels and tench, and duck eggs, water rats; but in bad times they would starve. It is wonderful to imagine the old-time fen with miles and miles of reeds and meres and waterways stretching half across England. The enormous flocks of wildfowl and the hordes of clanging skeins of wild geese. The ruffs and reeves, avocets and cranes, and perhaps the rare wandering pelican. But you would have to be a semi-savage to survive.

The last of the indigenous tribes of great bustards survived the build-up of the human population after the Great Plague of 1665 until 1838 when the remaining bustard of the British race was killed at Lexham near Swaffham in Norfolk. Formerly there were droves of great bustards roaming the unenclosed heathlands. They were almost as big as turkeys and lived a nomadic life in the arid, semi-desert country around Thetford and Brandon, where the wind blew the sand into hills and ridges and the rabbits were in thousands. One of the sports of the 16th century was chasing the young bustards before they could fly by the gilded youth of those times — on horseback and with running dogs. It must have been a pretty hazardous sport when one considers the wild heathlands where the bustards lived and the rabbit holes where a galloping horse could come to grief in a split second.

In those days the wild life of East Anglia could cope with the natural balance of nature without let or hindrance of man; it was only the growing population and the enclosure acts, and the greed of mankind that upset the balance of nature. The spoonbills that bred with the herons in the Reedham heronry and at Claxton in the Yare Valley were wiped out as British breeding birds, not because they were good to eat, but because their plumes which

Sciurus Vulgaris. This one likes apple trees.

adorned their heads looked nice on ladies' hats. The last pair of black tailed godwits lost their eggs to the egg collectors on the Buckenham marshes about the year 1828. These egg collectors collected for the London markets and sent hampers of eggs of green plover, avocets, terns, redshanks and gulls up to London by carriers' carts twice a week; and after a few years the birds just could not stand it and ceased to breed on the marshes round Potter Heigham. The ruffs and black terns ceased to breed in Broadland, and the bittern — which was a common bird during the 18th century — ceased to breed in Broadland in about 1868.

What the marshes were like in their heyday before the birds were shot out can only be imagined. Even the butterflies suffered from the collectors' greed. The British race of the large copper, which must have looked like a flying poppy, died out with the completion of the drainage of the Lincolnshire fens. I do not think it ever was a common butterfly as it has a difficult and tangled life-pattern, with a hibernating caterpillar in a rolled dead leaf of the water dock. The swallowtail almost went the same way with a price on its head for every specimen found by the broadsmen for his collecting clients. The bearded tit was shot to adorn a glass case.

In fact the greed of the collector just about put paid to the bird life of Norfolk and Suffolk. There were colonies of avocets at Salthouse and on the North Norfolk coast, and at Horsey and Hickling in Broadland; but they were shot for their feathers and their eggs taken for eating. The black tern went the same way; and the ruffs were trapped and fattened for food in little pens. The fowlers who did the trapping got a shilling a dozen for them. The avocets ceased to breed in East Anglia in 1824 and the black terns in 1858 — and the ruffs about the same time. It was the age of the collector and everything that moved was shot if it had a price on its head. There were people who did nothing else but watch out for wandering birds such as spoonbills on Breydon Water near Great Yarmouth, and during the autumnal migrations the slaughter of the warblers on the coast in the hopes of finding one rare one was tremendous. One man was reputed to have shot 500 small birds in the coastal belt near Blakeney just to obtain one rare-warbler for some client who wanted it stuffed in a glass case.

A dead bird in the hand could be positively identified, whereas a bird flitting about in the bushes could be anything from a chiffchaff to a bluethroat.

Towards the end of the 19th century England was a place to avoid by any form of bird or butterfly that flew or fluttered in the reed beds of East Anglia. Then the turn round came early in the present century. The museums were full of echoes of the past glories of East Anglian bird-life. Full to bursting point, and one could only sit and dream of the miles of primitive fenland where the wildfowl rose on thunderous wings and springtime was a glory of nesting colonies of black terns and avocets on the miles of semi-flooded marshlands. The Great War of 1914 burst on the world and the flower of English manhood died in the mud of Flanders. For four ghastly years the slaughter went on and during that time England almost bled to death. But the bird life gradually began to recover from the insane greed of the collectors, simply because there was no one to do the collecting. The bitterns bred for the first time again in Broadland at Upton in a vast tangle of sedge in a place near Upton Broad called the Doles.

I was staying at Upton as a schoolboy, and the keeper's son and I saw a pair of Montague harriers and heard the bitterns booming. We saw swallowtail butterflies in the reed fens, and there was a great crested grebe's nest on the big broad. I went off to Ipswich School soon after that year and the Suffolk countryside with its water meadows and clear streams and rolling linnet-haunted heathlands were a paradise. There was a pond near Claydon near Ipswich where the great crested water newt lived, the first I had ever seen, and the marshlands bordering the estuaries of the Rivers Stour and Deben and the Orwell were wild and unpopulated and rang with the bells of the nesting redshanks. There were stag beetles in Orwell Park if you knew where to look, and lime hawk moth caterpillars in the lime trees bordering the school field.

Just outside Ipswich, near Martlesham heath, was a lake called the Old Decoy Ponds. Once upon a time they had taken thousands of wildfowl in the old decoy days. Now the decoy pipes had gone and they were full of dead trees and a glory of birdsong in the spring and full of black cap warblers and whitethroats. There were great green woodpeckers nesting and spotted woodpeckers, and once I saw a pair of lesser spotted woodpeckers creeping about in an old rotten tree. There were nightjars on the heath in those days and sheld ducks nesting in rabbit burrows on the banks of the Deben near Woodbridge. Thankfully I grew up in an age before chemicals were considered as a part of modern farming. There were tractors on some farms, but horses did most of the work and there were ants' nests on the dry sandy banks, and insects in untold thousands that provided food for the myriads of song birds. The dawn chorus in the spring was really something to listen to. Bird photography was taking the place of collecting stuffed birds; it was not always a good thing because sometimes the birds were kept off their eggs by some clumsy photographer so long that she deserted her eggs. But the bitterns were back in Broadland in strength and great efforts taken to protect them. The Montague and marsh harriers came back to Hickling and often in the years between the wars spoonbills came to Breydon Water while on migration to Holland or Southern Europe and departed unmolested.

During the 1920s and 1930s black terns were seen each year on migration, but they did not stop to breed. The odd avocet looked in too, and so did the ruff, but they had had enough of England. A friend and I had an amazing morning with a party of avocets. We were, and still are, very keen wildfowlers and I had rented an area of marshland at the top of Breydon water by the side of the River Waveney. There was a little wall which kept the small tides off an area of mud flats and reeds and a big wall which stopped the rides from flooding the cattle marsh.

It was known as the Island and belonged to Sir Thomas Beauchamp from whom I hired the shooting rights. It was the most perfect place for a wildfowler naturalist. There were a nice lot of wild duck and teal early in the season and hundreds of snipe all season through. The first time I shot there I saw three bitterns and a party of bearded tits, and a Montague harrier turned up in the middle of the afternoon and proceeded to drive the snipe out of mud flats in the reeds. Every time I went there this harrier used to almost wait on me like an old time falconer. Several times he beat my dog in picking up a snipe I had shot, which I suppose was the whole idea. It sounds impossible, but it actually happened.

Then one August an old friend and I went early morning duck flighting there. It was an awkward place to get to as you had to have a boat and we were a bit late getting onto the marsh wall. But we got one or two mallard each which was enough. Then a black and white bird flew over us and settled on the mud about twenty yards away and started to wade about in about three inches of water and scythe the water with an upturned bill. We watched absolutely fascinated. 'Good heavens', said Jack, 'it's an avocet'. Well, that put paid to our shooting for the day as we did not want to scare it away. After a while it was joined by a small flock of avocets until there were 35, all as tame as chickens. This was in the year 1935. They came on a south easterly wind and they left next day.

There were a few ruffs on migration and one spoonbill that year. All

Oyster Catchers at Ramsholt.

using the tidal pools in the reed beds on my shoot. They stayed for a short time and then departed, but the snipe were in hundreds and the Montague harrier was there all season through. There were always bitterns in the reed beds and parties of bearded tits. Green shanks and green sand pipers used it as a staging post on migration.

As a shoot it was not very good as, apart from the reed beds and the salt semi-brackish pools between the little wall and the big marsh wall, there was little to attract wild duck. A few teal used to use the sea aster beds on the ronds at the top of Breydon, and there were a covey or so of partridges on the cattle marsh. But for me it was a place of delight because of the wandering migrants and the rare waders that used to drop into the salt pools.

In the deep winter-time there was always the chance of a wild goose, and great whistling hordes of wigeon used to come on to any fresh water pools left by rain on the marsh. It was as near to what the old brackish fenland and Breydon must have been like in the far off days when it was one of the best wildfowl haunts in England. In the spring the marshes rang with bell-like whistles of the redshanks and were aweep with the cries of nesting peewits. It wanted but little imagination to think of what the marshes were like a few hundred years ago when the black terns and the godwits were common nesting birds and the spoonbills nested in the garland of old trees that were blue in the distance where the misty uplands met the levels of the marsh by the Reedham heronry and the old marsh carrlands of Havergate and Wickhampton.

In all the dykes intersecting the marshes of the Yare valley frogs swarmed in the springtime and every pond and drain had its quota of spawning toads. The dykes near my home were covered in duck week and full of water snails and water beetles, water boatmen and every sort of fresh-water insect life. For eight or nine years after the Second World War small wild-life swarmed in the marshland dykes. Then the scientist, not content with the old time ways of washing up with soda and soap, invented detergents; they also invented DDT and a few more chemicals. Old-time farming with loads of animal manure was on its way out. The first things to suffer were the frogs and toads. They absorbed the detergents through their skins and within a year there was not a spawning frog or toad in any of the marsh dykes connected with the River Yare. The duck weed disappeared and all the snails with it. The dykes became lanes of polluted clear water that collected slime and undecomposed filth on the roots of the alder trees, simply because the tiny insects that — although horrifying to look at through a microscope — were the agents that kept the water clean and ate the decomposing weeds and dead fish, and in fact did a marvellous clearing up job in the natural way of life and death. The detergents killed them; and the water in the dykes and the river became sterile.

The DDT killed everything it came in touch with. I was told by a young marine biologist the other day that if all the DDT was destroyed today, it would take the natural balance of nature 10 years to recover from its effects. The chemicals on the land did a great deal of harm to the insect life of the countryside, and the grasshoppers just ceased to exist except on the railway embankments. Ants' nests died out in the fields, and in consequence the partridges became scarce because there was not enough natural insect food for the young ones. The swallowtail butterfly, although not so common as in the days before the Second World War, managed to keep a foothold in the reedlands of the Yare Valley, but the large copper that was introduced from Holland did not do so well, fading out after a season or so. Not because of pollution, but because of warbler persecution, strangely enough. It is a most spectacular butterfly and not too strong on the wing, and the whitethroats and sedge warblers would not leave it alone. It needs a lot of country to survive, and Broadland and what remains of the fens are very restricted areas to what they used to be before the drainage mills were built.

Common Tern with chick.

There were two colonies of natterjack toads in the Yare Valley, one at Reedham and one at Cantley. The natterjack does not hop but runs and is the demon toad of witchcraft. It was said in olden days that if you caught a running toad and put it in an ant's nest until all the flesh was eaten off its bones and then threw the bones into a running stream at midnight, one bone would glow with a blue flame and run against the current. You caught this bone and with it you could cast spells, such as turning the milk from your neighbour's cows sour, or otherwise ill-wish those you hated in the village. In the old times, when they hung a child of seven for stealing bread and burnt witches at the stake, anything seems possible.

Anyway, the detergents killed off the natterjacks and, as far as I know, there is now only one small colony somewhere behind the Winterton sandhills. But superstitions die hard and I can remember old marshmen with eelskins tied around their knees to keep off the rheumatics. There was a white hare too on the Acle marshes that always crossed a dyke in front of my hide in the early dawn where I waited for the wild geese to flight in from Scroby sands. I was told never to take any notice of it, certainly not shoot it, because if I did there was an old woman who would have been found dead of gunshot wounds in one of the nearby villages. She was a dear old village woman by daytime, but at night she roamed the marshes as a white hare. When she died some time during the last war the hare was never seen again. I laughed when I was told about her; but the old people only tried to laugh. They were even more scared than I.

1947 was one of the most ghastly cold winters in living memory and the small birds suffered terribly. The great green woodpecker almost died out and kingfishers had a very bad time; only a few pairs in the far West of England managed to keep the species going. The bearded tits of Broadland died out, but somehow managed to repopulate the reed beds of Norfolk and Suffolk by immigrants from the Continent so that now it is a comparatively common bird in the reed beds of Broadland and on the Suffolk bird sanctuaries of Minsmere. Philip Browne, the Editor of the *Shooting Times and County Magazine,* who was the prime mover in the organising of the bird sanctuary at Minsmere had the great joy of seeing the first avocets to breed in England since 1824, at Minsmere in 1947. They bred reasonably successfully for a year or so, and then deserted Minsmere for Havergate Island off the Suffolk coast near Orford. There was some trouble with raiding rats, but that was stopped and there is now a colony of avocets breeding on Havergate Island each spring.

Luckily the Wildfowlers Association of Great Britain and Ireland, The Society for the Protection of Birds and the Nature Conservancy and other interested societies have all got together and we are getting some of our lost breeding birds back again. There are a few pairs of black tailed godwits breeding in the fens, and on special sanctuaries on the East Coast. There are also a few pairs of black terns and a small colony of ruffs. There is a scheme afoot to reintroduce the great bustard. If they can adapt themselves to the modern way of man's civilisation, we may yet see droves of great bustards on Salisbury Plain, and a few on the linnet-haunted heathland of Norfolk and Suffolk. It would be a miracle if we ever see the spoonbills breeding in the trees with the herons at Reedham as they did in the 15th century.

I wonder what my old form master of Ipswich School would have written for his history tag for the year 2000. Perhaps it is just as well we do not know.

Alan Savory was born at Blickling in Norfolk in 1905. He was educated privately and at Ipswich School before spending three years as a farm pupil. He started writing as soon as he left school and sold his first article in 1928 — since when he has been contributing to the Shooting Times and Country Magazine, Country Life *and the* East Anglian Magazine. *Before the war he ran a wildfowl and fur farm in the Norfolk Broads area. During the war he served in the Royal Observer Corps before transferring to the Royal Air Force where he was attached to Air Sea Rescue. He saw active service in the second landing in North Africa. His first book, published in 1953, was called* Norfolk Fowler *and other publications include* Lazy Rivers *and* Thunder in the Air *— which was the result of a 12,000 mile safari in an old car from Cape Town and up the Zambesi. Hobbies include wildfowling and fishing and he has been a member of the Wildfowlers Association of Great Britain and Ireland since it started.*

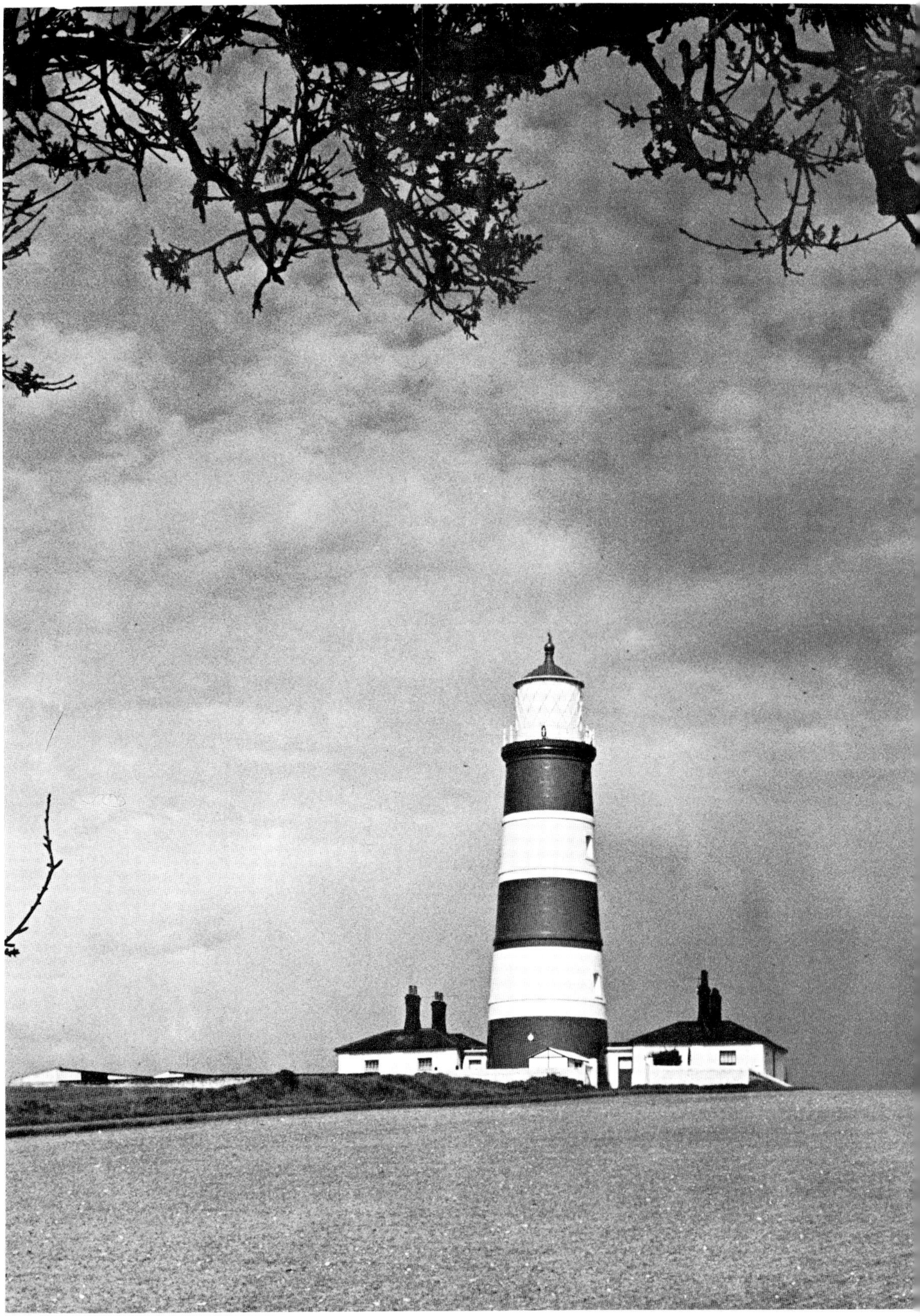

A.W. Roberts
The Sea

A WILD, restless sea washes the shores of East Anglia — shallower than most, saltier and more dangerous. There is a lack of easy harbours for the hard-pressed sailor, for once he leaves the spacious waters of Harwich Harbour for the north there is no easy run-in until he sights the mouth of the Humber; and that is sometimes an evil place to enter. The harbours of Yarmouth and Lowestoft are artificial ones, enclosed by stone walls through which the mariner must pick only certain states of the tide; and Southwold is unuseable except for very small craft.

The history of East Anglia is bound up with the North Sea. Over this turbulent waste came the Iceni from the German Rhineland, the English from their continental home of Angel, which place still exists and where the old deserted farms and villages have been excavated to show how a whole nation swept south-west to find new lands to conquer and farm.

The Anglians from Angel made East Anglia, their warriors driving all before them. They rowed across the North Sea in ships such as the one unearthed at Sutton Hoo, near Woodbridge, though many may have fallen by the wayside and gone ashore in Friesland, North Holland, to settle and farm there just as they do today. The Dutch Frieslander of today is closely related to the old Anglians who swarmed ashore between Orfordness and the Wash after the Roman Legions had departed. Not that they were afraid of the Legions, for they raided them continuously for hundreds of years, making swift attacks from their ships just as the Scandinavian Vikings did 400 years later.

The Romans had to appoint a 'Court of the Saxon Shore' to try and ward them off, but there is little doubt that many settled along the coastal areas as farmers and farm foreman under the Roman Regime and formed a 'Fifth Column' when the main English invasion began in 400-500 A.D.

In turn, the East Anglians were plagued by the Norsemen in their longships, killing, looting and burning the churches, towns and villages which the Anglians had so laboriously built. They came with the north-east wind in their square sails and even in recent times I have heard the term 'Norseman's Wind' when the seas thunder on the Suffolk shingle or Cromer cliffs.

When the main English fleet lay off East Anglia in Roman times, they were commanded by a famous leader called Uffa, whose family became kings of East Anglia. Places like Ufford and Offton remind us of this great seafaring chief of those ancient times.

The sea has brought more fame to East Anglia than anything else. Thomas Cavendish, second Englishman to sail round the world (after Drake), lived at Trimley in Suffolk and his navigator, Eldred, lived in Fore Street, Ipswich. On the banks of the Orwell stands the house of Admiral Vernon, Victor of Portobello. Almost next door is Broke House, home of Admiral Broke, who, although he regretted missing Trafalgar, won fame by his victory in the little frigate *Shannon* over the American warship *Chesapeake,* off

Left: Happisburgh Lighthouse.

Boston. The devastating accuracy of the *Shannon's* gunfire, followed by a courageous boarding party, utterly defeated the Americans in 15 minutes. Many of the *Shannon's* crew came from Broke's native Suffolk.

Another great Admiral rose from an East Anglian village named Burnham Thorpe in Norfolk. He was a slip of a lad named Horatio Nelson, and let anyone say a word against him among Norfolk seamen and he'll be dangerously near a punch on the nose (and rightly so!). Nelson went to school at Walsingham and used to sail paper boats down the roadside stream.

Captain Cook, although from Whitby, was well known in East Anglian ports when he served in the collier brigs which kept Norfolk, Suffolk, Essex and London supplied with coal. These brigs used to beach on open stretches of coast where there was no harbour, and unload their coal into tumbrils. Masters of these brigs were skilful and had vast knowledge of the tides and weather, so that in spite of the risky trade they engaged in, very few were ever lost. In the heyday of these brigs, a daily panorama of sail could be seen from almost any point on the East Anglian coast.

The last sailing vessel to bring coal from the north was the mulie barge *Cambria* which used to load at Keadby in Lincolnshire and deliver to gas works at Harwich, Colchester and Margate. In fact she was the last purely sailing vessel trading under the British Flag.

Spritsail rigged sailing barges were, in fairly recent times, a feature of the East Coast. They carried cargoes from London (mostly out of big ocean-going ships) to the millers and merchants of Ipswich, Lowestoft, Yarmouth and King's Lynn. Their red sails could be seen rounding Orfordness winter and summer, and many are the hair-raising manoeuvres they have been forced to carry out to take the pierheads at Lowestoft and Yarmouth on dark, bitter winter nights with the seas threatening to pound them to pieces in a few minutes if the helmsman made a mistake.

The last of them — the *Cambria* — went out of the trade at the end of 1970, after 64 years of continuous cargo carrying. She is now preserved by the Maritime Trust, who took her over, with other historic vessels, for 'care and safe keeping'. The Maritime Trust is the sea equivalent of the National Trust on land and both these organisations have found much in East Anglia which they will preserve as part of our national heritage.

When one realises the dangers ships must face in the North Sea, it is not surprising that the East Coast lifeboatmen have made a name for themselves which, I hope, will never be forgotten. All are volunteers, with the one exception of the crew at desolate Spurn Head. Probably the most famous coxswain was the late Henry Blogg of Cromer. Three times he was awarded the Royal National Lifeboat Institution's Gold medal for daring rescues, and he was also decorated with the George Cross and the British Empire Medal.

Once an East Coast barge named the *Sepoy* drove ashore in a wicked gale, and the crew clung desperately in the rigging as the seas crashed over the deck. There was only one way to save them before the mast came down. Blogg drove his lifeboat on the crest of a huge sea right across the barge's deck. The men dropped from the rigging into the boat and the next sea lifted them off and away to comparative safety.

Blogg has gone now, but he left a tradition at Cromer which will never die out.

His nephew, Henry Davies — better known as 'Shrimp' Davies — is now coxswain and used to be bowman for Blogg. Shrimp was out one night trying to rescue the crew of a ship on the Haisborough Sand. In trying to get across the sand the lifeboat struck and capsized. The crew were struggling in the water and the whole lot were related — brothers, cousins, uncles — so that for a time it looked as though all the menfolk of seafaring Cromer would perish together. But they scrambled back, righted the boat and not one of them was lost. Shrimp is a dedicated lifeboatman. If vicious gales come on with the darkness he does not go to bed, but sits up ready to don his seaboots should the maroon go up to signify distress at sea.

Asked once why he did it he said: 'The greatest reward of all is to stretch out my hand, feel a hand clasp mine, and pull him to safety.'

Another famous East Anglian lifeboat was the one at Caister. They were known as the 'Never-Turn-Backs'. This was because when the lifeboat capsized in the surf trying to get off to a ship in distress, nine members of the crew were drowned. At the subsequent inquiry one of the survivors was asked: 'If the conditions were so bad why did you not turn back?' The man's answer rang round the world: 'Caister men never turn back.'

The East Anglian herring fishery, famous and profitable for hundreds of years, has fallen now on thin times, largely because of modern 'mass-fishing' methods which destroy the spawn and young. But at one time a huge fleet of sail assembled in Yarmouth and Lowestoft in the autumn and the catches were prodigious. Salted 'red' herring were sold to Russia, Germany and the Baltic States; and thousands of barrels would be stacked along the quays waiting for ship-space. Kippers from East Anglia went to every corner of the British Isles and, in season, there was always a ready sale for fresh herring. In olden times herrings were used as tax-tribute to the Kings of England.

Herrings are caught by drift nets, rather like curtains hung below the surface of the sea. The shoals of herring 'gill' themselves into the meshes and thus are caught with the flesh unharmed.

In addition to the herring fishing, there was always (until recent times) a sizeable fleet of trawlers working out of Lowestoft, sailing out to the Dogger Bank and as far north as the Arctic. Many are the sea adventures Lowestoft men could tell. I know one who, after being dismasted and missing for four weeks and drifting nearly as far as Denmark, eventually arrived back in Lowestoft on the day that a memorial service for the crew was being held in Lowestoft church. A small boy ran into the church shouting 'The *Winnie* has been sighted' and the entire congregation streamed out of the church and down to the pier heads. Left alone, the parson could do no more than rush to the belfry and ring the bells with all his might. One of the survivors was my great grandfather — Charles Brown — and another relative named Utting. There are many Browns and Uttings in the churchyards of Kessingland, Pakefield and Lowestoft. My mother was a Brown of Kessingland and I wonder if it is mere coincidence that I — although born on the Dorset coast — have spent much of my life trading up and down the coast of my mother's birthplace.

Incidentally, strangers to our coast are often mystified by the terms 'up the coast' and 'down north'. To an East Anglian sailor the tides are far more important than the school map, which shows north at the top and south at the bottom. But the ebb tide out of the Thames Estuary runs away to the *north* along the Suffolk and Norfolk coastline and sailing vessels bound north come *down on the ebb*. The flood tide, sweeping through Pentland Firth from the Atlantic, runs southward, filling the rivers and creeks on its way to London and Dover. So ships from the north come up on the flood. So *up* is to the south and *down* is to the north. You can always tell a landlubber because he says he is going from London 'up the coast to Yarmouth'. But then, as an old Pin Mill skipper once said: 'Half the people ashore are as ignorant as hell — they're damn near as ignorant as the other half.'

In the two World Wars, the East Anglian coast was in the front line. Lowestoft Ness is the most easterly point of England and nearest to Germany. In the 1914-1918 War the German fleet bombarded Yarmouth and Harwich and in the second World War the ships on the east coast were under constant attack by aeroplanes and 'E'-Boats. North of Yarmouth was a stretch of coast called E-Boat Alley, where the fast German raiders lay in wait for British merchant convoys. Hundreds of British sailors met their death in the holocaust of machine gunning, bombs, mines and torpedoes, between Yarmouth roads and the Humber Estuary.

Today, the East Anglian coast bears little relation to its glorious past. Hardly a sail to be seen except the occasional pleasure yacht, one or two inshore fishermen, a handful of motor coasters — and that's about all. In the once busy and bustling ports there are caravan sites, fair grounds, vast car parks and beach amusements for people from the Midlands. Entertainment of the inlander has become the order of the day, rather than the old ideas of work and manual industry. Raucous canned music and the screams of the 'dolly birds' on the switchback have replaced the rattle of halyard blocks and the shouts of seamen. Perhaps it is all for the better.

But the sea that laps the sand and shingle or thunders along the shore under the lash of a 'Norseman's wind' still holds the greater part of East Anglia's history and East Anglia's secrets.

Although born in Dorset, in 1907, Bob Roberts is of East Anglian descent and has spent most of his life in coastal sailing barges carrying cargoes between London and the Humber, trading into Maldon, Colchester, Ipswich, Lowestoft, Yarmouth, King's Lynn and Hull. The tides and weather are much the same now as 2000 years ago, so he has become steeped in the history of the East Anglian coast, the elements of the sea providing a continuity over the centuries which is often obliterated on land. He has written three books about his voyages and is now engaged on a fourth.

John Steel
Things Antique

LONG before I ever thought of living in East Anglia, I was walking round the Great Room at the Grosvenor House Hotel, admiring the exhibits in the Annual Antique Dealers' Fair, when I saw a piece which caught my eye. It was a Queen Anne bureau bookcase of small proportions, being only 2'9" wide and a little under 6' high. The walnut was beautifully patinated and set off the carefully chosen grain of the wood superbly. The dealer noticed my interest and together we examined it. Amid the glittering treasures in this great annual event, the restraint, almost understatement, of the piece gave it an attraction which more than enabled it to hold its own against the opulence which surrounded us. The dealer must have felt this too, because we settled down happily to remove drawers, examine hinges and admire the finely cast handles. At length he observed that it was probably from East Anglia. He couldn't explain why. It had all the quality of a London piece, but was somehow just that little bit different.

Perhaps I should explain that London has for hundreds of years attracted the finest craftsmen from the rest of the country so that, although for example, Chippendale came from Yorkshire, no one would dream of calling his work 'North Country' or provincial, for these terms have the connotation of heaviness or inept design.

As walnut furniture rocketed in price, I turned my attention to oak of the 16th and 17th centuries which, until a few years ago, had been out of favour since the 1930's. The finest book on the subject, *Early English Furniture and Woodwork*, was written in 1922 by Herbert Cescinsky and Ernest Gribble. In 700 pages it traces the development of English furniture from the dissolution of the monasteries until the start of the walnut period in the 1680's. In selecting the hundreds of illustrations, a large proportion of the early examples used to come from East Anglia. There are dozens of photographs of fine woodwork taken from churches all over the area. By this time my interest in East Anglia was thoroughly aroused and when the opportunity of a suitable job arose I moved to Suffolk, anxious to discover what the area had to offer.

The fact that the area has a very great deal to offer, very little of it connected with antiques, does not detract from the delight of discovering that what has been discussed in books explores only the tip of the antiques iceberg in East Anglia. The commercial success of sheep rearing in the period from the 13th to 16th century provided the area with great wealth; almost as important was the existence of the ports which had close contact with Holland. I had not appreciated the extent to which maritime communications had existed in these early periods. The position of East Anglia when Europe was communicating freely gave it a great commercial advantage. By contrast, the relatively isolated position of Britain in the 18th century onwards until the present day left East Anglia on the road to nowhere, a position which is now being dramatically reversed.

House-hunting in East Anglia some years ago was fascinating to anybody vaguely interested in the antique. The absence of stone, or even bricks in any quantity, led to reliance on wood for the entire construction of the house, save for the footings and the main centre chimney which were made of the very red flat Tudor bricks. Wood, mainly oak but also elm and chestnut, must have existed in vast quantities in the early centuries. Beams a foot thick are standard and the reserves of strength are massive. The use of wood enabled decoration to be applied by the builder. On the huge early beams one sees interesting mouldings, some designed to lessen the appearance of thickness, others as in the case of rope-like mouldings decorated simply to enhance the appearance. As with such objects as table legs which the Victorians found offensive, so the crude strength of mediaeval beams proved offensive to them and was hidden by planking or merely boxed in. This was just as well, for the love of black oak in the 1920's resulted in the staining of those old beams which were exposed, thus robbing them of the faded silvery colour — their patina — which they had acquired over the last 300 to 500 years.

Patina on furniture must be one of the most valuable substances. Scraped off from, say, a bureau, it might weigh an ounce but would drop the value by £100. Fortunately, this is not the case with old houses, but nevertheless the rarity of beams in their original condition is a sad reflection of what Osbert Lancaster so happily refers to as the 'Stockbroker Tudor craze'.

Beams and studs (the vertical pieces which support the weight of the house) occasionally carry carvings, but in general this decoration was reserved for corner posts and wall plates — at least in the early years. Seeing the elaborate decorations on the corner posts of what appear now to be relatively humble houses, it is not hard to believe that the craftsmen who built the churches moved to domestic work when their ecclesiastical work was completed.

By the 16th and 17th centuries the amount of decoration increased, or was it merely that it became more commonly used? Whatever the reason, carved decorations and plaster mouldings make their appearance. Carved overmantels are still to be found. In the 1920's these were often ripped out and used to make bedheads for elaborate Tudor beds which commanded very high prices. By-products of this despoliation were small carved figures, heads and panels which can be bought for a few pounds and can be backed on velvet to produce a pleasant decoration.

In the 17th and 18th centuries East Anglia began the decline in prosperity, but money was still spent on decorative items. One of the features of the Suffolk house is the pine corner cupboard. When house hunting, it seemed that even the smallest workers' cottage of any age had one. I remember walking over ploughed fields to what was little more than a shell in my search for a house. Even the stairs had started to disintegrate, but tucked in a corner was a small two-shelf piece only two feet high with two panelled doors that had been painted inside originally and must have been attractive. I subsequently discussed these little cupboards with a dealer I got to know and he told me that he had realised their potential some years previously and offered a few shillings each. When the stripped pine boom came in the early 1960's he cleared his barn of several hundred for a matter of pounds a piece. He showed me two he had kept for himself. Both were standing cupboards —

one in particular was highly ornate with the inside fluted and formed in the shape of a shell at the back. Like the smaller edition I had seen, it too had been originally painted blue inside, but the dentil moulding and fine blind fret marked it as being a piece of considerable quality. It came from a Norfolk hall which had been heavily damaged by fire. The material to build these pieces was most probably imported from Scandinavia, with which Britain had had a flourishing timber trade in the various types of conifer commonly known as pine but which includes red deal.

Of the original furnishings of these 16th and 17th century houses, there is little left. Oak and elm would have been the principal woods used, though later yew and the fruitwoods would have been employed. The interest in oak was such that most of the quality oak has long since been identified and removed. The systematic and organised way in which yew wood Windsor chairs — a very much later Suffolk antique — were rounded up in the 1920's and 30's for dealers by the gipsies at a few shillings each suggests that the much more valuable early pieces would have been searched for very diligently. It is still possible to find odd items of 1630-1700 which have probably lived in East Anglia all their lives. It would still be possible to build up quite a selection of small, slightly damaged side tables for under £30. Odd oak chests are still to be found — one I possess was bought from the house where it has lain since it was made about 1690. There must also be plenty of coffers, though again exceptional pieces like the one I was offered for £120 and which subsequently sold for £400 in London, are rare. It has caryatids (carved figures) along the corners and sides and was probably made in the mid-17th century.

One interesting sidelight of the great craze for oak between the wars was that a supply of early oak was developed. Several factories in East Anglia produced fine imitation period oak furniture; indeed, so fine was it that large quantities were sent to America by agents unable to find sufficient of the original article. Amusing stories are told of old floor boards doing service for table tops, oak beams providing the raw material for trestle tables. It is interesting to note that the old oak with which the beamed houses were constructed was not matured before use. This explains the contorted shapes that many have taken up. It perhaps also partly explains why only the surface of these beams aged. Cescinsky, referred to already, had some beams cut to find out how they had changed over the years and was surprised to find that the centres were green. Faking furniture, therefore, is far from easy. Chemicals and wire brushes may be used to damage the grain, but the colour is hard to simulate.

Having bought a thatched Suffolk farm house and furnished it with oak and walnut furniture (most of it still needing at least some restoration, for cobblers' children do go barefoot) I contracted that fatal malady, a love of long case, or more commonly grandfather, clocks. For those who are not infected it should be explained that the long case clock is just about the perfect antique and attracts fervent admirers. The justification for such a boast lies in the fact that it is a pure example of the cabinet maker's art, actually does something, has the attraction of the automation and can, moreover, be made extremely accurate. The most loyal followers would claim that each clock has a distinct character of its own or rather its maker, for clocks by the same maker do have strong similarities.

Having started to collect grandfather clocks, it became apparent that East Anglia abounded with makers working during the golden period 1670-1720. Not only were there a large number of clocks produced, but a surprisingly large proportion were of high quality. As in the case of furniture, the distinction between London and provincial applies, but there is nothing in the work of such makers as John Smorthwait, Barnaby Dammant and Nathaniel Hedge which would make them unacceptable had they been London makers. In 1969 Bernard Mason produced *Clock and Watchmaking in Colchester* and one realised that there were not just one or two but nearly a dozen clockmakers working to high standards. Reading this fascinating book, one realises that it is again the proximity to Holland which enabled East Anglia to keep up to the quality of London work. It is interesting to read that one of the top early makers of long case clocks — a maker whose clocks fetch thousands of pounds at auction on the rare occasions when they appear — Ahasuerus Fromanteel, was apprenticed to a clockmaker in Norwich and went to London in 1629. He married Maria de Bruigne, a spinster of Colchester. Part of the Fromanteel family settled in Colchester and at least one apprentice from Colchester, Joshua Warnock, was apprenticed to Fromanteel. The development of the long or royal pendulum was started in Holland and Colchester clockmakers were using this and the anchor escapement as early as 1675-80, whereas other provincial towns did not use this refinement until much later.

Bernard Mason unfortunately writes only about Colchester clockmakers. Other schools of clockmakers existed in East Anglia — John and Roger Moore of Ipswich were good makers and there were several in Norwich and Bury St. Edmunds, as well as Cambridge.

Perhaps even more fascinating is to read that there is evidence of clockmaking having been carried on in East Anglia from some time before 1460. At this date clockmakers were rare in country areas — perhaps the combination of wealth from the sheep and the proximity to Europe mentioned earlier enabled this early development.

Unfortunately there are no records of furniture makers in East Anglia, at least none that I have come across. No doubt, as in all other provincial areas, cabinet makers carried on business in the main town. Indeed, from the evidence of the Queen Anne bureau bookcase which started these thoughts, there must have been some good makers. Other odd scraps of evidence exist to suggest that quality was always considered important — a sideboard of about 1770 with the flat edge to the top veneered right round the back as well; an early oak piece with exceptional carving.

One name does, however, survive; that of Day. John and Dan Day were chair makers — a distinctly different art from that of the cabinet maker — who lived at Mendlesham, about 15 miles north of Ipswich. Working in the early part of the 19th century, they produced a design of chair which at first sight looked like a form of Windsor or possible Lancashire chair, and which incorporated small turned balls in the design of the back. Chairmaking is far more difficult than the layman imagines, and although these are relatively simple country chairs, they are as good as anything produced elsewhere in the country. This is evidenced by the fact that the price of £60-£80 a chair for the top quality ones is higher than for any similar design. I met a dealer recently who claimed to understand which of the brothers had made which of the dozen or so basic designs. He had been taught this by his father who had learned it from one of the original workmen. When I can find sufficient of the various designs to photograph, it should be possible to put on record this interesting information which, if it is not captured now, will be lost for ever.

East Anglia even has its own porcelain which is highly treasured by collectors. Lacking the pretentiousness of some of its competitors, Lowestoft has a simple naive quality which is perhaps what makes it so desirable. Very few examples remain from the early period of the factory. All these are blue and white. Little or no polychrome was produced until 1772 and the early pieces have a dullish grey-blue, rather similar to Delft. The middle period was from 1761-1772. A wide range of items were produced including mugs, bowls, moulded cider jugs, tea bowls and saucers, creamboats and coffee cups.

Lowestoft had some special shapes, one design of cream jug being called sparrow-beak, after its resemblance to that bird. The handles of cups and jugs often have a characteristically Lowestoft kick. There were certain unique features in the pieces themselves — teapots often had seven holes in the strainers as well as a glazing on the inside of the teapot lid.

After 1772 the output of the factory increased considerably. Printing was introduced to produce the blue and white ware, and patterns similar to Worcester and Caughley were sometimes used. In addition to the normal items, such odd pieces as eyebaths, eggcups, bottles, caddy spoons and miniature teawares were produced. A pap-boat or feeding cup was also produced, which was unique in 18th century porcelain.

Polychrome wares were produced after 1772 and pieces by the anonymous worker, the tulip painter, are particularly sought after. His bold style of painting, often incorporating a full blown tulip, is of fine quality. Prices for Lowestoft are high. The rare birth tablets, which are peculiar to the factory, fetch £250-£300.

John Steel was born in 1934. Educated at St. Peter's School, York, and later at Campbell College, Belfast, he graduated in Economics at Queens University, Belfast, in 1952. Later he became a chartered and cost and works accountant, and for 10 years was a management consultant and subsequently consultancy manager in a City firm.

Together with his partner, Diana Thorpe, he set up the Antique Collectors' Club in 1965 with the objective of developing his own interest in antiques and related subjects. In 1968 The Price Guide to Antique Furniture *was published. This was the first of eight Price Guides that have now been published out of a full series of 30.*

Now 'retired' from consultancy, and living in the peace of Woodbridge, John Steel acts as Editor of the Club's monthly magazine 'Antique Collecting' and overall Editor of the Price Guide series. His main love is long case clocks, but he also enjoys sailing, riding and good food.

'... The old and ...'

Eldon Griffiths
The New East Anglia

EAST Anglia is one of the most agreeable places in all the world for a man to work and bring up his family in. That is why more people are settling here. East Anglia is also a part of the country which is likely to have increasing attractions for the businessman. That is why it has already felt, and will continue to feel, the pressure for greater industrialisation and urbanisation. So the question that arises, when considering East Anglia's future, is to what extent this region should, and can, respond to the pressure for growth — for pressures for growth — for more houses, factories, roads, transmission lines and sewage plants — while still retaining its character and charm. We cannot prevent East Anglia's changing; the challenge is to channel and civilize changes that are inevitable so as to improve, rather than disfigure, an environment that still is touched, at almost every point, by a calm countryside.

The protection of the environment has lately become one of the more fashionable clichés. Yet in this country, and especially in East Anglia, a recognition that nature is man's most precious possession, and that the quality of life depends very largely on our physical surroundings, is scarcely a new discovery. Those who built East Anglia's great churches or sited our villages were as much environmental planners as those who later and more self-consciously laid out the garden cities of the 1920's or designated the Green Belts of the postwar years. Today, however, we have something altogether bigger and more powerful, dedicated not only to conserving the natural and man-made beauties of those whose environment is good but to enhancing positively the surroundings of those whose environment is bad. I refer to the Department of the Environment which brings together, under single command, overall responsibility for the whole of local government, land-use and regional planning, for transport, building, water and sewerage, recreation and every aspect of pollution control. The new Department is charged simply, if overwhelmingly, with responsibility for making life better. One of its concerns will be to help the development of East Anglia to take place without defacing the countryside and defiling its market towns. This task will not be an easy one. Yet on its success, or failure, will depend in large measure how agreeable (or otherwise) life for the large majority of East Anglians will be in 20 years time.

At present, East Anglia enjoys, more perhaps than most parts of Britain, a landscape made better by man. Over wide areas, it presents a picture that breathes life into our social history. A picture of the Viking invasions and of the great medieval abbeys. Of Cromwell's prisoners reclaiming the marshes, and Constable painting his landscapes along the valley of the Stour. It is also a picture of farming, East Anglia's biggest industry. By no means all the accoutrements of the modern farming industry can be said to improve the landscape: sheet metal grain stores and concrete block pig palaces are scarcely the most graceful additions to the rural scene. Nor is the rooting up of hedgerows a specially helpful contribution to the balance of nature. Yet East Anglia's farmers contribute very substantially to the maintenance of our balance of payments and their industry does more than all others to keep East Anglia green — or golden — in the midsummer months.

Farming also provides not only a measure of stability but one of the main stimuli to change among East Anglia's people. The remarkable growth of its productivity has meant that the numbers engaged in agriculture are declining sharply. As a result, in some areas of East Anglia, the population is static or falling, and many market towns feel a loss of viability. It is in part because of this that some East Anglian towns see their future in town expansion schemes, negotiated with Greater London. Simultaneously, there has been a demand for more jobs to be located in rural areas to counteract unemployment, raise wage levels and halt the outward migration of young people. Overall, during the 1960's, East Anglia has shown great resilience in the face of this decline in farm employment. Between 1960-69, while 20,000 jobs were lost in agriculture, there was a growth of 48,000 jobs in manufacturing and 58,000 in services. More than half of these jobs were for women.

Such figures are an illustration of the extent to which industry and commerce (including the holiday trades) are now overtaking farming as the region's largest employers. This, indeed, is the shape of things to come in East Anglia. At present, it is true, industry is not moving into the expanding towns as rapidly as a few years ago. This is the result in part of an inadequate level of industrial investment naturally. For the moment, therefore, the pace of development in some of these towns has slowed down; but looking further ahead, to the recovery of the national economy, which I expect to be in full flood by the middle 1970's, there is every reason to believe that East Anglia will be well positioned to take advantage of an acceleration in industrial investment.

Among the numerous factors which favour the region's progress is the Common Market. Many industrialists already have transferred their export to Europe from the Port of London to Felixstowe and Harwich. Since 1961, the overall value of Britain's foreign trade has gone up by 60%; the corresponding figure for trade through the East Anglian ports is 515%. This trade to and from Europe seems certain to go on increasing; and it could bring with it a surge of investment from Europe. It seems likely that more industry and more services will wish to establish themselves in or within reach of East Anglia's principal ports.

A third and related development bringing new pressures to bear on the East Anglian environment is the sheer growth of its population.

In no other region in Britain is the population growing so fast in percentage terms. To some extent this is the product of deliberate planning — the creation of the New Town at Peterborough, and the development of the expanding towns. Sensibly handled 'overspill' can bring a fresh injection of human vitality, and new standards of expectation. But a considerable proportion of East Anglia's increasing population is made up of voluntary migrants — of people choosing to live and work in an attractive environment, or to retire in it. Hence the exploding demand for moderate-priced homes to buy. New housing estates thicken around the edges of the old market towns. The gaps in village streets, are 'infilled' with bungalows and shops with plateglass windows. Everywhere the pressures are increasing for new planning permissions in East Anglia's scheduled villages. To give way may be to risk the spoliation of the rural scene — yet to resist inflexibly may equally be to consign a living village to stagnation, as its population ages, the school and the shop close down, the bus service becomes uneconomic and the doctor's surgery is closed. One aspect of the house-hunting pressure shows signs nevertheless of being an unqualified success. The increased availability of improvement grants is enabling young couples, all over East Anglia, to 'fix up' old country cottages, many of them left semi-derelict by farmworkers leaving the land. The thatching industry has revived. Tree-planting is catching on fast. Seldom if ever have so many delightfully colour-washed cottages stood out in such well tended gardens as one sees in Suffolk these days.

More people, more industries and more trade inevitably mean more pressures on East Anglia's transport system. Unfortunately, increasing costs are making the public transport, whether by train or bus, incapable of competing with the ubiquitous motor car. Many branch line railway services, which were running at considerable losses, have already been terminated. The case for subsidising others must be looked at with care. Meanwhile the rural bus, packed with passengers at rush hours, trundles round country lanes all but empty (and profitless) on its off-peak journeys. To take just one example, the number of Eastern Counties bus passengers fell by close to one-fifth in the 1950's and by a further quarter in the 60's — while the area's population rose sharply. Meanwhile, in West Suffolk the number of cars registered leapt from less than 10,000 in 1952 to more than 45,000 in 1971. The same trend seems certain to persist all over East Anglia for as far as one can see into the 70's and 80's. And alongside the car is the lorry, too often pounding down roads that were built for nothing heavier than a drayman's cart.

Soon there will be more lorries, carrying their giant containers to feed the expanding ports. And with the lorries will come more noise, vibration and fumes. Fortunately for East Anglia, environmental considerations coincide here with economics. The Department of the Environment's new road-building strategy will take account of the need to expedite traffic to and from ports and to by-pass historic towns. On both counts, East Anglia will benefit. By the early completion of dualling from London to Ipswich along the A12. By the building of the Stumps Cross motorway, linking London to Cambridge. Above all by the decision, held up throughout the 1960's, to create a major strategy routed from the Midlands to the East Coast ports. Few things will do more to improve the environment along the line of the A45 than the expediting of bypasses around Cambridge, Newmarket, Bury St. Edmunds, Stowmarket and, eventually, Ipswich.

Obviously, it is essential that these new roads should be landscaped sympathetically. Important, too, that tomorrow's new factories and housing estates should be sited with a regard for their impact on the environment. By all means, let there be new industries and gas pipelines, bigger and better ports, fast motor roads and all the rest. But let it never be forgotten that these are the means, not the ends: they have value only insofar as they promote a better way — and a higher quality of life for individual men and women. East Anglians know only too well what happened to the coal fields during the first Industrial Revolution. Vast areas of England still bear the environmental scars of indiscriminate industrial development and jerry building.

There is no need for anything like that to be repeated in East Anglia in the late 20th century. If the region is to play a part in the Second Industrial

The Ipswich Underground Car Park in 1965 – at that stage the largest hole in Europe.

Revolution, this one based perhaps on less polluting materials, we must be careful to ensure that it enhances, and does not destroy, the heritage that the countryside has given us.

The fact is that many people in East Anglia have chosen to live here because they prefer peace and quiet. They do not necessarily wish for fast cars and supermarkets. Only for respite from the noise of the internal combustion engine and transistor radios. They want the undisturbed beauty of their gardens and surroundings, and their pride in their own homes. Such people feel apprehensive for the East Anglian environment. They fear the East Anglia of the 1980's may be one they will dislike — that they may yet find electricity pylons blocking their front windows, diesel fumes in their bedrooms, vast new housing estates covering every hill.

We must prevent this happening. Not by standing in the way of progress but by using every resource of environmental planning to see that the new factories are situated so as to avoid abusing the countryside; that the new estates are laid out intelligently; the new roads landscaped so that they become a pleasure to behold, as well as to drive along. Given the co-operation of the new local authorities, to be established by 1974-75, together with overall environmental leadership from a Department of the Environment controlling transport, land-use and all aspects of physical planning, I believe East Anglia can do this. For in our efforts to civilise the region's development, we have some clear cut advantages.

First, East Anglia starts with a more or less clean slate. Because it missed the early impact of the steam and coal revolution, its new industries can be based on the later, cleaner and, let us hope, better designed methods of the late 20th century.

Secondly, East Anglia's towns can expand without having to demolish vast areas of slums. Bad property abounds in Norwich, Ipswich and Peterborough but on nothing like the scale of Liverpool or Leeds; while in the market towns expansion in East Anglia starts more or less from scratch.

Third, East Anglians are aware — and so is central Government — of the price that was paid elsewhere for neglecting the environment in the interests of uncontrolled growth. Let us learn from the lessons of back-to-back terraces, ribbon development and urban traffic jams: by welcoming technical change but keeping it as the servant, not the master of man.

If East Anglia can do these things — seize hold of the new industrial and technological opportunities yet civilize them for the benefit of ordinary men and women living in the midst of a still unspoiled countryside, then indeed it will qualify as Britain's new frontier. It will be showing the way not only to a brighter economic future but to better and more civilised living. In that way, the new East Anglia can do more than achieve success. It will deserve it, too.

Eldon Griffiths was appointed Joint Parliamentary Secretary, Ministry of Housing and Local Government, and also Minister with responsibility for sport in June 1970. He has been Member of Parliament for Bury St. Edmunds since 1964. Born in 1925, he was educated at Ashton Grammar School and Emmanuel College, Cambridge; he was also a Sir John Dill Fellow at Yale University. He served in the Royal Air Force from 1944-45. From 1949 to 1956 he was a correspondent, and later an editor for Time *magazine. In 1959 he became foreign editor of* Newsweek *magazine, and from 1961 to 1963 was Chief European Correspondent. He also wrote an 'Opinion' column for the* Washington Post. *During his journalistic career he covered crises in Budapest, Cyprus, Jordan and South East Asia. He is also an experienced broadcaster both in Europe and America. Greatest distinction of all, perhaps, is that he is a member of the Lords' Taverners.*

Paul Jennings at East Bergholt.

Paul Jennings' publications include Oddly Enough, Even Oddlier, Next to Oddliness, I said Oddly, Diddle I? *and* Oodles of Oddlies. *There is a* Jenguin Pennings. *Born in 1918, he was educated at King Henry VIII School, Coventry, and Douai School. While still a lieutenant in the Royal Signals he began to write for* Punch *and the* Spectator. *He joined the* Observer *in 1949; but is now a freelance writer. He is married to the daughter of the distinguished music critic, the late Eric Blom, has five children and lives at East Bergholt in Suffolk. He believes, with a kind of mad poetry, that tube trains have a low level consciousness, 'a worm soul': 'you can cut a tube train in half and it wouldn't mind.' He reads the top row of keys on a typewriter as a pronounceable word,* qwertyuiop, *and thinks it would make a good onomatopoeic word for corkscrew,* qwe-rt *being the squeaky noise of the cork turning round and the* yui-OP *being it coming out. On average each of his books sells 4,000 copies which, he estimates, is about 3,496,000 fewer than* Lady Chatterley's Lover.

Paul Jennings
The Suffolk Settler, Crabbewise

THOUGH saints and scholars try with all their art
To give man peace from his own restless heart
The fact remains, and surely can't be missed
By e'en the dimmest sociologist,
That man can't find, when all things whirling be
The rock which yet demands his loyalty:
How, if he's on the go for all he's worth,
Can man revere one chosen spot of earth?
When all (to quote old Heracleitus sage)
Is flux, what stirs his patriotic rage?
How should a man love London in these days
Which houses nothing but lewd films and plays?
Beaumont and Fletcher's happy 'prentice boys
From a fair city, not a hell of noise
Fared forth to holidays of mirth and ale,
Not stuck in stinking traffic, nose-to-tail.
Above the ground exhaust fumes fill the air;
Below, all ads for female underwear.
Now Culture from her capital has fled
And left mere Mechanism, swift but dead
Which rightly made C. Connolly declare
The village idiot is in Leicester Square.

So, the stout Settler takes the better part
Who, loving England with a faithful heart,
Casts on the counties round a searching eye
To find the best wherein to live and die.
Surrey? He tries, but soon stops talking
On seeing what the prices are in Dorking.
A Sussex oast-house? Only in the range
Of men from sordid bucket-shop or 'Change.
Berkshire is better; but no rural steading
Is worth dependence on a place like Reading;
Nor Hertfordshire could hold his heart in fee
Whose fields contain so much light industry.
Essex? Ah, well, of course, there's lots of that;
But *live?* Near *Chelmsford?* (And it's all so *flat*) ....

Well may the Settler's drooping spirit rise
When beauteous Suffolk he at last espies.
What moves him first? Her quality of light
Shining through air supremely clear and bright?
Her calm slow rivers that go windingly
Through herbal marshes to the pebbly sea
Past villages where luminously glint
Her noble churches, marvels made of flint?

What more inducement, or what further proof
Could any want than Needham Market's roof?
What other county could the Settler choose
Who once has seen the ends of Blythburgh pews,
Why longer hover on decision's brink
When ochre-ish houses (though they call it pink)
Folded in farmland or in secret vale
Fill him with hope that one might be for sale?

So: it is done. Although he's on his knees
After the agent's and the lawyers' fees
His humble sticks of furniture now can
Be stowed in this enormous yellow van.
But though the Settler (and the Settler's wife)
Have rightly done this thing, and changed their life
Does no tear fall, no wrinkle crease the brow
At leaving everything they've known till now?
Do not the warnings echo in their ears
Of those who confidently said, 'my dears,
You must be *mad* to leave your friends and go,
For Suffolk people all take *years* to know.'

......Oh, *piffle*, thinks the Settler, as they never fail
To tell this old but quite unfounded tale,
Where is the Suffolk village where they act like this
And ban the stranger from their pastoral bliss?
Though Suffolk people do not gush or flap
He is a fool who falls into the trap
Of thinking calm is cold, or who would try
To misinterpret that calm Suffolk eye
Which (if he did but know) can also gaze
On boon companions known from childhood days,
Thus: two old codgers in a public bar,
One with a face that length of nose doth mar;
'Jim, thar's a drop a-hangin' on yar nose!'
What doth the friend reply, do you suppose?
Only in Suffolk could the answer be
'Yow wipe it then; it's nearer yow than me.'
He is a fool ever who tries to swank
To men like this, impervious to rank,
Or prematurely, anxious to impress,
Attempts a hearty, instant mateyness.
But the stout Settler, having much more sense,
Finds in this very trait his recompense;
No brass-band welcome, flower-bedecked,
But clear regard and courteous calm respect.

So, as his roots push down in Suffolk earth,
He earns their sober smile, their decent mirth.
Though he, long nurtured in another place,
Will never be a member of their race
Will not his children bear the sacred sign
Who soon say not 'at home', but 'down at mine'
And in that slightly sing-song voice proclaim
(Though rarely) 'Ipswich *won*! A super game!'

Say then, does nothing mar the Settler's peace
Whose joy in Suffolk doth each year increase?
Ah, naught is perfect in this vale of tears!
Behold the Settler now beset by fears
That he alone, of all the human race
Will fight with passion for this chosen place;
That he alone (for instance) will protest
When faceless men attack the *Sailors' Rest*
(A splendid house in Ipswich which some men
From London want to pull right down and then
Put up the usual concrete office block
Too hideous to bore, too dull to shock,
Not beautiful or useful, simply meant
To stuff some greedy pockets with its rent).
And if in Ipswich, (after all, a town
Of little architectural renown)
The Settler sees the menace of the age ......
......Developers' Greed and Money-grubbers' Rage ......
How much the more he feels *he* must defend
The country beauties that They mean to end.
Will the stout Settler stand up there alone
To stop Them flooding quiet Tattingstone
(Though Alton Mill, They say, with any luck
Will be removed to safety on a truck),
And try to make Them see the plan is bosh,
Our one real hope a barrage of the Wash?

Why, thinks the Settler with a wild surmise,
Do natives stare at him with glassy eyess
When he, with argument and marshalled fact
Rallies them all to talk no more, but act?
Perish the thought that their support is dim
Because the change he fights began with HIM;
Still will unravished Suffolk be his hope
And he her liege, more Catholic than the Pope.

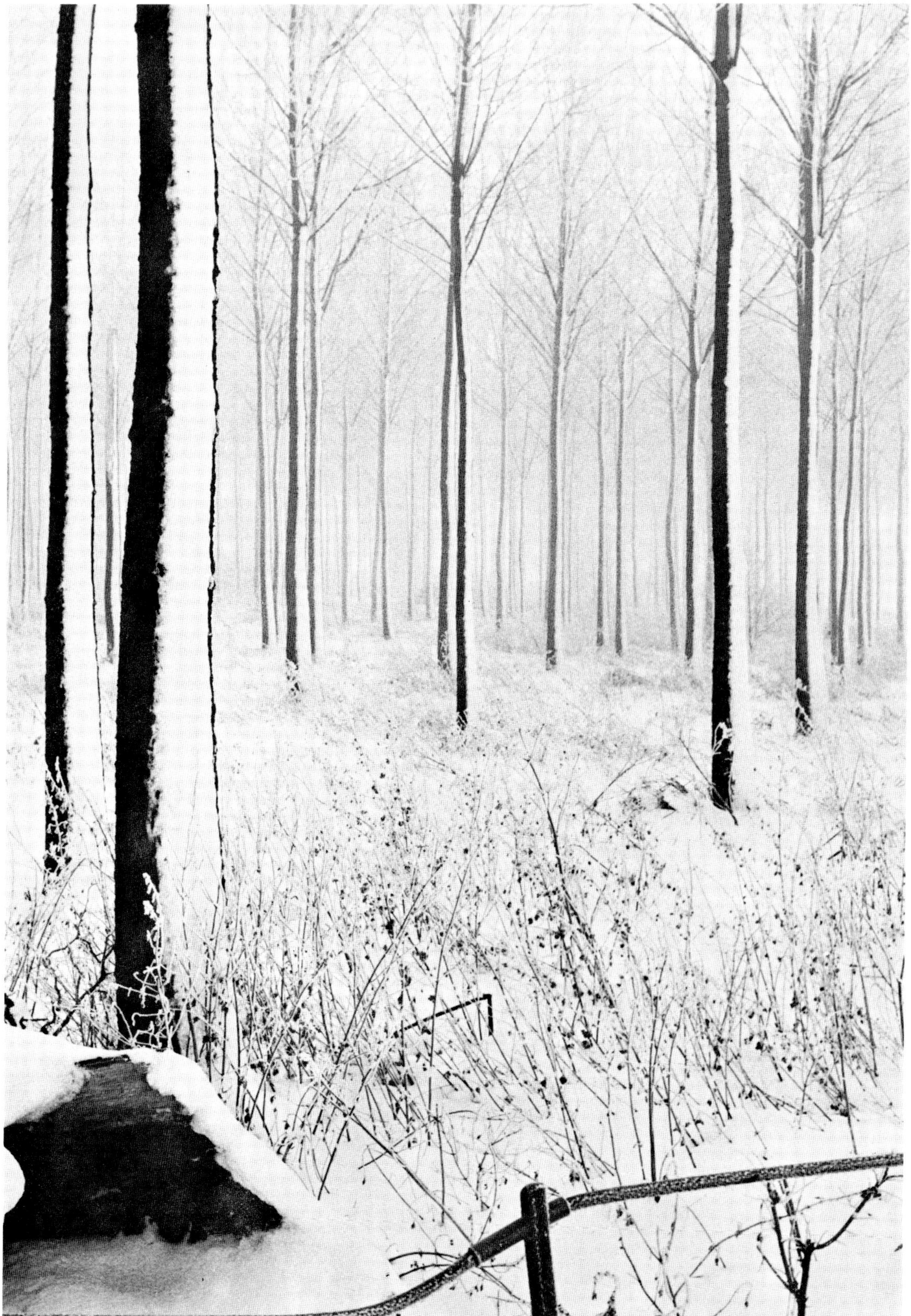

Logie Bruce Lockhart
Eastward Ho! For Sport

I AM writing this in a nostalgic mood. The familiar notice *'Chasse gardée'* is the only sign of life except for a small lizard rustling in dessicated pine leaves. Pleasant though it is to close one's eyes and daydream of Norfolk frets with the smug coziness of Provençal sun toasting one's back, the immeasurable superiority of East Anglia as a sporting paradise is nowhere more evident or harder to bear. Provence is the most wonderful place in the world to do nothing in, but for the sporting male, who still likes to do things in his spare time after the glory of two or three sizzling and inactive days, what can it offer? Underwater fishing for pulpy octopus and brightly coloured little fish, more suitable for *bouillabaisse* than for specimen cases? An occasional opportunity to rattle one's bones water ski-ing on the choppy Mediterranean? As for these notices of *'Chasse gardée'* on scrubby slopes and peach orchards, they are more productive of snails and frogs than of wild boar or deer. Partridge and pheasant? It is more likely to be larks and fieldfare: anything down to and including sparrows. If glamorous game should find its way into the Frenchman's bag, it is more likely to be hoopoes or golden orioles than capercailzies.

εἴθε γενοίμην — would I were, not, perhaps, in Granchester, but somewhere in the East Anglian marshes. What part of Britain, what part of the world exceeds East Anglia for the variety and verve of its sport? 'Marshes' is an oversimplification. Lagoons, broads, heaths, flint villages, bricks, pine forests, vast open skyscapes, dunes, shingle and meadows, no wonder there is variety.

Apart from the pheasant shooting, it may not be the greatest in any one department, but it has a genuine rusticity, a kind of amateur bounce, an abundance of little known treasures which ensure that it has more to offer the all-round sportsman and games player than any other part of England.

It is both feudal and democratic; the word class is seldom heard and the conception is little thought about. The secret, of course, is that the middle classes have not yet reached East Anglia in force; they eke out a precarious existence in isolated outposts of what is mistakenly held in other parts of Britain to be civilization — like Ipswich, Norwich and Cambridge. The East Anglian proper is squire, gamekeeper or gardener or some other sub-species of the genus farmer. They wear tweeds of uniform shabbiness and have pheasants swinging from their hips. Apart from the fact that the first sub-species wears an Old Etonian tie, and keeps *Plato's Republic* beside *Beet Weekly* in his loo, they are indistinguishable.

Not even in the Borders do pheasant pullulate to such an extent. They are more of a hazard to driving than wheeled traffic. Nowhere else have partridge recovered so swiftly from the over-cutting of hedge buttom grass and from the disastrous winters of 1957 and 1963. Nowhere else do the skeins of geese come in over the marshes at dawn in such quantity. I doubt if a dozen different species of duck can be seen in a single day in any other part of Britain.

Left: Woods near Heveningham Hall, Halesworth.

The secret of the continued richness of East Anglia's wild life lies in the respect and love of the countryman for his land. It was, until recently, fashionable to laugh at the traditional lore of the muck farmers who prophesied doom and dust bowls at the advent of D.D.T. and the quick, slick new farmers. More modern science has proved the wisdom of those who over the centuries have learned to live in harmony with nature rather than to exploit her.

Not without hard work and loving care, have the North Norfolk Bird Sanctuaries remained the best places for seeing wild birds not only in Britain but, perhaps, in Europe. Even Norfolk, however, is not completely secure against pollution. The increasing flow of inconsiderate holiday-makers on the Broads has not helped their wild life, or their famous fishing; but great pike still lurk in Barton and the bitterns boom like foghorns on a calm summer's day. The little Glaven and Stiffkey rivers bear quite good trout; but the danger signals are there: the mussel beds at the mouth of these rivers are suspect pending a year's investigation.

On the whole fishing flourishes. Along the shores weekenders pursue the temperamental dab or an occasional specimen cod. In remoter parts, these fishermen are replaced by a peculiar race of thigh-booted, semi-professionals with more than a hint of smuggler or pirate in their appearance if not in their descent. They hunt for bigger game: tope, skate or mackerel in the daytime, and, at night, secret summer expeditions after the most lovely of all fish. When the winds are gentle and the tides just right they drag the shallows. There the sea trout lie, in no more than a foot of water, allowing the rolling of the waves to scrape away their sea lice on the pebbles. When the net hits them, they jump, an unbelievable silver intensified by the moonlight and splashes of phosphorus, which spurts like Christmas sparklers from the heels of the fishermen on the wet sand. The sea trout run big along the Anglian shores, and the longshore men tell tales of 19 pounders.

Unfortunately they do not, as yet, run up the rivers between Trent and Test. Brown trout, however, are plentiful. Apart from the gravel pits, which offer big fish to those who practise the sink and draw techniques, it has not, thank goodness, generally been realized that there are dry fly streams in the East which offer as good sport as anywhere in England. Less sophisticated and over-fed than the Test trout, harder to get at than the Highland trout, an abundance of three-quarter pounders lurk in the gin-clear waters of the Wensum, the Nare, the Wissey, the Bure and the Glaven; and these rivers hold a few giants. A nine-pounder was landed near the end of the 1970 season. More important, the solitude of the rivers, wending their way round Breckland, and the difficulty and variety of their banks, means that a trout weighing a pound affords a memorable struggle to anglers with eight foot rods and light tackle. Such equipment is necessary to negotiate the tangle of undergrowth where nature is still at its richest, where kingfishers flash and sedge warblers burble.

Sport is a wide term and any glimpse of East Anglian sport cannot pass over the great traditional British games. Football seems to set the pattern. There are four or five very good clubs which stop short of a permanent place amongst the greatest, but have a devoted following and are liable to produce sudden, amazing feats of giant killing, or even one immortal season. Such was Norwich City's season of 1958/9, when they had that glorious run which almost took them to Wembley. They claim some of the most loyal and best behaved supporters in the country, and they occasionally remind their fans that the great days may not be far off again — as when they beat Manchester United at Manchester in the F.A. Cup.

Peterborough United is another team which has periodically excelled itself. In 1960/61 they set up a new scoring record for the League: 134 goals. In 1964/65 they beat Arsenal by 2—1 in the Cup and reached the sixth round. Arsenal must find East Anglia tiresome: in 1957 they could only draw with Colchester in the Fourth Round. Colchester must rank amongst the greatest giant killers of all time; their remarkable feat in 1971 in disposing of the mighty Leeds United by 3—2, at a time when Leeds were favoured by many for the Cup and League double was as unexpected as it was well deserved.

Not even the record of these clubs can exceed the sheer unpredictability of Ipswich, which has a good claim to be considered the leading East Anglian team. Their moment of glory was the season of 1961/62 when, under the great Alf Ramsay, they won the League by team work and will to win. I hope it would not be thought rude to the great goal scoring efforts of Phillips and Crawford to say that it was a team without stars.

It took them only two seasons to swing right back and to be relegated, and yet by 1967/68 they were champions of the second division. The fact that they earned a replay in the fifth round of the Cup in 1970/71 shows that they are still a force to be reckoned with.

Rugby is on the increase in the East. Although there are no top ranking clubs — distances and sparseness of population make it very hard to break into the first class circuit — a great deal of cheerful, vigorous second class rugby is enjoyed as only Anglian farmers can enjoy life. A little market town like Holt, where rugby was only started a few years ago, puts three teams into the field on most Saturdays. There is a case for saying that English rugby owes more to Cambridge University on the one hand and Dicky Jeeps on the other than to anything else, even if some will feel that English rugby owes little to anybody.

Cambridge University... of the many wonderful athletes and sportsmen produced from Cambridge, a whole host have disappeared into East Anglia, preferring to enjoy their sport and to share it with East Anglians than to seek fame which many of them would undoubtedly otherwise have earned in the hard and often bloody-minded competition of international sport. Of nothing is this so true than of cricket. Like East Anglian hockey, cricket has often been a family affair: the Pilches, the Edriches and the Rought-Roughts. David Armstrong's splendid little book on Norfolk cricket reveals that there were a dozen clubs as far back as 1788. A Norfolk team played the rest of England in 1797, and three Pilch brothers were playing by 1826. In 1885 Norfolk scored 695 against the M.C.C. at Lords. Towards the end of the century Lincolnshire, with two demon bowlers, deprived Norfolk of the position of Cock of the East; but they climbed back again under the long and often brilliant captaincy of Falcon who skippered the team from 1912 to 1946. If Falcon had played for a first class county there is no knowing how far he might have gone, as his seven cheap wickets against one of the great touring sides showed.

The reign of the Edriches is known wherever Wisden is read. The return of Bill Edrich in 1959, after he had retired from Middlesex, transformed the fortunes of Norfolk County. In the 11 seasons before his return they had won 12 matches. In the next 11 seasons they won 42.

In 1959 Ted Witherden topped 1,000 runs in 10 matches, and in 1960 Norfolk topped the table. Ian Mercer, Richard Jefferson and Billy Rose have all been useful bowlers in recent years, and Moore collected six cheap wickets against Yorkshire in the Gillette Cup. Even as late as 1970 the Edriches would not lie down. Bill finished his top scoring effort for Norfolk against Middlesex with 22 runs off seven balls — at the age of, I believe, 54.

They last well, East Anglians. Their swiftly drying, beautifully flat hockey pitches encourage veterans' teams of sprightly performance and venerable appearance as well as a crop of great hockey schools: Felsted, Gresham's, Framlingham, The Leys, and Culford, where such outstanding players and coaches as A.J. Cockett and Norman Borrett ensure that the skills of a great generation of artistic players are not forgotten.

Squash and tennis, too, are growing. The new courts of Lime Tree Road have done a lot for Norwich in this respect, and while no squash player of international class has yet emerged, the general level has risen so sharply that Norfolk was able to beat Cambridge University this year by four matches to one. There must be half a dozen players around now in Norfolk, any one of whom might have been county champion a few years ago. Men like David Wild, Malcolm Willstrop and Malcolm Clarke are capable of surprising any but the very best.

Messing about with boats, for which Britain is famed, is a sport which must surely have its headquarters around Blakeney, Burnham and the Norfolk Broads. It is the kind of leisurely individualistic and skilled sport at which East Anglians naturally excel.

So one could go on. There is no space to dwell on the sport of kings, of which the headquarters is on the borders of East Anglia; the hunting, the coursing, the beagling, the lovely inexpensive golf, or the strange local sports like the Fens skating races. A complete list would be impossible.

The true character and distinction of East Anglian sport lies not so much in facts, figures and achievements as in its amateurishness in the best sense of the word: the capacity to enjoy sports and games as art forms, to love exercise and fresh air in beautiful places, to achieve occasional flights of inspiration, to reverence the company of some real personalities and to feel at one with the rough old land which produced them.

Logie Bruce Lockhart was educated at Sedburgh and at St. John's College, Cambridge, where he was awarded the Larmor prize for the outstanding all-round undergraduate of his year. He played for Cambridge University at rugby and squash and for the Crusaders at cricket. During the war he served with the Sherwood Foresters and the Household Cavalry. He was capped five times for Scotland. Mr. Bruce Lockhart was appointed headmaster of Gresham's School in 1955. He is a lifelong devotee of fishing, and fond of music.

Ronald Blythe
Who Are We?

ONE hot summer's day during the 30's my aimless bicycling through the Stour Valley lanes brought me to Higham and to an inquisitive penetration of yet one more cool old church. I was 12 or 13 and churches were the only hard and fast things which I accepted on otherwise exquisitely pointless journeys. The date of this particular ride, like nearly all the really important records of childhood, is hazy and must always have *circa* fixed before it. But I can remember its tarry, flowery smell and its solitude. A man was cutting the churchyard grass and there was the usual, satisfying damp hollow crunch as his scythe brought down the thick-stemmed umbelliferae. I can also remember the bicycle, which had curiously armour-thick ridged mudguards.

Unforgotten too is the unreligious excitement with which I let myself into the church and began, in my usual fashion, a delicious kind of exploration which was based on a highly romantic notion of history inaccurately archaeological and vaguely sensual. One of the things which most people would like to retrieve from their personal oblivions is what they really felt when art first invaded their innocence. The boy who used Suffolk like a private terrain, wandering about in the colourful tangles of pre-chemicalised fields or who clambered about guiltily in belfries, had not yet reached the stage which demanded actuality. What was this countryside without Perp. or Dec. or agricultural facts and figures? Somewhere which subsequent knowledge was bound to destroy, of course.

Looking back — it had no significance at the time — I find it piquant that one of the first people to substitute experience for ignorance in my vision of East Anglia should have been none other than Dr. Havelock Ellis. Before this pale old man, dressed in what I suppose must have been one of those cream linen suits and carrying a straw sun-hat, began to point with his stick at the arches in Higham Church and to talk about architecture, I would have found it difficult to tell anyone why I was in the building at all. Did he sense this, or was he simply pleased to have someone to talk to? What he said has vanished; I shall never be able to recall one word of it. But the occasion itself remains vivid. The extreme whiteness of the hair and beard, and the lightness of the clothes together proclaiming someone exceptional. The unapologetic instruction — I later learned that he had once been a 16 year-old schoolmaster in Australia — and the odd feeling I had that from now on I should have to begin to use my wits, instead of my dreams, when I next went on one of these outings, puzzled me. It was the man cutting the grass who put me right, as they say in Suffolk. 'You've been having a word with Dr. Havelock Ellis then?' he called out as I rode away. So that was what I had been doing.

It was only recently that I discovered what had made this slight encounter possible. Searching through material for a study of the beginnings of the Fabian Society in the library at Nuffield College, Oxford, I came across the autobiography of Havelock Ellis and, in it, a long account of how, at the end of his life, he had returned to Suffolk to find his origins and to see what it was in these origins which had formed his own personality. And, with hindsight admittedly, I find myself dating my own conscious identity with East Anglia from this time.

Unlike Havelock Ellis's search, mine has never been overt or deliberate but a long, slow recognition brought about by mainly accidental agencies. While I was about to embark on a life of study and the imagination in my own scrap of the English countryside, he had returned to this very same place at the end of the day. He, too, wandered about, and at Great Waldingfield he found memorials to his mother's family, the Peppins, and in Sudbury he saw that he was descended from a staymaker named Ellis who was a contemporary of Gainsborough's father.

But it is the by-product of this genealogical investigation which is of such special interest, for it contains a striking assessment of Suffolk which, coming as it does from someone uniquely skilled in making assessments, offers a professional verdict on the people as they were just before the full onslaught of 20th century change.

After saying of his father's family that 'their energy is always fairly adequate to carry them along the path of life in which they find themselves, but they are never troubled by any surplus of unused energy. *In medio tutissimus ibis*, that is the truth they know by instinct. My own temperament has in it elements of an extremely other sort, and I owe much to the Ellises for a good dose of this beautiful mediocrity, to me a harmonising influence of the most precious character,' he analyses the inhabitants of the region thus:

'East Anglia, as I have found, has some claim to be a focus of English genius. Much that is most typical in English politics and adventure, thought and science and art practice, has come out of East Anglia. The people of Suffolk, sometimes apparently slow, are yet ever exuberant in energy, often bright of eye and quick of action. Cautious, patient, pliant, conciliatory, they can yet be forceful, independent, obstinate. Not superficially brilliant like the people of the south-west, they are not so impenetrably reserved beneath a hard rind like the people of the north; there is a strong emotional undercurrent which makes itself felt, even though it may not be visible, so that they are a friendly people whom it is not difficult to get on with. Women play a large part among them. The solidity these people of Suffolk owed to their Dutch and Flemish affinities has been modified by French Huguenot and other foreign elements. They are a practical and materialistic people who delight to make their surroundings spacious and beautiful, a religious and benevolent people, indeed, yet by no means ascetic, scarcely even, in the narrow sense, a severely moral people; their instincts in life, as in science and art, tend to direct them towards Nature.'

O sapientia! In the first place, what a comfort it is to know that any inherited recklessness is likely to be counter-balanced by an equally inherited 'dose of beautiful mediocrity'. And what a rehabilitation for a degraded noun! But the writer has managed to put his finger on the elements which have produced Suffolk's particular brand of sanity and rationality. However, Havelock Ellis does not attempt to describe the often explosive condition of a personality made up of a serene kind of commonsense and a high, though repressed, imagination. Julian Tennyson, writing at about the same time as Havelock Ellis, though with the eagerness and freshness of a very young man, senses mystery and certain intangibles. 'Not only are the people shy, but the spirit of the county itself is independent, capricious, elusive — if you don't treat it properly it will, like an unresponsive tortoise, retire to the seclusion of its own shell and escape you for ever. That slight animosity of Suffolk attracts the right people and repels the wrong ones. It is a country for the individualist, for the explorer and the lover of loneliness.'

Julian Tennyson's phrase 'slight animosity' remains for me one of the best warning shots across the local ethos ever made. When one first meets a stranger here his nature is not to offer some conventionally courteous *entrée* to friendship, but to set in motion a gentle but noticeably active resistance to one's request for sociability. It is essential to defeat this, though at the same time not to appear to be in too great a hurry to do so. In East Anglian villages, getting to know one another can still be, in spite of the speeded-up times we live in, a cool, rather mannered business.

Neither suspiciousness nor out-and-out hostility have any place in this animus; one is simply meeting some ancient reflex by which a man once protected his precious individuality from those who saw him simply as a work or fighting machine. One is also encountering someone who can be loquacious when he likes but who thinks it is poor taste to 'be all over you' at the start. Thus, the very sparseness of the language adds to the feeling of indifference. It is a fascinating thing to watch two elderly farm-workers, each unknown to the other, reach the point of candour in a public bar.

Of course, all attempts at describing the traits of a particular piece of country soon run into generalisations. Once, before cars and electronics opened up the secret villages, and when nothing more than the tales of a returning sailor or the oratory of a politician or evangelist disturbed the dull peace of the parish, and when the cycles of the natural year and the human year were still in close correlation, and — to face facts — the majority of people were too exhausted by labour to do much in the way of developing their potential as individuals, there *did* exist certain shared basic attributes which gave each region its strong communal character.

Whether such obvious characteristics can be traced now is doubtful. What most people do when they think of themselves as 'Suffolk' (or Cornish or Kentish) is to associate themselves with the generalisations which have been superimposed on conclusions drawn from the ancient patterns of life in the area. It has also become normal to accept the great artists and writers of the county as remarkable extensions of one's self. Suffolk people, unless they happen to live in Sudbury, accept John Constable as the most brilliant synthesis of their personality and imagination.

Two factors have intensified county self-consciousness since the last War. The first is the rapidity of change and the guilt with which a region which has produced an inimitable architecture, local methods of agriculture and a rich culture, watches all this being superseded by things which *immediately* invalidate all the old values. Hence the growth of conservation, particularly during the last decade. The changes are far from being all malign. And anyone knowing the realities of rural existence up to the 1940's is not going to shed many tears for the housing, schooling and wages of those days. But is Suffolk less 'Suffolk' because of Telstar, North Sea Gas, the Rolling Stones, sliced bread, the Aldeburgh Festival, the tractor-driver returning home in his Mini, the 'death of God', the consciousness of the Third World, the sexual revolution, the chemicalised fields, the animal factories, the nature reserves, higher education or easy transport? The blessings and curses equal out but, even so, can the local spirit survive under their pressures? It is too early to say. All that we understand at present is that the threat to our county identity has become so tough and multifarious that it has put us on our guard, and also made us intelligent about the actual meaning of the heritage which we could so easily lose.

The second factor, this time an entirely benign one, which has sent county-self-consciousness soaring, is the modern guide-book. By this I mean everything from Pevsner to television documentaries, from local social studies to local memoirs; a vast outpouring of regional literature and comment which, apparently, will never be vast enough to satisfy our narcissism. There is unlikely to be a county in Britain which does not produce a similar industry.

It is naive to imagine that this mass of topography exists for the visitor: it exists because we have this passion for ourselves and our land, and can never hear enough about either. Here, set out with great skill and in all their exact particulars, are our local assets and when we read them, or see them handsomely photographed, the menace of Telstar, chemical farming, etc., recede — and we breathe again. The church masterpieces, the fritillary fields at Framsden, Britten's operas, *The Hay Wain*, the mysterious horsemen from the old farms, the direct descendants of the Sutton Hoo king, the holy ones from Selig Suffolk, the inhabitants of Chelsworth or some equally perfect place, the origins of New England, the *Rubaiyat of Omar Khayyam*, and the view from Letheringham Hill, *Cornard Wood,* the bones of Dunwich, the Blythburgh angels, the stones of Shingle Street, the miles of corn in July, the huge trees, the bitter winds, Ipswich on Saturday night — *this* is what we are! 'It says so here.'

The formative influences of place on genius is a question which leads one to a very interesting inexact science. There are writers and artists whose work is rooted in their birthplaces, and others whose birthplaces have had little connexion with their books and pictures. But regional pride lumps them all together, though I can never quite understand why a guide-book muster of celebrities generally should prove anything significant. Suffolk certainly made Constable but did it make Gainsborough? Or Wolsey? Sometimes its peculiarly suitable-for-working-dreamers climate turned Irishmen translating Persian into Suffolk poets. I never read,

   With Earth's first Clay They did the Last Man's knead,
   And then on the Last Harvest sow'd the Seed ......
without seeing Fitz plodding across the fields between Boulge and Debach. But, on the whole one should be wary about what the Victorians called Great Shades. To claim them exclusively can only add vanity to the list of our attributes.

It leads one to George Crabbe. And here the gain is unique. No other English county has anyone anything like him. Which means that no other English county has ever had to endure so total a self-analysis. E.M. Forster, who loved the Suffolk coast, said that to talk about Crabbe was to talk about England. 'He never escaped from Aldeburgh in the spirit, and it was the making of him as a poet. Even when he is writing of other things, there steals again and again into his verse the sea, the estuary, the flat Suffolk

Right: Dinner time.

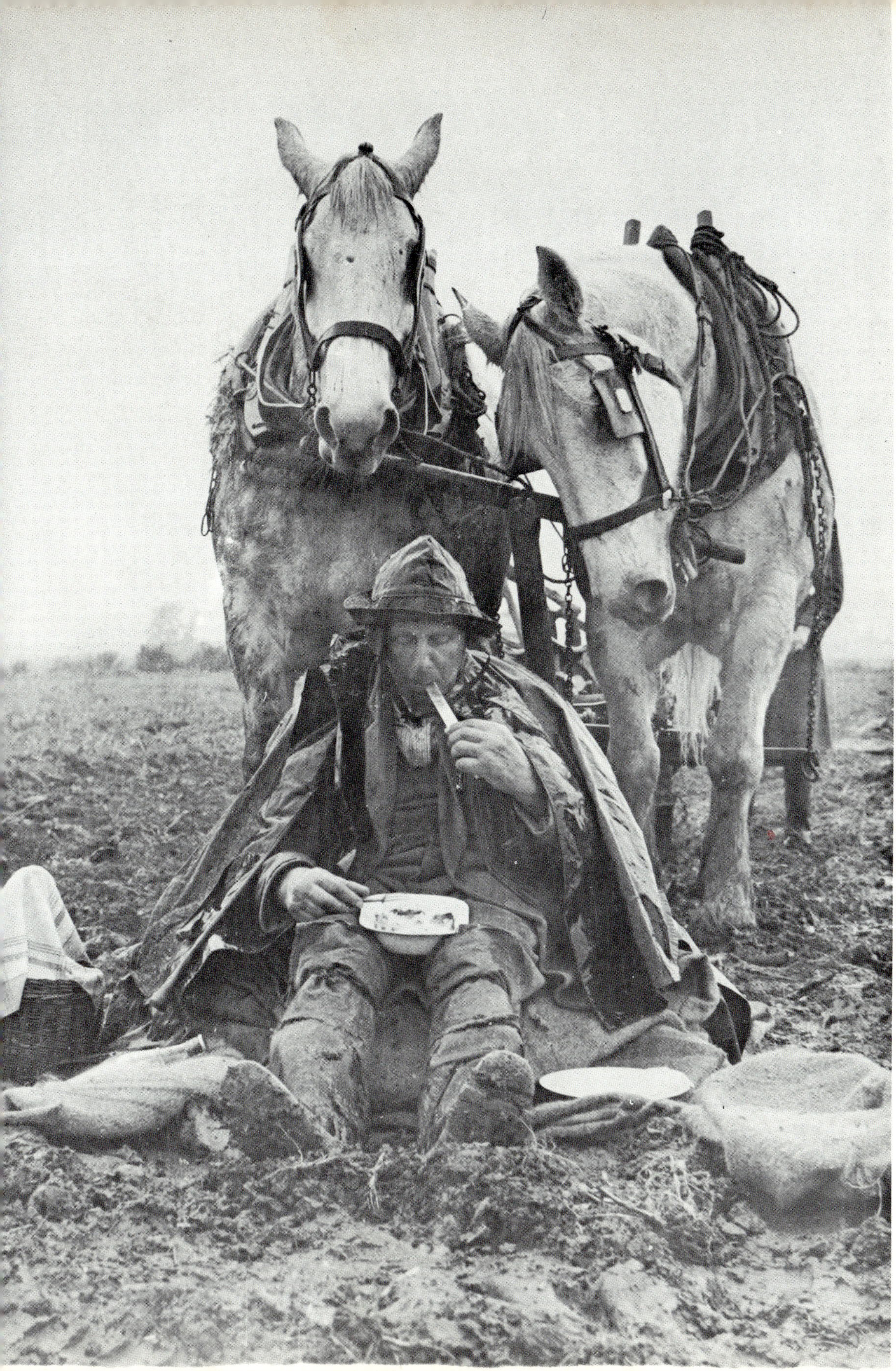

coast, and the local meannesses, and an odour of brine and dirt – tempered occasionally with the scent of flowers ...... Crabbe is a peculiar writer: some people like him, others don't, and find him dull and even unpleasant. I like him and read him again and again; and his tartness, his acid humour, his honesty, his feeling for certain English types and certain kinds of English scenery, do appeal to me very much. On their account I excuse the absence in him of a warm heart, a vivid imagination and a grand style ......'

Crabbe's birthplace.

I like him very much, too. If anybody has managed to nail us down to what we really are, Crabbe has. But that was donkey's years ago, some will say. We have improved (or got much worse) since then. Not in Crabbe's eyes. His is the speaking likeness of Suffolk for other times as well as his own. It is significant too that this county should have produced one of the first great anti-romantics of modern literature. Plodding on, using a style that was years out of date, he was saying things about human nature in an idiom which we now find psychologically fascinating. For us, Crabbe's remorseless eloquence lays down the determining factor. His verse-tales contain, in effect, our genetic faults and gifts, though mostly the former, I fear.

When Forster looked around for a word in which to sum up Crabbe in the most complimentary manner, he chose 'provincial'. And it is in discovering our exact kind of provincialism that we shall find out who we — the still fairly sparse inhabitants of some 50 miles of most beautiful land between the Stour and the Waveney — really are.

This provincialism has its roots in the Suffolk soil and the faster we move away from all genuine contact with the fields around us, the faster it will vanish. Urbanism is not only the physical approach of the concrete, it is a non-rural — or sentimentally rural — way of looking at things and living life. More and more people, although they live in the heart of the country, are beginning to think in urban terms. And if or when this process becomes complete, then our county character will be something for the folklorists to excavate from the handful of us who plough or fish or even garden in the old manner.

That wonderful Orkney writer George Mackay Brown said that the farmers and seamen in his remote island no longer told each other tales when they met, or discussed the local experiences in dramatic terms. Their talking point was last night's television, a game of football played 400 miles south, a disaster on the coast of India, a packaged song. If this sounds depressing, it is true to say that more and more of us can get to a concert at Snape, or on the rivers in boats, or on the marshes with field-glasses. We can also get away. And this is why we shall never be the same again.

Ronald Blythe was born in Suffolk and became a full-time writer during the 1950s. His work includes:
- A Treasonable Growth *(Novel)*
- Immediate Possession *(short stories)*
- The Age of Illusion: England 1919-1940 *(history)*
- Components of the Scene: An anthology of The Prose and Poetry of the Second World War *(Penguin)*
- Emma by Jane Austen *(Edited, with an Introduction for the Penguin English Library)*
- Akenfield
- William Hazlitt: Selected Writings *(Edited and with Introduction for the Penguin English Library)*

His stories, essays and literary criticism have been published in The Listener, The Observer, Sunday Times, The London Magazine, New World Writing, New Statesman, Harper's Magazine *(New York),* The Countryman *and in various anthologies.*

His television documentaries include films on John Nash and John Constable for the BBC.

He is at present working on a study of the early Fabian Society and also a book on the history of the Aldeburgh Festival for Benjamin Britten.

In 1970 he won the W.H. Heinemann Award for Akenfield *and was made a Fellow of the Royal Society of Literature. He was also recently awarded the Society of Authors' Travel Scholarship.*

He lives at Debach, near Woodbridge.

John Stannard
The Craftsmen

Mr. Herbert Grapes of Ranworth swinging his scythe on the marshes during the winter harvesting of Norfolk reed.

Mr. Henry King of Ashwell Thorpe in Norfolk was for a time shepherd to the Queen on the Sandringham Estate.

Mr. Victor Minns of Hethersett likes a hand-operated forge best. His forge is still in regular use.

Mr. Samuel Braybrook, a gun-smith at Downham Market in Norfolk. By the time Samuel was 12 years old he could handle and fire a 12-bore shot gun as well as any grown-up.

The mystery of Sutton Heath.

Eric Rayner
The Haunted Places

WITH no more precise date than that it was during the reign of King Stephen — 1135 to 1154 — William of Newburg set down that, on one harvest day, reapers saw a boy and a girl, 'completely green in their persons', emerge from the ancient excavations that gave the village its name of Woolpit.

Months later, when they were once again the colour of normal human beings, and eating and talking like them, they told a tale of a far off St. Martin's land where there was perpetual twilight, and 'a considerable river' beyond which was brightness and daylight. They had heard church bells, and then remembered nothing more until they were amongst the harvesters.

Lodged in the house of Sir Richard de Calne, at Wyke, they were eventually baptized but, alas, the younger of two children, the boy, died shortly afterwards. The girl, however, grew up and eventually married a man in Lynn.

Honest, thoughtful William ended his narrative with the resigned remark that everyone could think and say what they pleased, but that he had no regret at having recorded the 'prodigious and miraculous' events.

Looking at the map, the story is not so remarkable for eight miles west of Woolpit is Fordham St. Martin and the river Lark, and all within the sound of the bells of Bury St. Edmunds. The real conundrum is not the children's odd green hue and their long silence afterwards — two things which would come from wandering in the terrifying twilight solitude of the woods — but why were they never claimed by their parents or guardians?

Wayland is a hamlet near Watton along the Wymondham Road. A Norfolk Gentleman dying there, by his *Last Will and Testament,* confided his two babes to the care of their uncle, but that uncle, seeking their estate, paid two ruffians to take the children into Wayland Wood and kill them.

Maybe the two men were 'felowes fleshed in murther' but on this occasion at least one of them had a change of heart and could not bring himself to slay such innocence. This led to a fight, and the killing of the other man, where-upon he went off, leaving the children to wander and fare as best they could.

And so they went in and out amongst the towering trees, through the sunlit glades:

> *Their pretty lippes with black-berries*
> *All besmeared and dyed*
> *And when they saw the darksome night*
> *They sat them downe and cryed.*

But, unlike the wandering innocents of the *pantomime,* there was no happy ending: they died in each others arms, receiving no burial:

> *Till Robin red-breast piously*
> *Did cover them with leaves.*

But murder, even by proxy, must have retribution if not vengeance, which is 'Mine sayeth the Lord', and in the course of time the wicked uncle's barns were fired, his fields made barren, and his cattle carried off by the murrain. His two sons were drowned on a voyage to Portugal and he, himself, died a beggar in gaol.

As for the 'prettye babes', when the wind is wild amongst the trees, and Wayland wood shakes with its thunder, they go wandering hand-in-hand piteously calling out for the big, broad, strong knave who never returns. Go back to your bier of leaves, my darlings, he will never come again.

What are storm winds if they are not the accumulated chorus of centuries of those unjustly done to death or slain in battles such as Assandun, when the Danes and Saxons fought, in 1016, from sunrise to glorious sunset and on until the moon was flooding the Essex marshes with silver. Oh yes, the Essex marshes have enough dead to fill the wind with such an immense clamour of shrieks and groans as to make your backbone ice. On such a night of disembodied agony witches could ride on broomsticks, and eyeless ghosts stand beneath every leaf-stripped, stunted oak.

These marshes, and Canewdon's in particular, are witch country, but oddly enough the witches of Canewdon always preferred bath-tubs or hurdles to broomsticks when crossing the River Crouch. There have always been witches in Canewdon, three in silk and three in cotton, and when one died and another took her place a stone fell from the massive tower of St. Nicholas' church.

The masons who built the tower — put up to celebrate Agincourt so it is said — must have known all about the witches for, up on the parapet, they stuck gargoyles: three-toed, hairless, malignant, spitting, cat-like witches' creatures. However, having fallen down one day or night they are now in the north aisle of the church.

Also inside the church are other, much later, reminders of Canewdon witches, hatchments of the Kersterman family who settled here from the Netherlands about 1700. Anyway, of the 19th century progeny two, old Lady Eliza Lodwick, and her sister, Mary Anne, were accounted witches and treated with the caution and deference due to such callings.

On one occasion the villagers of Canewdon petitioned Mr. Atkinson to allow James Murrell, the 'Cunning Man' of Essex to whistle up the witches and make them confess themselves by dancing round the churchyard. But the parson never did, and everybody was sure that it was because he didn't want to see his own wife cavorting round.

A 'Cunning Man', by the way, was a white wizard who could whistle all the witches to him, and even conjure them up on his 'magic' glass, and if he branded a woman as a witch, as Murrell did to a Mrs. Eves at Hadleigh, her life would be made miserable. Whether George Pettingall was a white wizard I don't know, but he is said to have whistled the last sheaves of the harvest into a wagon one evening, without any visible aid apparent.

Silk draperies rustling by a man as he went down to the ferry, old women sitting in darkened rooms and mumbling incantations while they burned hair and nailparings of their intended victim, geese that sickened and then grew splendidly and magically fat again — life in Canewdon was never dull.

But all this was small magic compared to that rummaged out by Master

Matthew Hopkins, Witch-Finder General, in 1644 and onwards. A most diligent man this, riding, riding through all East Anglia, getting as many as 29 condemned in one batch; after their memories had been jogged by hours of darkness, bound cross-legged on a table, starvation, and walkings until blisters and blood smeared their feet.

Bitter weepings, denials, cryings-out for pity, it was no use, they had to confess: how they had sent their 'imps' to murder, to sink ships, or even to make a horse lame and emit noises 'as of a foul chimney on fire'. And those

The babes in the wood — Rendlesham Forest.

'imps', they had names: *Elemawzar, Pyewackett,* and *Griezzell Greedigutt,* etc, etc, which, as Mr. Hopkins so rightly said, 'no mortal could invent'.

Alas, alas, as is so often the case with men who toil for the common weal, Mr. Hopkins was misunderstood and accused of being a witch, himself. Some say he was 'swam' and then hanged, but anyway, he was buried at Mistley on 12th August 1647.

On Sunday, 4th August 1577, between the hours of nine and 10 in the morning 'whilst the minister was reading the second lesson in the parish church at Bliborough a strange and terrible tempest of lightenings and thunder strake through the wall of the same church unto the ground almost a yard, drave down all the people on that side above twenty personages, then renting the wall up to the Revestrie, and left the dore and returning to the steeple rent the timber, brake the chimes and fled to Bongay six miles off'.

Half an hour after that calamitous invasion of storm, people were found

A witch hunter and his victims AD 1647,

grovelling on the floor. Some were scorched and two, a man of 40 and a boy of 14, lay stone dead.

At Bungay there was 'such darkness, Rayne, Hayle, Thunder and Lightning as was never seen the Lyke, Never to be forgotten', with John Fuller and Adam Walker struck dead in the belfry.

That last was in St. Mary's, Bungay, where 'a black dog or the divel in such likeness' ran down the nave 'with great swiftness and incredible haste' and wrung the necks of two men. Maybe, children dancing round the Druid's stone on the west side of the north porch had, indeed, raised the Evil One; but Bungay has certainly commemorated the event in a lead panel on the lamp standard:

> *All down the Church in midst of fire*
> *The hellish monster flew,*
> *And passing towards the Quire*
> *He many people slew.*

That black dog of Suffolk has no name, but the one of Norfolk has. He is Black Shuck, a huge beast that prowls along dark lanes and over lonesome field footpaths, his footfalls soundless but his howling unearthly and spine-chilling. If you meet him you will know him as long as you are on this earth — not very long because he is the harbinger of death within a 12-month — by the one fiery eye in the middle of his broad forehead. Like all hell-hounds he is only abroad on wild nights, when the sea and the winds are roaring and all nature in turmoil.

There seems to have been nothing ghostly or supernatural about the 'wonderful sea monster' dredged up in an Orford fisherman's net. According to Ralph de Coggeshall, a 14th century abbot, the creature, in size and shape something resembling a man, had a hairless crown and a long ragged beard. It ate whatever was offered, be it cooked or raw, but talk it would not; no matter how the Governor's servants ill-used it.

Then, one day, a fisherman took it out to sea, first spreading his nets so that it should not escape. But once in the water, its natural element, the creature found no difficulty in diving below the nets and re-appearing some distance off, grimacing, so the fisherman thought, in derision. Having thus shown its independence, it followed the fisherman's boat back to the shore, and allowed itself to be taken once more into captivity.

But then, one day, the call of the sea was strong, and the bald-headed, bearded, man-like creature slipped back into the salt briny, never to be seen again.

North of Wroxham, still on the River Bure, is Blickling Hall. It also has its stories of ghosts, and grim and ghastly those ghosts are: no less than a black hearse-like carriage drawn by four headless horses, driven by a headless coachman and, all-dressed-in-white, Anne Boleyn inside, her dainty hands on her knees, holding her own severed head.

The whole gory apparition appears just before midnight, the 19th of May, goes slowly up the broad avenue, and then vanishes at the doors. Inside, along the corridors, headless spectres glide with a rustle of ghostly garments, and vanish.

When the news of the executions of Anne Boleyn and her brother, Lord Rochfort, was brought to Blickling:

> *That very time at dead of night,*
> *Four headless horses took their flight,*
> *Dragging behind them as they ran,*
> *The spectre of a headless man.*

> *Beneath his arm his head he bore,*
> *Its tangled hair all wet with gore.*
> *Pursued he was by demons foul,*
> *With piercing shriek and dismal howl.*

Such is the cortège of Sir Thomas Boleyn which goes hell-belting across 12 bridges, along roads and byways, over hedges and ditches, and through gates and fences in a round of that night countryside that must be completed before cock-crow; the time when all phantoms must go back to their graves, some in sulphur and brimstone and blue fire.

Midway between East Dereham and Thetford, in the lanes and two miles south-east of Stow Bedon, George Mace, 'a mysterious sort of man', and other poachers met in a plantation by Breccles Hall, once an Elizabethan manor house. The night was still and quiet, and a serene moon floated in the heavens. They deliberated in low voices and then, promising to meet at the back of the Hall and 'settle up before the moon was down' they went off in two parties; furtively and without noise.

At 'settling time' the two parties met at their rendezvous, but Mace was not amongst them. Mace was the leader and so the gang waited for him, a little uneasily since the moon was already waning. Suddenly there was a rumbling of wheels in the still night, and a few moments later a great flashing of coach lamps through the stained windows of the old hall: such a great flashing, in fact, that 'the very coats of arms on the windows were painted on the hoar frost' at their feet.

The coach came round the house and stopped at the door. Steps were let down, doors opened, closed again with a slam and then... the lamps went out, the moon was gone, and the coach vanished in the utter blackness without a sound.

Unnerved by it all, the poachers waited no longer, but slipped off in the darkness to their various homes. Next morning 'Jarge' Mace was found lying on his back at the front door of Breccles Hall. Not a mark was on his body, nor a stain on his clothing, but his body was stiff and cold, and dead as any body could be.

Two or three miles due East of Great Wymondham is Stanfield Hall, the home, in the 16th century of Sir John Robsart and his daughter, Amy, due to die in most mysterious circumstances in Cumnor Hall, Oxfordshire — with her husband the Earl of Leicester, and Elizabeth I of England, under dark suspicion.

In 1848 the Hall was occupied by the Recorder of Norwich, Mr. Isaac Jermy who, for some time, had been at loggerheads with one of his tenants, a man named James Bloomfield Rush. Rush, violent, vindictive, and cunning, forged the Recorder's signature and then, well acquainted with the habits of the household, stationed himself outside the door one November night; disguised and armed with a double-barrelled shot-gun.

As usual, Mr. Jermy, after his dinner, came out for a short stroll. But he never got beyond the doorway. Rush, discharging both barrels, killed him on the instant. During the terrible commotion that ensued Rush shot and killed Mr. Jermy's son, wounded Mrs. Jermy and a female servant, and then ran out of the Hall. Behind, he left a document implying that the shootings had been

committed by two men, known to be claimants to the Stanfield estate.
　　But the girl with whom he was living at Potash Farm, under questioning, destroyed his alibi and he was hanged outside Norwich Castle in the presence of a great crowd from all parts of the county. No one ever said ghosts walked, but for a full half century afterwards men would go out of their way to avoid Stanfield Hall, a tall house with several gables, and tall, corniced chimneys, and no woman or child would venture abroad in Hethel, where Rush had lived, after nightfall. The evil men do lives after them.

Execution of witches.

　　Spain's Hall, near Finchingfield, Essex, is a red-bricked mansion with mullioned windows, wrinkled roofs, and eight-sided chimneys. In the year of the Armada 33 year old Kemp brought his bride Philippa Gunter there. Three decades later, on 8th June 1621, pacing in his grounds, bitterly repentant of having accused his elderly wife of infidelity, he vowed aloud that, to punish his so hasty tongue, he 'would not speak again for seven years'.
　　The birds, the trees, the flowers, all nature heard the outrageous vow and so, too, did a certain 'Raven' Foster; so called from the fact that three of those black-plumaged birds had croaked on a tree all the night long of his birth. The seventh son of a seventh son, a gatherer of herbs, a 'fey' man, at home with the wild creatures of the woodland, he sternly warned Kemp that

such a vow would bring nothing but sorrow and calamity.

But Kemp made no reply and, 'swallowed up with a Melancholy Phrensie', remained silent whilst his physician reasoned, his wife pleaded, and a parson prayed that God might change his, Kemp's, mind.

There had been plans for the making of stew or fish ponds. Now, William Kemp decided to construct one for every year of his self-imposed silence, and by the May of 1622 the first one was completed. And in that same month three of his servants, two men and a woman, were found floating in it: quite inexplicably drowned.

The next year his wife, Philippa, broken hearted by her husband's conduct, died; with Kemp by her bed, but never offering a word of comfort or love to see her into the beyond.

The year after that, 1624, on a wet June evening, Kemp suffered his own personal misfortune. Falling from his horse he broke a leg, and because he would not shout out for help he laid on sopping, saturated ground the night through. Early next morning labourers found him; but he was ill for months afterwards.

In the late Autumn of 1626, restored to good health once more, he was on his way back from Halstead when the long-portended thunderstorm broke with shattering violence. The sheets of rain, the frightful flashes of lightning, and the thunder cracking and rolling overhead made the horses unmanageable and so he and his groom — with whom he communicated in sign language — took shelter in the tower of a castle fast falling into ruin.

A place of cobwebs and bats, the two men found first ashes and embers of a fire on an ancient hearth, and then heard men's voices from a chamber above: two things with sinister connotations for it was known that vagrants and robbers frequented the tower.

Lying full-length on the floor of a third chamber Kemp listened and heard, so it turns out, an unspecified number of men plotting a raid when the storm abated: on Spain's Hall. The groom, down below, knew nothing of this, but the drawn horror on the face of his master warned him that something dreadful was afoot. Here, indeed, was a time to speak, but William Kemp said no word as they spurred through the streaming blackness of the storm. And neither would he speak when, with despair in his heart, he saw the swollen river — the Blackwater? — racing too fast for an old man like himself to get across.

Still ignorant of what was afoot, the groom begged Kemp to go the long way round, whilst he forded the river with his horse with a written message. Whatever Kemp put on that paper the groom could not read, because he had never been to school. And neither could anyone in Spain's Hall read it: the river water had rendered the writing illegible.

Came a hurried, anxious conference, and every man, mounted and armed, rode out to protect William Kemp from whatever peril threatened him. When they returned, with their master, they found battered down doors, broken furniture, débris; and in an upstairs room of the south wing a dead, eight-year old boy. Silverware, money, finery, everything of value had gone.

By the June of 1628 the last of the seven fish-ponds was completed, and on the eve of the 8th June William Kemp went to bed, obviously in high spirits. Tomorrow, his self-imposed vow would be ended. He slept well enough through the night, but towards morning he groaned and rolled his head as though there was some nightmare in his brain. And when he did wake up he looked a very sick, old man.

Now, the whole household, servants as well, gathered round his bed: for the moment of speaking. But William Kemp could not utter a word. From a tongue, wilfully silent these seven years, came barely audible incoherencies, and the hand that had served him in lieu of a tongue was nerveless.

That evening, with the last flush of sunset still in the sky, William Kemp died. A day or two later he was laid beside the wife he had wronged, in the Kemp Chapel which stands on the north side of the chancel in Finchingfield's church of St. John the Baptist. And there, on the wall, a marble tablet put up by his nephew and inheritor relates of *William Kemp Esq., pious, just, hospitable: master of himself so much, that what others scarce doe by force and penalties, he did by a volountary constancy hold his peace for seven years...*

A century or so later the last Kemp died, and Spain's Hall had new owners, but for many years afterwards there were whispered rumours of a small ghost, a phantom as insubstantial as mist which, on turbulent nights, wandered restlessly from chamber to chamber in the south wing.

Only when that wing was burned down, and replaced by the present Georgian one, did the unquiet spirit go to that other realm.

An old drawing of three witches and their imps.

Eric Rayner has been a freelance writer since 1955. Specialises in cricket, local history, and his travels in the Mediterranean and Europe. Prefers most of all to write about the English countryside, particularly Norfolk and Suffolk; and he contributes regularly to the East Anglian Magazine. *There can be very few villages in East Anglia he has not wandered through, sometimes on a bicycle, most times on foot, invariably toiling under the weight of a rucksack. Likes country pubs and country churches — and has an uncanny skill for discovering places where he can get bed-and-breakfast for less than £1.*

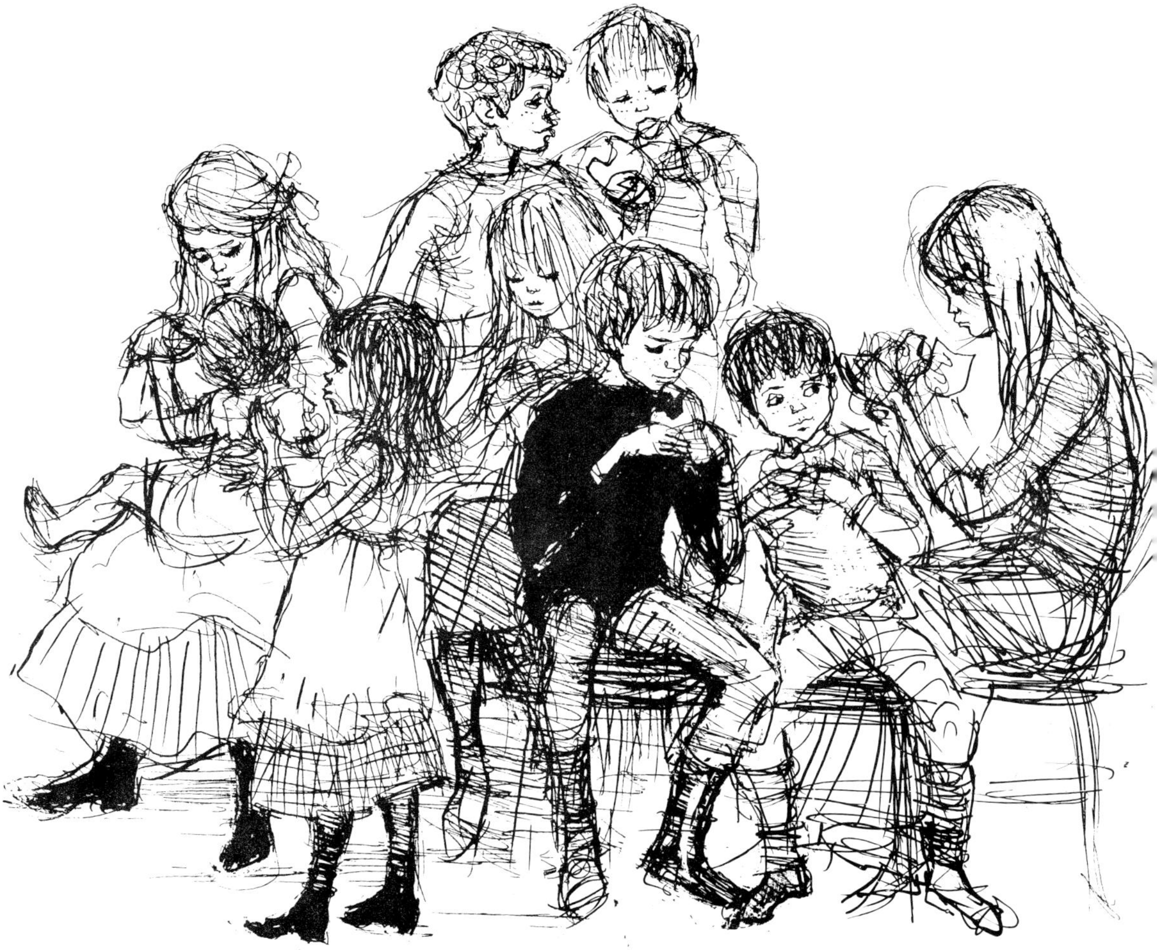

mrs. a. woods

(We have never met Mrs. Woods, who sent a typewritten manuscript, with a pen-written note 'typing excuse I have only recently learned', to the East Anglian Magazine; *but we think she must be one of the most delightful characters alive in East Anglia today. We reproduce extracts from her story exactly as it was submitted, except that we have broken it up into paragraphs. — M.W.)*

BETTER known as pat or murphy; age 82 years; my life began the twenty-sixth of juanary 1899 as the clock chimed midnight the old woman that attended my mother to bring me into the world said she is dead; so i was laid out on the table as such; but i must have had different idears; so i was registered as marther ann ketteringham by john thomas egarr at terrington st clements in norfolk; and me born at midnight my mother said i should always be in trouble and quite true i always have been;

my mother was a very good living woman; she had thirteen of us kids to bring up; my father was a clever man; but one fault drink; times were very hard thoes days; our cheefly food was bread and lard; throu fathers drinking habits we never stayed long in one house; mother hated the moving but us kids loved the novelty of it;

as far back as i can remember we lived in a big old house called the union we dident have such things as carpets we used to strinkle sawdust on our floor; now father decided to move to another house much smaller one; that was far to small for our famialy two weeks and we move againe to a bigger house called fourscors we did not stay there long we soon moved on to dawsmere bank this time there was no exitment for us kids we were scared; a man had cut his head off in the lavetory;

all to soon we moved to a house called the mill pad the old mill was very near our house and in the mill house mothers used to take there babies to have there tongues cut; from there we moved to a house in lutton marsh when the boss see family he soon put us in a big farm house; and the roof of the old house was full of honey; my we lived on honey for long enough;

mother used to say come on you wenches and go to chapple on sundays never mind about being a bit raggy; our chapple was a kitchen at guys head the pulpit stood in the fire place and the pots and pans hung all around;

we only stayed there about two months; so off we go again; right into cambridgeshire a distance of fourty miles; throu wisbeach march and chattris untill we came to a little village called mepal the house we went in was so small we could hardly see it just like a heap of straw sticking out of a swamp; next day father had to take the doors off to get our things in; ten of us kids had the upstars leanto thatched roof; i well remember the night the roof blew off and us kids were bare to the sky;

mother and fathers bed room was downstars a room just big enough to put one bed in and that filled it; so father had his barrel of bear on the foot of the bed; he always sat on the side of the bed and had a tot when he went to bed; outside the dirty swamp water splashed up the walls; but i never

195

remember it getting in the house i expect it was built that way; we had to go to the toilet by boat;

i loved and longed to be a nurse i did get a nurses help job with nurse meekley at sutton bridge i was very happy then; now i was coming the age of twenty; truly all my life i had never been interested in the opperset sex but one day this charley woods came along and changed my life completely and i was married within the year; i loved him very dearley and hoped i should spend the rest of my life as his wife; and i did; we had eight babyes all my own feeding no bottles never and all perfect from them; we have twenty five grandchildren and twenty five great grandchildren; my kids are all around me and they are very good to me i also took a baby girl when its mother died at her birth;

we were married at long sutton registra; i had to buy my own wedding ring charley was to shy; and in my condition i got flustered and got the ring stuck on my finger and had to have help to get if off; i had three shillings left over from the golden soveren that father lent us to get married with; so i bought calico to make myself another shirt i onley had one; our best man was swinging a babies tete in front of uor faces and sure the next day we needed it;

off we go to charleys parents for our wedding dinner; no jolly fun no nothing; we just sat not to close; his mam was looking at us we stayed the night there; but earley next morning i relised i ought to be going to my own home where i lived so of me and charley goes walking all the four miles to sutton bridge; i was then having the usual pains that a woman has at thoese times all the way; and charley held my arm every time i felt quer it took me a long time to get home; soon as we entered the door i remember my mother saying; come on i know whats the matter with you; she had so many she knew the signs; and in an hour i had a son;

at the end of may charley had a chance of a good horsemans job but we must live in large house that was once an hotel; our few things looked lost; i was very unhappy there i had neioubours that loved my charley; to much for my liking so we moved to lutton marsh where my seckond baby was born; in that house a man had bashed a womans head in only just before we moved in; that made me scared in that house too but the work i had to do seemed to forget the horror of it;

i had five lodgers and eleven paddies to look after; and had time to help a poor woman that lived near she was horribly poor she layed on an old iron bed with only straw on and old coats; and a new born baby in her armes; i took her one of my beds and made her comfortable; altho i could ill afford it; she was very grateful to me, that is my nature i just carnt pass by a wanting being;

again charley move to a new job; he got more money being head horseman; our house stood in a forty acre field with little lakes dotted about and trees of every discription it was georgous; charley used to put me a swing on the big chesnut and swing me i was very happy then;

then my therd baby came along what a place to have a baby no proper road to the place only across fields; when the time came and i needed help charley went to an old gipsey camp; she dident stop to go across the field she went strait thro the river; when she got to me and my baby was being born the water was running out of her cloths; and a more horrible face i never did see; gipsey leach; lived in an old caravan with an old tin trunk as a lav; its true one half of the world dont know how the other half lives;

there were no pills those days; we had to have babies as they came; the night before my fifth baby was born the celing of my bedroom fell in and nearly smothered me; my mother dragged me out and then layed my bed on the floor of the other room; that same day my luciee was born; her black hair stood strait up she must have felt the shock as much as me the troubles i have been thro; and i have lived to be eighty;

after the war charley went back to work for his boss mr smith; charley used to say his horses knew he was home; his horses would on accasions break out of the field and come in front of our window and winney for him at four oclock in the morning; his brasses always hung shining on my wall;

charley got on well with the smiths at monks house and he stayed there the rest of his life; we were a very happy family by now the older kids were marring age; the clock of age one carnt stop and the grandchildren began to arrive and who better to have them home than mam so i piled the bits of furenture in the corner and a bed in and made a room for babies to be born with mam in attendance;

I had a large tea hurn which i kept shining, no use for it now; so charley as burried it under our concreat yard to earth the wireless in this house where we live now;

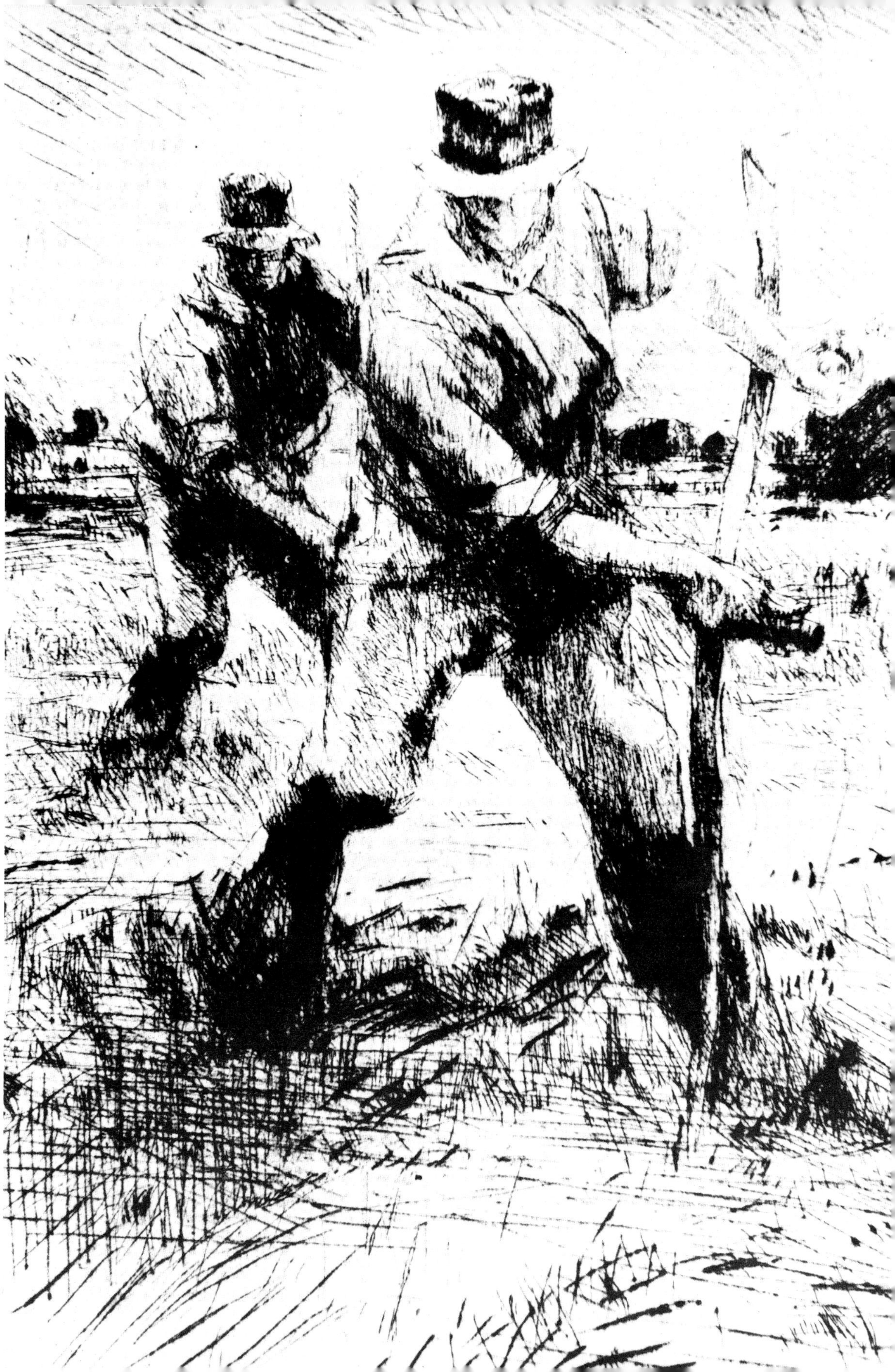

Harry Becker

Of the countless mute, inglorious Miltons unmentioned in this anthology, we should most like to pay tribute to Harry Becker. Born in Colchester, Becker studied at the Royal Academy in Antwerp before working at the studio of Carolus Duran in Paris. Here he came under the influence of the Impressionists, viewing the work of Manet and Degas with particular admiration. Returning from the continent, Becker settled at East Bergholt before eventually making his home at Wangford in Suffolk.

He found inspiration almost exclusively in the countryside surrounding Wangford and would go into the fields with the workers at 5 a.m, drawing endlessly in notebooks, sketching men at work, cattle, sheep — often annotating his drawings with time of day, date and weather conditions. His draughtmanship and concern with the physical expression of labour are strongly reminiscent of the early van Gogh. In the above etching one can sense the urgency of haymaking, a race against the elements as rain slants down from a peevish sky. Even the horse is straining.

Becker died in Wangford in 1928, leaving in disordered piles and bulging folders his life's work — several hundredweight of drawings, etchings, lithographs and paintings. All too few have been seen by the public.

Haymaking.

Left: The fellows who cut the hay.

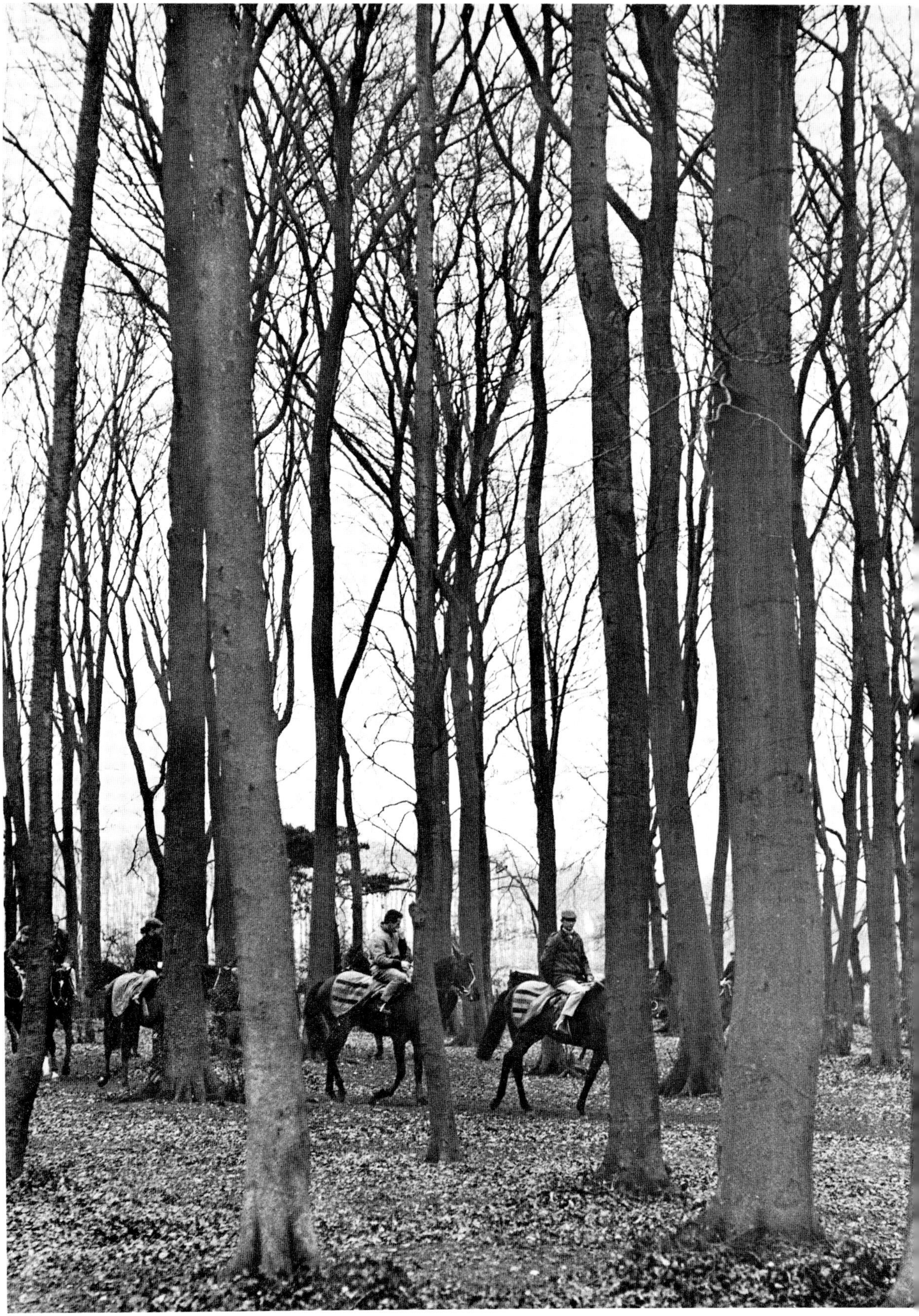

John Seymour
Gone Away

A MAN with no roots is a poor tool. Even a gypsy has roots — not in any particular country, but in his family, culture and race. I spent the first half of my adult life travelling, working and soldiering in a score of different countries, in Europe, Africa and Asia, but at no time did I ever think of myself as anything but an East Anglian.

My childhood had been spent on the Essex-Suffolk border, my early friends had all been East Anglian country people, and I still found the East Anglian language (which so far no East Anglian has ever been able to reproduce) the most beautiful sound on earth. I remember once when I was squatting over a little fire in the pouring rain of the monsoon in Burma with some wild East African tribesmen, the lobes of whose ears hung down to their shoulders, a white man came up to me and asked me the way to a certain British artillery unit. 'Blast Bor!' I replied. 'I reckon you'd a sight ruther be a 'gooin' to Swaafham!' After he went away — in an hour or two's time — my African sergeant said: 'That man is your *Ndugu*,' meaning brother. I said 'yes', although I had never seen him before in my life. If he had come from Surrey I wouldn't have wasted two words with him.

Why then, people may ask, leave East Anglia which is the only place where you can ever have any roots, and go about as far away from it as you can in England and Wales without actually falling into the sea?

Well, how can I answer this question honestly — even to myself? Land at £60 an acre instead of £300 is perhaps part of the answer; 'overspill' another; too many people; too many motor cars; too many aeroplanes, all come into it. I am a countryman, have *never* lived in a town, and I am only happy if I can keep a good distance away from cities and their spin-off. The East Anglian, like every other kind of person in the British Isles, has always been ready to emigrate: to go away and cut a life for himself in another country. The people who crossed the sea 1500 years ago from Friesland and south Denmark to settle in East Anglia came because they were adventurous and wanted to pioneer in a strange land.

But having made the move — what are the pros and cons? What is better — what is worse?

I love North Pembrokeshire, and Wales. My neighbours are kind and cooperative — we still farm on the old mutual helping basis, where we make each others' hay, or shear each others' sheep, in happy beer-drinking gangs, and money does not seem very important to us. My neighbours are my friends, they are merry men, they are great singers, they are poets. My children have put down roots here — they will grow up to look at North Pembrokeshire as their land, the people as their people, Welsh as their second language. Maybe they will be singers and poets too. I shall never be part of the land, though, no matter how long I stay here, or how well I am accepted, I shall always be the stranger: the foreigner. And I shall always miss what is really my native land — not England which is just an abstraction — but East Anglia, which is a real land, and East Anglians who are a real

Left: To Newmarket heath.

people, different from any other people on earth.

What is it about the East Anglian countryman which makes him different from anybody else? Is it a kind of wry, unsmiling humour (or smiling only with the eyes), a taciturnity, a tendency to under-state everything — to accept everything — to play everything down? 'Well now's the time to laarn!' shouted the old Suffolk barge skipper to his mate, when the latter fell overboard yelling that he didn't know how to swim. But I'll bet the old boy got him out of the water again, and without panicking or flapping, and very probably without removing his pipe from his mouth.

If I take something to a tradesman here, where I live now, and ask for it to be mended, he will promise me anything: 'Yes, yes! Tomorrow you'll have it! It will be ready for you then! Early!' A fortnight later I'll go to get it, and find it is still not done, and the tradesman and I will both go down to the pub and have a marvellous afternoon, when the pub really ought to be shut, ending up by singing 'Bread of Heaven', in Welsh.

If I took the same thing to an East Anglian craftsman he would shake his head, and look solemn, and say he was up to the eyes in work, and snowed under. I could leave it if I liked, but he wouldn't promise anything — could look in next Saturday if I liked, if I happened to be passing by, but — 'mind you, I arn't a-gooin' te promise naathin!' — and I could go away feeling absolutely sure about three things. One, that the job *would* be finished 'a' Saturday'. Two, that it would be honestly and well done. Three, that I would not be overcharged.

Of all the people in the world I have worked with, I have found the East Anglian the most utterly reliable. When the seams of the world begin to crack I'll bet some East Anglian, somewhere, will pull a pipeful of shag out of his mouth, spit, say: 'Blast if that in't a rummun!', put his pipe back and go on hoeing his sugar beet. I think my photograph of Mr. A. Balls outside his Garden House captures some of this spirit. If you told a 'furriner' that Mr. Balls was laughing when this photograph was taken, he'd think you were mad. But he was — an East Anglian laugh.

Everybody tells me the world is changing, and East Anglia is changing as quickly and as much as anywhere else. Maybe it is — maybe that's why I left it. But somehow I think the change is only on the surface. The wheat will still be growing on the Fens in a thousand years time, so thick that if you throw your hat on it, it won't reach the ground; the North Sea will still be flowing in and out of muddy Norfolk harbours; someone very like Johnnie Burrell will still be baiting long-lines at Aldeburgh — no matter how out-dated people tell him this form of fishing is. The Normans came and built Framlingham Castle. The Normans have gone, but Mr. Keeble, the East Anglian, is still there.

John Seymour, author of 'The Companion Guide to East Anglia' and many other books, has chosen for a change to capture the study of East Anglia with the camera lens rather than the pen. The photographs he has taken on the following pages are particularly evocative of the countryside in which he spent so many years. His captions bring his pictures further to life.

Right: That lovely stuff mud, and salt tidal water, and gently sloping arable fields bordered by woodland. The best of the Norfolk scene at Brancaster Harbour.

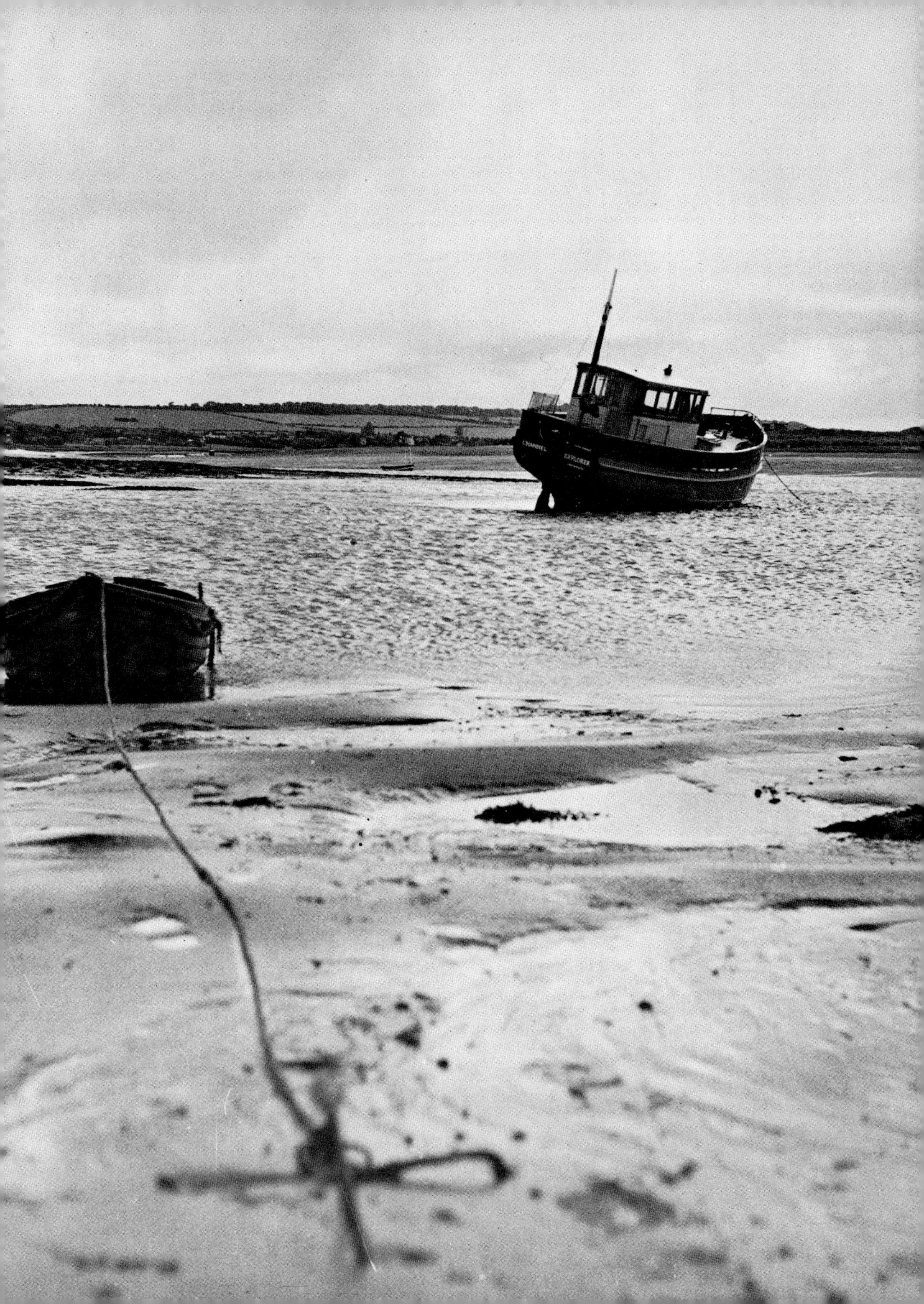
CHANNEL
EXPLORER

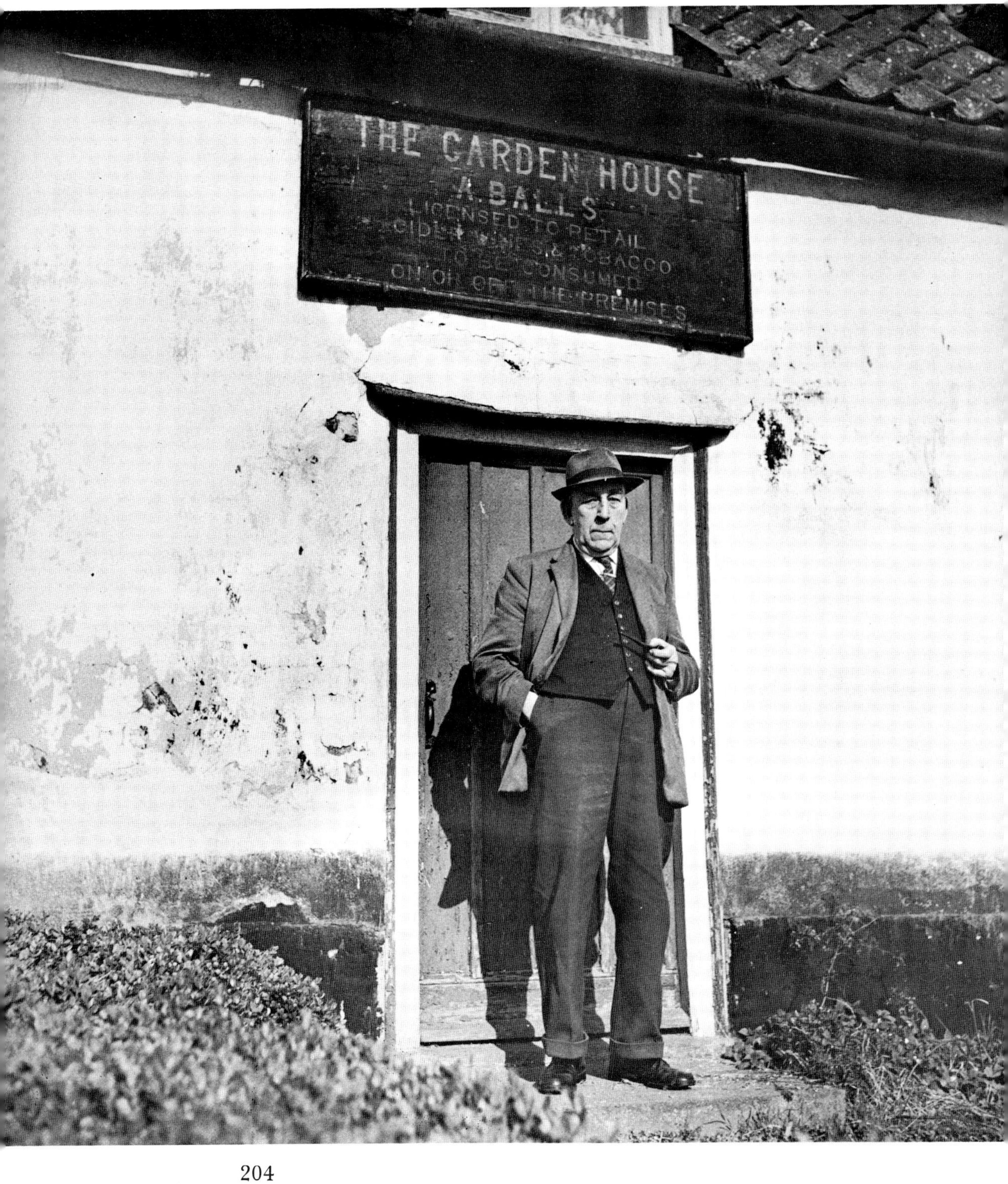
THE GARDEN HOUSE
A. BALLS
LICENSED TO RETAIL

Mr. John Burrell snoods his long-lines ready to put off the Aldeburgh beach to catch codling and skate.
Left: There is something foursquare and unchanging about the true East Anglian man. The landlord stands outside one of the few remaining cider and wine houses in England: at Old Buckenham, in Norfolk.

The Normans built Framlingham Castle, the Ministry of Works keeps it from falling down, but the East Anglian countryman continues as he has done for a thousand years: clearing the land and tilling the soil.

A small boy with a snowball guards the keep of Orford Castle.

John Seymour was born and brought up at Tendring in Essex, and spent his childhood there, at Frinton-on-Sea, and as much of it as he could sailing the Suffolk and Essex estuaries in a small boat and working on farms, including Horsey Island. He went to Africa at 20, earned his living in various ways between the Cape and the Congo for six years, served in the King's African Rifles for the six years of the war, in Abyssinia and Burma. After the war he was a District Labour Officer for the East Suffolk War Agricultural Executive, then spent several years exploring East Anglian waters in a Dutch fishing boat, which was his home, got married and moved ashore to a smallholding near Orford. After eight years of this he migrated to Pembrokeshire, where he now farms.

illustrations

	Page
Fred S. Curtis	146
John Donat	128
Courtesy East Anglian Daily Times	162
Courtesy Eastern Daily Press	131
R. B. Fleming & Co. Ltd.	114
John R. Freeman	117
Giles *(reproduced by courtesy of the Sunday Express)*	15
Peter Keen *(reproduced by courtesy of the Weekend Telegraph)*	20
Jennifer Kent	49, 194, 197
Paul H. T. King	177
Marlborough Fine Art Gallery	116, 119, 120
Caroline Odgers	8
Keith Pilling	11
Hazel le Rougetel	158
Dennis E. Scammell	94
John Seymour	203 - 7
Ann Stainton	6, 50, 51, 53, 126, 136-7, 141, 144, 184, 187, 200
Julian Stainton *(aged 16)*	17-19
John Stannard	180 - 3
Rosamund Strode *(reproduced by courtesy of Arup Associates)*	132
Clive Strutt	131
John Wallace	42, 52, 75, 106, 111
Michael Warren	86, 88, 91
John Western	68, 70
Jeffrey W. Whitelaw	134

Negatives and plates by Typerian Ltd, Greyfriars Works, Cecilia Street, Ipswich.

The chapter heading drawings, book design and layout are by Margaret Pocock.